Rational Powers in Action

Human actions unfold over time, in pursuit of ends that are not fully specified in advance. *Rational Powers in Action* locates these features of the human condition at the heart of a new theory of instrumental rationality. Where many theories of rational agency focus on instantaneous choices between sharply defined outcomes, treating the temporally extended and partially open-ended character of action as an afterthought, this book argues that the deep structure of instrumental rationality can only be understood if we see how it governs the pursuit of long-term, indeterminate ends. These are ends that cannot be realized through a single momentary action, and whose content leaves partly open what counts as realizing the end. Sergio Tenenbaum argues that we need to focus on temporal duration and the indeterminacy of ends in intentional action, even to explain the rational governance of relatively simple actions. Theories of moment-by-moment preference maximization, or indeed any understanding of instrumental rationality on the basis of momentary mental items, cannot capture the fundamental structure of our instrumentally rational capacities. Tenenbaum provides a new theory of instrumental rationality as rationality in action.

Sergio Tenenbaum is Professor of Philosophy at the University of Toronto. He is the editor of *Desire, Practical Reason, and the Good: Classical and Contemporary Perspectives* (Oxford, 2010), and the author of *Appearances of the Good: An Essay on the Nature of Practical Reason* (Cambridge, 2007) as well as numerous articles in ethics, practical rationality, moral psychology, and Kant's practical philosophy.

T0346926

Rational Powers in Action

*Instrumental Rationality
and Extended Agency*

SERGIO TENENBAUM

OXFORD
UNIVERSITY PRESS

Great Clarendon Street, Oxford, OX2 6DP,
United Kingdom

Oxford University Press is a department of the University of Oxford.
It furthers the University's objective of excellence in research, scholarship,
and education by publishing worldwide. Oxford is a registered trade mark of
Oxford University Press in the UK and in certain other countries

First published 2020
First published in paperback 2023

Published in the United States of America by Oxford University Press
198 Madison Avenue, New York, NY 10016, United States of America

British Library Cataloguing in Publication Data

Data available

Library of Congress Control Number: 2023936359

ISBN 978-0-19-888956-4

Printed and bound by
CPI Group (UK) Ltd, Croydon, CR0 4YY

Contents

Preface

While on the subway to work I space out and, before I know it, I've reached my destination. But there were many things I could have done between the time I boarded the subway and my final stop. At each moment, I could have chosen to grade a paper from my bag, or to read the fiction book that I downloaded to my tablet, or play some electronic games on my phone. There were also slight improvements that I could have made to my seating arrangements—I could have gone closer to the door, or away from the noise bleeding from my neighbour's headphones—improvements that I could have weighed against the inconvenience and effort of moving from one seat to another.

On many views of instrumental rationality, especially those that take orthodox decision theory as their starting point, my failure to consider these options, or at least to act on them if they would turn out to be preferable, shows that I have fallen short of ideal rationality. Of course, everyone will rush to add that given our limitations, we should not engage in trying to maximize utility at every moment; we're better off using heuristics, or tried and true strategies that allow us to approximate ideal decision making as much as possible given our limited rational capacities. On this view, an ideally (instrumentally) rational agent chooses the best option at each moment at which she acts. I argue in this book that this is a fundamentally flawed picture of rational agency given the structure of human action.

We are often (indeed, arguably always) engaged in actions that stretch through extended periods of time in the pursuit of less than fully determinate ends. This basic fact about our rational existence determines a structure of rational agency that is best captured not in terms of the evaluation of moment-by-moment choice, but rather by the (attempted) actualization of various ends through time. The point is not that, given the vicissitudes of the human condition (that it takes time to deliberate, that our calculating powers are modest, and so forth), it is too demanding to evaluate our choices in terms of moment-by-moment maximization of utility (let alone to enjoin agents to be explicitly guided by an ideal of moment-by-moment maximization). Rather, given the nature of *what* we pursue and *how* we pursue it, a theory of moment-by-moment maximization, or any understanding of instrumental rationality on the basis of momentary mental states, cannot capture the fundamental structure of our instrumentally rational capacities. Instrumental rationality is rationality *in action*, and, in particular, in action that extends through time.

The book aims to provide a systematic account of the nature of instrumentally rational agency in the pursuit of long-term, not fully determinate ends; that is, ends that cannot be realized through a single momentary action and whose content leaves partly open, at least to the agent herself, what counts as realizing the end. The restriction of the scope of the theory to these kinds of ends does not represent a significant narrowing down of the realm of rational agency; at least as far as human agents are concerned, most, if not all, of the cases in which someone exercises her capacity for rational agency are instances of rational agency in the temporally extended pursuit of indeterminate ends.

Chapter 1 presents what I take to be the general structure of a theory of instrumental rationality, and lays down some of the main ideas and motivations for the extended theory of instrumental rationality (ETR) developed in the book. I characterize the content of a theory of instrumental rationality in terms of its given attitudes (the "inputs" for a theory of instrumental rationality), its principles of coherence, its principles of derivation, and what counts as the conclusion of practical reasoning or the exercise of our powers of instrumental rationality (what the theory of instrumental rationality takes to be the "outputs" of practical reasoning). I then provide a way of distinguishing the domain of instrumental practical rationality from the domain of substantive practical rationality. Chapter 2 starts presenting the main tenets of, and the initial motivation for, ETR. According to ETR, both the given attitudes ("inputs") and the conclusion of practical reasoning ("outputs") are actions (more particularly, the intentional pursuit of ends). The principle of instrumental reasoning, which tells us (roughly) to adopt means to our ends, is the only principle of derivation, and a principle (roughly) requiring agents not to pursue incompatible ends is the only principle of coherence. The chapter also presents one of the main theses of ETR; namely that the rationality of an agent through an interval t_1-t_n does not supervene on the rationality of the agent at each moment t_1-t_n (what I call the "non-supervenience thesis"). In other words, someone may be irrational over a period of time without there being any moment during that time at which they were irrational. The main contrast to ETR in Chapter 2 is with a version of orthodox decision theory; contrasting the view this way helps us understand some of the most important potential advantages of ETR.

Chapter 3 continues developing ETR, and starts the proper positive argument for the theory. ETR takes the intentional pursuit of ends to be the only relevant attitude for the theory of instrumental rationality, and takes the principle of instrumental reasoning to be the only principle of derivation. However, isn't practical rationality essentially comparative? Doesn't a rational agent choose the *best* alternative among a set of options? In particular, it seems that if the agent has more than one end, we'll need to introduce comparative or graded attitudes, such as the preference orderings in orthodox decision theory, in order to explain the rationality of her choices in contexts in which the agent needs to choose among competing ends. The chapter argues that the lack of comparative or graded attitudes does not prevent ETR from providing an adequate account of rational agency in contexts in which an agent has multiple ends that can be distinctly pursued through different actions. In fact, ETR does better than theories that rely on comparative and graded attitudes in accounting for the fact that, given our pursuit of indeterminate ends through time, in many, if not most, situations, there is no "best" option. I argue that in these situations our only option is to "satisfice". At the same time, the chapter explains how some comparative attitudes, such as preferences, can be incorporated into ETR in specific contexts.

Chapter 4 looks at Quinn's puzzle of the rational self-torturer in order to establish the truth of the non-supervenience thesis. The puzzle presents, in a rather simple and stark way, a structure that pervades our pursuit of ends through time. I argue that that a proper solution for the puzzle (and thus a proper account of instrumental rationality that applies to extended action) must accept the non-supervenience thesis. But given that long-term actions are pursued through momentary actions, we need to understand how the agent's *extended perspective* (the perspective of the pursuit of long-term ends) and the agent's *punctate perspective* (the perspective of the pursuit of momentary actions) interact in realizing the agent's indeterminate ends. This chapter presents ETR's account of this interaction. Since extant theories of instrumental rationality cannot do justice to the non-supervenience thesis, and a fortiori, to the structure of agency illustrated in the puzzle of the rational self-torturer, this chapter represents an important argument in favour of ETR.

Chapters 5 and 6 consider whether introducing future-directed intentions in our account of instrumental rationality can do a better job than (or at least complement) ETR in accounting for extended agency. Work on the relevance of future-directed intentions to rationality would seem particularly promising in this context, as future-directed intentions are often introduced exactly to do justice to the temporally extended nature of our agency. I argue in these chapters that attempts to rely on future-directed intentions can do no better than ETR in explaining rational agency through time and often end up generating spurious requirements. I argue that these theories try to understand the structure of rational agency through time as a *diachronic* structure rather than a properly *extended* structure, and therefore these attempts are bound to fail.

Most theories of rationality take it for granted that rationality is always a matter of conformity to certain principles, or responding to reasons. In Chapters 7 and 8 I argue that (non-trivial) principles of rationality cannot fully capture the nature of our instrumentally rational powers. There are also what I call "instrumental virtues". An agent suffers a defect of rationality insofar as she fails to have one of these virtues, or insofar as she manifests one of its corresponding vices. However, an agent can manifest instrumental vices without violating any principle of rationality. Chapter 7 proposes that courage is one of the instrumental virtues, and shows how one of its corresponding vices, cowardice, must be understood as a defect of our rational powers. Chapter 8 argues that ETR gives us the tools to account for an overlooked instrumental virtue, which I call "practical judgment". An agent exhibits the virtue of practical judgment insofar as she can pursue long-term ends without relying too much on restrictive implementation policies. The account also allows us to understand ordinary phenomena such as procrastination as manifestations of practical judgment's corresponding vices.

Chapters 1 through 8 proceeded mostly assuming that the agent has all the relevant background knowledge that she needs to pursue her ends. But this raises the question of whether the theory can be extended to contexts of risk and uncertainty. This is particularly important given that orthodox decision theory provides a powerful account of the rationality of choice under risk. Chapter 9 argues that ETR can provide a satisfactory account of rationality in these contexts and that it can actually co-opt the resources of decision theory exactly in the cases in which the theory seems most plausible; namely, the pursuit of what I call "general means" (such as the pursuit of health or wealth). Moreover ETR plausibly renders coherent certain ubiquitous choice dispositions that seem incompatible with orthodox decision theory.

Many people have helped me in the course of writing the book and developing these ideas; many more than I can presently name. But I would certainly like to thank for their invaluable feedback, Chrisoula Andreou,

David Barnett, Christian Barry, Michael Bratman, Mark Budolfson, Ruth Chang, Philip Clark, Brendan de Kenessey, Matthias Haase, David Horst, David Hunter, Thomas Hurka, Douglas Lavin, Erasmus Mayr, Julia Nefsky, Sarah Paul, Juan Piñeros Glasscock, Douglas Portmore, Diana Raffman, Arthur Ripstein, Karl Schafer, Michael Thompson, Benjamin Wald, and Jonathan Weisberg. Alice Pinheiro Walla organized a workshop at Bayreuth for the book manuscript that not only pushed me to complete a draft of it, but also made me rethink many of the ideas of the book. I am immensely grateful to her and the other commentators at the workshop: Franz Altner, Luca Ferrero, Erasmus Mayr, and Franziska Poprawe. Luca Ferrero and Jonathan Way refereed the manuscript for OUP, and their thoughtful and insightful comments made me rethink many of the book's arguments, and greatly helped making them clearer, and hopefully, more compelling. Peter Momtchiloff at OUP was amazingly supportive and helpful through the entire process. I feel truly fortunate to have worked with him.

Many ideas of the book were developed and discussed in the annual workshop meetings of the Practical Thought and Good Action Network (later Action Network). These events were models of philosophical discussion and interaction, and I greatly benefitted from all our meetings. I would like to thank all participants and especially Matthias Haase, who kept the network going throughout the years.

I started worked on the book in the 2011–12 academic year. I received a fellowship for the Institute for Advanced Studies at the Hebrew University of Jerusalem for the Fall term of 2011, and I was a fellow at Magdalen College at Oxford University during the Trinity term in 2012. I made the final substantive revisions during the Summer and Fall of 2019, when I was a Research Fellow at the Australian National University (Summer) and received a fellowship from the Jackman Humanities Institute at the University of Toronto (Fall). The research on this book was also made possible by grants from the Social Science and Humanities Research Council of Canada (SSHRC). I am very grateful to all these institutions for their generous support.

Earlier versions of some of the material in this book has appeared elsewhere. An earlier version of parts of Chapter 3 appeared as "Acting and Satisficing" in *Legal Normativity and the Philosophy of Practical Reason*, edited by Georgios Pavlakos and Veronica Rodriguez-Blanco (Cambridge University Press, 2015), 31–51. Earlier versions of Chapter 4 appeared as "Vague Projects and the Puzzle of the Self-Torturer" (with Diana Raffman), *Ethics* 123 (October 2012): 86–112. An earlier version of Chapter 5 appeared as "Reconsidering Intention", *Noûs* 52 (June 2018): 443–72. An earlier version of Chapter 6 (except for Section 6.5) appeared as "Minimalism about Action: A Modest Defence", *Inquiry* (special issue on Choice Over Time) 57 (April 2014): 384–411; an earlier version of Section 6.5 appeared as "Self-Governance Over Time", *Inquiry* (September 2019): 1–12. Finally, an earlier version of parts of Chapter 8 appeared as "The Vice of Procrastination" in Chrisoula Andreou and Mark White (eds), *The Thief of Time* (Oxford University Press, 2010), 130–50. I am very grateful to the feedback provided by all of those I have mentioned in these publications. I would also like to thank here the various audiences that provided invaluable help with various versions of "Instrumental Virtues and Instrumental Rationality", which makes up the bulk of Chapter 7 and has not previously appeared in print: the material there was greatly improved by the feedback I received from audiences at Australian National University, Florida State University, the Halbert Network Meeting at the Hebrew University of Jerusalem, Universidade de Caxias do Sul, University of Michigan, the Workshop on Normativity and Reasoning at NYU, Abu Dhabi, and my commentator on this occasion, Eric Wiland.

My sons, Alexander Tenenbaum and Leonardo Tenenbaum, have put up with their father asking them bizarre questions about practical rationality on way too many occasions. People unavoidably judge their children to be exceptionally wonderful human beings, and I feel so fortunate that in my case this is actually true. My greatest debt is without a doubt to Jennifer Nagel. If any thought in this book is worth anything, it is because it has been improved beyond recognition through Jennifer's incomparable wisdom (and patience!). Moreover, if you write about ideal agency, it cannot but help to live with someone who so closely approaches this standard.

1

Extended Action and Instrumental Rationality

The Structure of a Theory of Instrumental Rationality

1.0 Introduction

The aim of this book is to provide a systematic account, or at least the beginnings of a systematic account, of the nature of instrumentally rational agency in the pursuit of long-term, not fully determinate ends; that is, ends that cannot be realized through a single momentary action and whose representation leaves partly open, at least to the agent herself, what counts as realizing the end.[1] The restriction of the scope of the theory to these kinds of ends does not represent a significant narrowing down of the realm of rational agency that it covers. Nearly all, and arguably all, of the cases in which human agents exercise their capacity for rational agency are instances of rational agency in the pursuit of indeterminate ends through an extended period of time. Thus the more ambitious aim is to provide a theory that encompasses the entire domain of instrumental practical rationality, or, more precisely (and moderating the ambition somewhat), a theory of the basic foundations of instrumental practical rationality.

Suppose, for instance, today is Monday and I am engaged in making the house look nice for a visit from my aunt, who will be arriving some time Wednesday afternoon. My having this end leaves various things indeterminate. Should I hang paintings on the wall, or put flowers at her bedside, or both? At some point, I might form a more determinate conception of what counts as making the house nice for my aunt, but it seems that I can

---

[1] Of course, this is not supposed to be a very precise characterization of these notions. I'll start by relying on an intuitive understanding of these notions, and try to provide more precise characterizations as the book progresses.

have the end of making the house look nice for my aunt without having settled this question. Similarly, what counts as achieving this end can be vague in many ways. How nice is nice enough for my aunt? If there is a small corner of my bedroom that has some dust in it, does it count as being nice enough? How much dust in the house will be enough to determine that the house is not nice? At precisely what time should everything be ready?

Moreover I can't just make the house look nice in one magical momentary twitch of my nose. I have to engage in various actions at some point between now and Wednesday afternoon, but there are (almost) no specific points in time at which I will be presented with a precise set of options such that I must choose a certain alternative if I am to make the house nice for my aunt. Everything (or at least nearly everything) I do could have been done slightly later, with slightly less effort, and so forth. Given these facts about the indeterminacy of my project and the way it stretches over time, what exactly am I rationally required to do at various moments or intervals in light of this project? How do the requirements generated by this end interact with requirements generated by other ends that I am pursuing at the same time (I am also writing a book, I need to teach Tuesday evening and be prepared for it, etc.)? What would be the virtues of character of ideally rational agents (and what would be the corresponding vices in less ideal agents) who can efficiently pursue ends of this kind?[2] This book will try to answer these questions and related ones.

On the view I defend here, instrumental rationality is, roughly, a relation between intentional actions. More specifically, it is the relation of the pursuit of some actions as a means and the intentional pursuit of an *indeterminate* end *extended through time*, in which the latter explains the former in a particular way. So my writing this sentence is a means to the intentional pursuit of writing this book, while writing a book (and also writing this sentence) is something that I pursue over an extended period of time. Moreover, the end of writing a book is indeterminate; in pursuing the end of writing a book, I do not (necessarily) specify the precise quality, length, or completion time, even though not all combinations of quality, length, and completion

---

[2] It is worth noting that indeterminate ends are not like "gaps" in a preference ordering. Gaps seem to imply that there's something missing there; an agent with a complete preference ordering has, as it were, made up her conative mind about a larger number of things than the agent with gaps in her preference ordering. But there's nothing missing in an indeterminate end; though we can talk about acceptable and non-acceptable determinations of an indeterminate end (and, as we will soon see, distinguish different ways of specifying the end), a determinate end is a different end, not a more "complete" one.

times are acceptable realizations of my end.[3] Note also that "pursuing an end" is not essentially graded or comparative. That is, pursuing an end does not come essentially in degrees. You do not pursue an end to a greater or lesser extent; you are either pursuing it or not. Or at least, I will not rely on any assumptions that ends are pursued to different extents; if there is sense to be made of the idea of "graded pursuits", it will be irrelevant for our theory. In contrast, on some views of beliefs and desires, beliefs and desires come in degrees, and the theory of rationality depends not only on the content of these attitudes, but also on their degrees. Similarly, the central category for my theory is "pursuing the end E", rather than "pursuing an end E^* to a greater extent than $E^\#$" or "pursuing and end E^* over $E^\#$". In contrast, a number of extant theories of rationality give attitudes that are essentially comparative, such as preferences, a starring role.

More specifically, the opposing views take instrumental rationality to depend on (i) comparative or graded attitudes, and to concern (ii) relations between mental states that are (iii) momentary, and (iv) whose objects are, in the relevant way, determinate. Not all opposing views need to accept all four parts of this claim. I'll start in the first two chapters contrasting the theory I'll develop here, the extended theory of rationality (ETR), with orthodox decision theory. Orthodox decision theory is obviously an important and influential view, but, more importantly for our purposes, it contrasts *in all these aspects* with ETR, and so it is an ideal contrast with the theory.[4]

In Section 1.1 I give a very rough outline of the contrast between orthodox decision theory and ETR, as well as some initial motivation for ETR, focusing on the contrasts marked as (iii) and (iv).[5] After this initial contrast, I move on to more structural questions. Sections 1.2, 1.3, and 1.4 introduce some important terminology and develop a general understanding of what a theory of instrumental rationality is. Section 1.2 aims to develop a neutral framework that can be used to compare and contrast different theories of instrumental rationality. Section 1.3 then puts forward some basic criteria for evaluating theories of instrumental

---

[3] More on the notion of "acceptable realization" below.

[4] Not all versions of decision theory fall into the category of a theory of instrumental rationality as I understand it here. So not all of them compete with ETR. More on this point below.

[5] The contrast with (i) is discussed in more detail in Chapter 3 and (ii) in Chapters 4 and 5. Of course, since the book aims to give an account of instrumental rationality that generalizes to extended actions with indeterminate ends, the contrast with positions that accept (iii) or (iv) is discussed throughout the book.

rationality. Finally, Section 1.4 proposes an explanation of the difference between instrumental rationality and "substantive" rationality.

My approach to the theory of instrumental rationality is in some ways different from a number of contemporary approaches to the theory of instrumental rationality, so it is worth saying a few words about it at the outset.[6] There has been a flurry of recent work on "coherence" and "structural" requirements of rationality and the normativity of the principles of rationality.[7] Often, these philosophers will start with principles of coherence and ask questions about whether we have reason to conform to the principles, whether there's value in a disposition to conform with them, and so forth. My starting point is the idea that we have certain rational powers and capacities to act, and the theory of instrumental rationality is the theory of a subset of these powers. The principles of rationality are thus the principles that, in some sense, explain the agent's exercise of such powers. In the good case, a rational action is one that manifests this power. Cases of irrationality will be cases of failures to exercise the power, or improper exercises of the power. Of course, at this abstract level of description it is hard to see how this distinctive starting point makes a difference, and I hope the answer to this question becomes clearer as the book progresses. However, two points are worth noting. First, although questions about the normativity and the value of rationality are important, they are not the only ones. I think much is missed about the nature of instrumental rationality if we focus mostly on these questions, and taking the question about the nature of a rational power as our starting point allows us to circumvent these issues. This is, of course, a methodological point. There is no commitment here that the same views would not be accessible if we were to start somewhere else. Conversely, insofar as this book yields insights about the nature of instrumental rational agency, we have good reason to accept that taking rational powers or capacities as our starting point is a fruitful line of inquiry.

Second, understanding rational agency in this way helps identify the kind of theory of rationality that I am proposing here. There are different types of theories of rationality. One can have a purely "evaluative" theory whose principles simply evaluate actions or mental states of the agent as rational or irrational, while making no claims about whether an agent is, or ought to be, guided by such principles. That is, the theory only speaks about

---

[6] More on this approach in Section 1.4.

[7] For a few recent examples of book-length works in this tradition, see Broome (2013), Kiesewetter (2017), Wedgwood (2017), Lord (2018), and Brunero (forthcoming).

principles *in accordance* with which a rational agent should form a mental state or act, but makes no claim about principles *from* which a rational agent ought to form a mental state or act. Though more common in economics, theories of rationality can also be purely descriptive: they can aim simply to explain human behaviour on the assumption that people by and large act rationally. Finally, a theory of rationality can be "action guiding". Such a theory tries to describe the principles *from which the agent acts* insofar as the agent is rational.[8] Since my interest is a theory that explains what it is to manifest these particular rational powers, it seems clear that the project falls roughly within the third type of theory of rationality. However, it is importantly related to the second: in the "good" case in which the agent's exercise of her rational powers is flawless, the theory of rationality provides also the *explanation* of the agent's behaviour. When a rational agent, for instance, believes *Fa* because she believes *(x)Fx*, the fact that *Fa* follows from *(x)Fx* fully explains the agent's belief, and Universal Instantiation is the specific principle that explains why the agent believes *Fa* (together with the known fact that *(x)Fx*). And, similarly, cases of irrationality will be cases in which the agent failed to manifest this power when she could or when the manifestation was in some way defective (that is, when the resulting belief or other attitude cannot be fully explained in terms of the manifestation of a causal power).[9] Here too the choice is methodological. I'll not try to defend this conception of rationality in any detail;[10] it'll prove its value if it produces new insights in the theory of instrumental rationality.

1.1 Indeterminate and Long-Term Ends

During my morning subway ride, I was just daydreaming. But there were so many things I could have done between the time I got on the subway and the final stop. At each moment, I could have chosen to read a paper from my bag (which one? I brought my colleague's book draft on Thales' moral theory, the latest issue of *The Philosophical Journal*, and a student paper on Eurovision aesthetics). I could have read the fiction book that I downloaded to my tablet—although the tablet also had some electronic games that I

---

[8] See Bermúdez (2009) for a similar classification in the case of decision theory.
[9] See Marcus (2012) for a very interesting attempt to provide an explanatory theory of action and belief in terms of rational abilities and their manifestations.
[10] However, a possible advantage of this approach, given what I said above, is that it has the potential to provide the tools for unifying evaluative and explanatory theories of rationality.

could have been playing without feeling guilty about engaging in this vice during work hours. Between the third and fourth stop, there was a chance to glance over the headlines of the newspaper that the person in front of me was reading, and between the fourth and the fifth stop I could have struck up a conversation with the intelligent-looking fellow seated to my left. If I decided to start a conversation, there were many ways I could have proceeded: I could have started with the weather, or taken his baseball hat as a lead to talk about our hopes for the Blue Jays, or just dared to express my discontent with our current mayor. Moreover, I chose not to make stops, but this was not necessary; I have a subway pass and it would have cost me nothing to just get out at the first stop to buy bread at that lovely bakery, or to acquire some cheap comic books at the used bookstore at the second stop, or to get an espresso and reply to a few emails at a Groundless Grounds franchise at each station. It is not clear that any of these stops would compensate for the twelve-minute reduction in my planned eight-hour-and-six-minute workday, but I never even considered them.

Does my failure to consider these options, or at least to act on them if they would turn out to be preferable, really show that I have fallen short of ideal rationality?[11] Of course, everyone will rush to add that given our limitations, we should not engage in trying to maximize utility at every moment; we're better off using heuristics, or tried and true strategies that allow us to approximate ideal decision making as much as possible given our pathetically feeble rational capacities. Yet, we might ask in what sense and why this is an ideal of rationality. Let us say that the Vulcans realize this ideal; a Vulcan, say, always has a preference ordering that conforms with the axioms of decision theory, her choices always conform to these preferences, and her preferences have all the bells and whistles we'd want from a preference set (they are considered, well-informed, etc.). Why are the Vulcans more ideal than I am, at least as far as my subway ride is concerned (doubtless we'd find much to deride in my employment of my rational capacities in other parts of my life)?

One answer would be that they actualize more value, or respond better to reasons, than I do. This answer might be correct (though I don't think so, or at least not necessarily so), but examining this type of answer is outside the

---

[11] This claim (and some of what I say below) needs very many caveats. There are many interpretations of decision theory and its relation to normative theory. I discuss these issues in greater detail later in the chapter, so for now I offer the bold, though vague and possibly imprecise, unmodified claim.

scope of this book. It pertains to the *substantive* rationality of the Vulcans, rather than their *instrumental* rationality. I'll discuss in greater detail below what counts as instrumental rationality, but for now, we can say that this alleged greater realization of value is not a difference in how the Vulcans succeed in realizing what they care about or what they're trying to achieve; instead, it is a question about whether the Vulcans are pursuing the right thing. But even within the realm of instrumental rationality, it might seem obvious that the Vulcans are doing better: after all, they follow their preferences, and thus they expect to do better even when we take their own attitudes as the standard. In my subway trip I often failed to pursue my most preferred option, and thus to choose what I most wanted. So have I not failed by my own lights?[12]

However, this thought makes two assumptions, neither of which I think is ultimately correct. First, it assumes that I have the relevant preferences. It is rather implausible that I have determinate preferences for each possible choice situation that I can concoct. But, more importantly, I will argue that it is not true that an instrumentally rational agent always chooses the most preferred option. The main reason for this conclusion is that we often (arguably always) are engaged in actions that extend through arbitrarily long periods of time in the pursuit of less than fully determinate ends. This basic fact about our rational existence determines a structure of rational agency that is not best captured in terms of moment-by-moment choice, but rather by the (attempted) actualization of various ends through time. This structure will often permit, and at some level require, that sometimes I choose a less preferred option over a more preferred one. As we will see in Chapter 4, the point is not that given the limitations of the human condition (that it takes time to deliberate, that our calculating powers are modest, and so forth) it is too demanding to evaluate our choices in terms of moment-by-moment maximization of utility (let alone to enjoin agents to be explicitly guided by an ideal of moment-by-moment maximization). But rather given the nature of *what* we pursue and *how* we pursue it, a theory of moment-by-moment maximization cannot capture the fundamental structure of our instrumentally rational capacities. Roughly, my subway ride is rational, or as I prefer to say, an expression of my rational powers, because through this extended action I have non-accidentally actualized one of my ends (my arriving at work in time) without undermining any other end of mine.

---

[12] To paraphrase Donald Davidson, I'd be losing by my own standards. See Davidson (1980b), p. 268.

Questions of moment-by-moment maximization do not even come up in accounting for my rational agency in this case. As will become clear later in the book, this is not to say that preferences and decision theory play no role in our understanding of instrumental rationality. Given the structure of some of our ends, and of some general means we use to pursue them, preference orderings will have an important role to play, even if a much more specialized and subordinate role than often assumed in the theory of instrumental rationality.

For orthodox decision theory, ideal rational agents have no indeterminate ends (preferences),[13] and the rationality of their long-term actions supervenes on the rationality of their momentary decisions.[14] The axioms of orthodox decision theory[15] guarantee that nothing relevant to one's rational choice is left indeterminate. Second, orthodox decision theory takes the rationality of actions that require the exercise of agency through time to be determined by the rationality of each momentary choice; the extended action is rational if and only if each momentary decision maximizes utility. This is not to say that, on this view, our extended plans and ends play no role in our decision, but their role is exhausted by their contribution to the expected utility of each of the momentary choices that I make. As Paul Weirich puts it,

> A wide variety of acts, such as swimming the English Channel, take more than a moment to complete...How does the principle of optimization address such acts? It does not compare the extended acts to alternative extended acts. Instead, it recommends an extended act only if each step in its execution is an optimal momentary act. Swimming the English Channel is recommended only if starting, continuing moment by moment, and finishing are all optimal.   (Weirich (2004), p. 18)[16]

---

[13] And for other theories as well, especially those that modify in some way or another orthodox decision theory. But focusing on orthodox decision theory has the advantage of letting us engage with a very clear and simple model.

[14] More on these commitments of orthodox decision theory below.

[15] For example, the axiom of continuity and the axiom of completeness, axioms that, roughly, require that the agent has an attitude of preference or indifference for any two possible options. More on these axioms below.

[16] For an interesting, similar idea in a different context, see Portmore's defence of maximalism in Portmore (2019) (especially chapter 4). For Portmore the evaluation of the extended action is prior to the evaluation of the momentary actions, but a similar biconditional still holds.

However, these two points express assumptions that are far from obvious. The assumption that rationality requires a complete ordering finds few adherents. Even philosophers who are sympathetic to normative versions of decision theory tend to reject the claim that ideal rational agents must satisfy the axioms, such as the axiom of continuity and the axiom of completeness.[17] Indeed why should fully determinate preference ordering, or fully determinate ends, be a condition of instrumentally rational agency? As Cindy Lauper has wisely pointed out, sometimes rational agents (or at least some rational agents) might "just wanna have fun", and it is not clear that this end requires a determinate conception of what counts as fun. The assumption that principles of rationality apply primarily or fundamentally to momentary actions has been mostly taken for granted in the philosophical literature,[18] but it is far from intuitively obvious. If my ends extend through time ("having swum the English Channel") and are pursued through means that extend through time ("swimming through the English Channel"), why would the rationality of these pursuits reduce to moment-by-moment decisions? Of course, these rhetorical questions are not a proper argument against these assumptions and quite a great deal of the book will try to present a compelling picture of instrumental rationality that does not depend on these assumptions. But it might be worth keeping in mind that instrumental rationality should, by its very nature, make as few substantive assumptions as possible. It leaves such assumptions to a theory of substantive rationality (if there is such a thing) and only looks at what a rational agent must pursue given what the agent is either already inclined to pursue, or committed to pursue, or simply pursuing.

1.2 What is a Theory of Instrumental Rationality?

The awkward disjunction at the end of the last sentence in the previous section is a symptom of a more general difficulty in understanding the subject matter of a theory of instrumental rationality. In a traditional conception, instrumental rationality was understood in terms of the principle of instrumental reasoning, a principle which connects ends with means. Having ends and taking means can be understood as certain kinds of mental states

---

[17] See, for instance, Joyce (1999) and Weirich (2004) itself.
[18] In fact, even Weirich's explicit acceptance of the assumption is relatively rare. Most of the time, the assumption is not even mentioned.

(intentions), activities (willings), or even kinds of actions (intentional actions). Such conceptions, however, might seem quaint and antiquated to our post-von Neumann and Morgenstern gaze. A conception of instrumental rationality as utility maximization is one in which one kind of mental state (preference) relates to another kind of mental state (choice); such a conception underlies the remarkably fruitful orthodox decision theory of von Neumann and Morgenstern (2007) and Savage (1972).

Traditional and contemporary theories not only have different conceptions of the entities that are relevant to a theory of instrumental rationality but, under certain understandings of the former, they might disagree even about the ontological type of the entities in question. Although some philosophers view decision theory as a theory about how the agent effectively pursues her ends, the notion of an "end" does not appear in the theory; neither utility nor preferences map unobtrusively into the notion of an end. It would thus be helpful if there were some general way to characterize instrumental rationality that is neutral between these various versions. What I propose below is a rough way of doing this. I'll not try to say much in defence of this framework, as I only intend it to be a useful way of capturing a wide array of different views under the same rubric of a theory of instrumental rationality. I doubt that any of the arguments of this book will depend on this particular framework.[19]

Let us start with an ideally (instrumentally)[20] rational agent. Our ideal rational agent must be finite. After all, God does not take means to ends or need to make choices in light of her preferences; God's representation of the ideal world directly causes it. Our ideal rational agent will have some representational attitudes[21] that will cause or explain[22] her actions. Among these attitudes that can cause the agent to act, there will be kinds of representational

---

[19] Of course, someone might disagree that orthodox decision theory and the principle of instrumental reasoning even share a subject matter. Hampton (1998) makes a suggestion along these general lines. Even this position is compatible with the aims of the book, however, since the arguments of the book ultimately don't depend on the assumption that they share a subject matter. For a view on the relation between the axioms of decision theory and the means–end principle that clearly implies that they do share a subject matter, see Nozick (1994). At any rate, not only do I believe that it is implausible to reject this assumption, I also think that it makes for much easier presentation to accept it.

[20] I will often drop the qualifier "instrumental" (and related qualifiers) when the context makes it clear that we are talking about instrumental rationality.

[21] I'll try to avoid talking about "propositional" attitudes as I do not want to take a stand on whether the attitudes in question take a proposition as their content. But they'll have *some* representational content.

[22] I am not committing myself to causalism here (the "cause" in question need not be efficient cause).

attitudes that are such that they always motivate an agent insofar as she is instrumentally rational. In other words, a rational agent will make the content of these attitudes actual if it is within her power to make it actual and nothing interferes (possible interferences include adverse conditions, ignorance and error, or simply the existence of other attitudes of this kind with incompatible contents). Let us call these attitudes "motivationally efficacious representational attitudes", or just "efficacious attitudes". An intention, for instance, would be a candidate for this kind of attitude. A rational agent would make the content of her intention actual if nothing interferes, and so forth. Among motivationally efficacious attitudes, there will be some that are, from the point of view of instrumental rationality, given or basic (I'll call them just "given attitudes" or "basic given attitudes"). The given attitudes provide, in some way, the standard of success for the theory and are not subject to direct evaluation in the theory of instrumental rationality. So if intending something (as an end) is the given attitude for a certain theory, then, first, the correct principle of rationality must be somehow connected to (the expectation of) making the end actual. Second, in itself, the fact that an agent intends an end is not a subject of evaluation for the instrumental theory of rationality. And as long as the object of intention is a coherent object to be made actual (it is not, for instance, a logically impossible object), the theory of instrumental rationality does not evaluate the intention as either rational or irrational.

Suppose desires are our given attitudes. In this case, the content of desire would provide a *basic standard of success* for the theory of rationality; when everything goes as well as possible,[23] the rational agent satisfies her desires. One can now have many reasons why desires provide this standard of correctness; one might have a Humean view of the relation between passion and reason, one might think that desires when working properly disclose what is valuable to us, and so forth. Other candidates for taking the role of given attitudes are preferences, (evaluative or practical) judgments, intentions, and intentional actions.[24] It is worth noting a few things: nothing I said commits us to accepting that a theory of instrumental rationality can allow for only one type of given attitude. A theory might allow multiple attitudes of this kind: arguably, philosophers who defend the importance of

---

[23] Of course, once we allow for the possibility of risk, rational agency cannot guarantee that things go as well as possible. In such cases, moving from the content of the given attitudes to what counts as success is significantly more complicated. But I'll ignore this complication except when I explicitly discuss cases of risk.

[24] This is not meant to be an exhaustive list.

future-directed intentions in a theory of instrumental rationality will accept that both preferences and intentions are given attitudes. On the other hand, we also do not rule out in advance the possibility that only members of a subset of attitudes count as given attitudes. So one might allow only informed preferences into our set of given attitudes, or only intentions for permissible ends. Such moves would rule that an agent could not count as instrumentally rational when responding to, respectively, misinformed preferences or evil intentions. This qualification is particularly important if one takes the principles of instrumental rationality to be "narrow scope",[25] in which case failing to limit their application in this way might have counterintuitive consequences. But it also makes it possible to allow for various principles proposed even by "myth theorists"[26] to constitute a theory of instrumental rationality. For we could allow that the given attitudes are "knowledge (justified beliefs) about reasons", as long as the "facilitative principles" proposed by philosophers like Raz (2005) and Kolodny (2018) imply similar principles governing how an agent correctly responds to facts that stand in instrumental relations to the reasons they have. An instrumentally rational agent, on such a view, would be one who responds to the reasons they know (justifiably believe) in accordance with (or based on) the Facilitative Principle.[27]

Finally, one might object to the inclusion of intentional action[28] as a possible given attitude; after all, intentional actions are not usually regarded as attitudes. Since this is the view I favour, I should say a few words about it. It is certainly correct that intentional action is an event or process in the external world.[29] However, what constitutes it as an intentional action is in

---

[25] For discussion of the scope of the principle of instrumental reasoning, see, among many others, Greenspan (1975), Broome (1999).

[26] Kolodny (2005, 2007), Raz (2005).

[27] A similar formulation could be given by using Lord (2018)'s conception of a possessed reason.

[28] I'll often just refer to "action" as opposed to "intentional action". Hyman (2015) warns that philosophers run together the distinctions between action and non-action, voluntary and involuntary, and intentional and non-intentional, but I'm not sure that this is entirely fair (for an earlier careful discussion with some of these issues, see Anscombe (2005)). At any rate, my usage will be restricted to cases in which the action (or refraining, or omission) is a manifestation of our will, considered as a rational faculty (although I agree with Kant that the "will is nothing but practical reason" (Kant (1996), Ak. 6: 412), alignment to the party line is unnecessary for the argument of the book). In the language we are about to develop, what matters for our purposes is that the relevant attitude is the outcome of the exercise of (or failure to exercise) the relevant rational powers relative to a given attitude.

[29] I am not settling the issue about the correct ontological category of actions, though a view of actions as processes is more congenial to the view I defend here. See Steward (2012).

part, on any view, a representation of the agent's. On Davidson's view (Davidson 1980a), these are beliefs and desires that predate the action, and on some Davidsonian views, intentional actions are constituted by certain mental states that causally sustain the action.[30] On an Anscombean view,[31] practical knowledge, understood as the agent's knowledge of what she is doing and why, is constitutive of intentional action. On a more classical view, animal action in general is the effect of the action's representation in the faculty of desire,[32] and at least in some of these views, rational action in particular is determined by an attitude that represents the action as good.[33] Although in the Anscombean view, intentional action parallels most clearly the structure of other propositional (or contentful)[34] attitudes, all these views accept that intentional actions share with mental attitudes an important feature for our purposes: they create opaque contexts that track the agent's point of view; what the agent does intentionally depends on the agent's perspective on the action. I cannot be intentionally ϕ-ing if the fact that I am ϕ-ing is in no way available to my mind.[35] This is just Anscombe's (later endorsed by Davidson) classic observation that actions are intentional only under a description[36] (and that the correct description depends on the agent's point of view).

A theory of instrumental rationality also needs to identify what counts as an exercise of the relevant practical capacity, or more generally it needs to specify the nature of the practical capacity it governs. If God desires light, that very representation will assure that there is light; even the command "let there be light" seems an unnecessary adornment: at best, it is a kind gesture to less powerful beings like us who would otherwise fail to recognize light as the effect of divine judgment. But finitely rational beings cannot always bring things about merely by desiring, intending, representing as good, and so forth. Finite beings must (often) exercise some active power to make the content of their given attitudes actual,[37] and the business of a

---

[30] Setiya (2007, 2011).   [31] Anscombe (2000).

[32] "The **faculty of desire** is a being's faculty to be by means of its representations the cause of the reality of the objects of these representations" (Kant (1996), 5:9n).

[33] "It is an old formula of the schools, *nihil appetimus, nisi sub ratione boni . . .* [This] proposition . . . if it is rendered: we will nothing under the direction of reason except insofar as we hold it to be good . . . is indubitably certain" (Kant (1996), 5:59–60).

[34] This clause allows for views in which the content of the attitude is not a proposition.

[35] This is much weaker than the "belief" condition on intentional action; namely, that I can only ϕ intentionally if I believe I am ϕ-ing intentionally.

[36] Anscombe (2000) and Davidson (1980a).

[37] On some conceptions of the given attitude they will themselves to be exercises of some active power (this will actually be the view proposed here). But even such views will need to

theory of instrumental rationality is to explain what counts as the proper exercise of (some of) these active powers. In orthodox decision theory, for instance, when outcomes are certain, an agent *chooses* the most preferred outcome (and more generally she *chooses* to maximize expected utility). In orthodox decision theory, the active power that is exercised is the power to choose. If "active powers" sounds too medieval, we might talk about dispositions and capacities, whose exercises are the proper objects of the principles of instrumental rationality. An agent is not instrumentally rational solely in virtue of the fact that, say, her desire to eat chicken soup for lunch gets satisfied. If this happens by the fortuitous and unexpected interference of her uncle who force-feeds her his famously delicious broth, her eating chicken soup is not the exercise of any rational capacity. For her to count as instrumentally rational, she must have prepared the soup, or invited her uncle over (knowing he'd bring the soup), or bought it from the store, or even just moved some chicken broth from the vicinity into her mouth; in sum, she must have exercised some capacity that she knew, or expected, would end up satisfying her desire to eat chicken soup.

It might seem obvious that the relevant active power or capacity is the capacity for voluntary action, and that instrumental rationality tells the agent that she should *do* something. Here, I'll try to argue that this apparently obvious view is also the correct one. However, far from being obvious, this view is implicitly rejected by most theories of instrumental rationality. As I said above, in standard decision theory, what counts as a practical exercise is a *choice* (or a similar state), not the action itself; more particularly, in most versions, a choice of a lottery. A choice is not, or at least not necessarily, a bodily action. Some believe that the conclusion of practical reasoning is an intention[38] or a decision,[39] and in such cases too, the relevant practical capacity will not be the capacity for voluntary action. Of course, one might think that this is an artificial distinction; these are, after all, *mental* actions. It is exactly due to their status as mental actions that they can be practical exercises; were they out of our control, there would be no sense of having them as the targets of our theory of instrumental rationality.

Doubtless, such states are candidates for practical exercises because we are not passive in relation to them. Still, many mental actions are significantly

---

postulate that sometimes further exercises of this or some other active power are necessary in order to make the content of the given attitude actual.

[38] Audi (1989), Paul (2013).   [39] Pollock (2006).

different from their bodily counterparts and it is worth keeping them apart in our taxonomy of theories of instrumental rationality. First, many kinds of mental actions need not be pursued by means of further actions. If I build a bridge, I do it by laying the bricks, mixing the cement, and so forth. Moreover in attempting to build a bridge, many things might go wrong. Many mental actions do not have this structure, and thus it is not clear that they are the same kind of act.[40] Of course, not all mental actions differ from bodily actions in this manner. Mental calculation, mental planning, and so forth seem to share these features with bodily actions, and the absence of bodily movements might be the only essential difference between these actions and intentional actions.[41] But decisions, intentions, choices, and so forth, the main candidates for non(bodily)-action causal powers, are not like that. In fact, their momentary nature and their impermeability to the vicissitudes of the external world is exactly what make them seem attractive as the main targets of our evaluation of the (instrumental) rationality of an agent.

For the purpose of proposing and evaluating a theory of instrumental rationality, we should think of intentional actions as primarily bodily actions. Many things can count as action on a broader sense of "action", which includes mental actions such as choice and intention. Beliefs, or at least (theoretical) judgments, are certainly candidates to be classified in this manner. But obviously beliefs should not count as the exercise of a *practically* rational power for the purpose of a theory of instrumental action. Rational belief is governed by the rules of epistemic, not practical, rationality.[42] And even in the cases in which mental actions look most like bodily actions, we have vexing questions about whether principles of instrumental rationality apply to them. As I do mental calculation, can I knowingly fail to take the necessary means to my end of calculating? Are there akratic mental planners, and those who fail to maximize utility in relation to their preferences regarding mental counting? I don't mean these questions as rhetorical questions; to my mind, these are genuinely difficult questions. So it seems a promising methodological choice to put them in a separate column from

---

[40] Boyle (2011) argues that beliefs etc. are within the genus of mental activity, but his view leaves it open whether mental acts are essentially different from bodily actions. For a similar view see Müller (1992). Peacocke (2007) argues that there is no important difference.

[41] If refraining is a degenerate case of bodily action, then even the absence of bodily movement is not a distinctive feature of such mental actions.

[42] Not all agree with this claim, but it is beyond the scope of the book to examine it. For a particularly radical dissenter, see Rinard (2017).

bodily intentional actions in our preliminary taxonomy of the basic categories available to a theory of instrumental rationality.

At any rate, it is uncontroversial that the principles of practical rationality should govern, directly or indirectly,[43] *at least* the bodily actions of the agent. And to the extent that someone chooses a mental act rather than the capacity for intentional action as the active power in question, it is likely because she thinks that the "movement" from this mental act to bodily action is no longer the manifestation of a rational capacity. Such a view might say, for instance, that although intentions are formed by employing our rational capacities, the *execution* of such intentions is not a matter of rationality. On such a view, the execution of an intention is a matter of skill or a causal process not under our rational control and thus not something that a theory of instrumental rationality should bother with. But this certainly represents a commitment that is worth marking explicitly; in particular, a commitment to the claim that practical rationality does not reach all the way down to, for instance, the movement of one's limbs. There seems to be in this position something analogous to the claim that the principles of rationality govern the formation of belief rather than the acquisition of knowledge. The idea on the theoretical side of the equator would be that the agent can, by her own powers, arrive at most at a justified belief, at least with regard to the external world. Whether it is knowledge or not depends on whether nature is in a cooperative mood.[44] On the practical side, the idea would be, similarly, that our rational powers extend only to our choices, decisions, or intentions. Once I formed a justified intention to go to the store, the job of practical reasoning and rationality is done; after this point, it is up to nature whether I actually reach the store, or I am struck by lightning, or I am tied down by anti-capitalist terrorists.[45]

A theory of instrumental rationality also needs to say something about the relation between the exercises of active powers (or "practical exercises" for short) and the given attitudes. In the simplest form, the practical exercises make actual the content of the given attitudes. For instance, on a view in which that practical exercises are the *choices* the agent makes, I would realize my intention to swim (given attitude) by choosing (practical exercise)

---

[43] Even philosophers who think that the principles of practical rationality govern, say, intentions, rather than intentional actions directly, still accept that in normal cases the action is rational or irrational insofar as the intention it executes is rational or irrational. See the discussion of the adequacy constraint below.

[44] See McDowell (1995) for a rejection of this picture on the theoretical side.

[45] See Broome (2013) for a version of this argument.

to swim. In the view that I will favour in this book, both the given attitudes and the practical exercises are actions; the given attitude will be in its more general form the intentional pursuit of an end. The relation will be a relation of "being means to", which includes both causal and constitutive means. So, for instance, the following would be an instance of (instrumentally) rational agency: I am putting my running shoes on as a means to going for a run. The relation between practical exercises and given attitudes is more complex in some theories. In orthodox decision theory the relation between my choice and preference ordering is not one of "making the content of the preference ordering actual", but, if anything, the realization of the greatest expected satisfaction. Still, the important point is that, in orthodox decision theory, the standard of success for choice is determined by one's preference ordering.

We can now say that a theory of instrumental rationality is a theory of the principles governing exercises of a (finite) rational agent's active powers in light of her given attitudes. There are at least two kinds of principles that a theory of instrumental rationality might have. First there will be *principles of coherence* among the (content of the) given attitudes. These principles determine which sets of given attitudes can be jointly rationally pursued, or which sets of given attitudes are possible for an ideally rational agent. A theory that takes intentions as the given attitudes might have a requirement that all one's intentions be jointly realizable. Second, a theory might have *principles of derivation*, principles that explain how the given attitudes determine the exercise of one's active powers. A principle that tells a rational agent to form an intention (practical exercise) to bring about the object of her strongest desire (given attitude) will be a principle of this kind.[46]

Some theories might have trivial principles of one kind (or none at all) and substantive principles only of the other kind. For orthodox decision theory, the substantive principles are all principles of coherence, principles that determine which preference sets can be represented by a utility function. If orthodox decision theory has a principle of derivation at all, it is simply the principle that says "choose so as to maximize expected utility".[47]

---

[46] Lately, philosophers often talk about requirements of "structural rationality" (see Scanlon (2007)) more generally, rather than just the principles of instrumental rationality. My focus on our rational powers makes this language not particularly suitable, but most of the requirements would have, arguably, correlates as either principles of derivation or principles of coherence. I discuss these issues in a bit more detail in Chapter 5.

[47] Even this principle will be dispensable in some versions of decision theory. If the preference ordering is determined by our choices, then there is no such principle. For a very helpful discussion, see Dreier (1996).

The view I favour, the classical theory of instrumental rationality, has one principle of each type, but the principle of coherence is to some extent a consequence of the principle of derivation. The principle of derivation says that a rational agent pursues all the necessary (and some sufficient)[48] means to her end. The principle of coherence forbids intentional actions with incompatible ends.[49] These are, of course, not unrelated. The pursuit of incompatible ends guarantees that at least for some of the ends you pursue, you'll not take sufficient means. Thus, in order to accept the principle of coherence, all we need to add is the assumption that an ideally rational agent will not have a set of given attitudes that makes it impossible for her to be guided by the principle of derivation in pursuing her ends.

Finally, by framing our issues in terms of the exercise of an agent's rational powers, we avoid difficult questions about how, or whether, rationality is normative, and various issues related to whether we have reasons to be rational. We are concerned in identifying among the agent's actions those that manifest a subset of the agent's rational powers, in particular, the agent's instrumental rational powers. This allows us also to look at various issues which might be overlooked on an exclusive focus on questions about normativity or rational requirements. For instance, if I right now decide to check my references as means to my end of writing my book, I am certainly exercising a rational power.[50] My preferred way of stating this is the following: in such a case I am acting on an efficient representation of checking my references as good for writing my book. Few will agree with this formulation, but the general idea should be relatively uncontroversial: such cases are instances of exercises of rational capacities. But obviously, I am not doing something that I am normatively *required to* do. And it is also not necessarily true that I am doing something that I have reason to do; whether this is true or not will depend at least on the question of whether I have reason to be writing my book. Moreover, an agent who fails to take some sufficient means to her ends fails in the exercise of a rational power, whether or not there is any reason to be rational. Ideally rational agents never fail to

---

[48] Given that "taking some sufficient means" is among the "necessary means" and that no means is sufficient if it does not also include all necessary means, mentioning both parts is redundant, but it makes for clearer presentation.

[49] Of course, you can have disjunctive ends ("go to Harvard or Michigan for Law school") or backup plans or conditional ends ("I'll try to get into Michigan Law School, but I'll apply to Harvard just in case it doesn't work out"). These are not cases of adopting incompatible ends.

[50] To make things simpler, I will assume that there is no end of mine that I am undermining in doing this.

exercise these powers at the right occasion in the right way, and thus at least a certain form of criticism applies to such an agent: the agent has fallen short of such an ideal. And, for this reason, we can also talk about violating "instrumental requirements" or "requirements of instrumental rationality" insofar as a certain agent fails to conform to principles that an ideally rational agent would. The significance of these criticisms and requirements, of course, might depend on answering questions about the normativity of rationality, but insofar as we want to understand the nature of instrumental rational agency, we can postpone this issue.[51] Similarly we can sidestep concerns about whether the principle should be understood as wide scope or narrow scope.[52]

The wide- and narrow-scope versions of the principle of instrumental rationality can be formulated roughly as follows:

WS [It ought to be the case that (If A intends end E and believes that E will be brought about only if A intends M, then A intends M).]

NS [(If A intends end E and believes that E will be brought about only if A intends M), then it ought to be the case that A intends M.]

There are well-known problems with both versions: NS seems to give us reason to pursue means towards ends we had no reason to adopt. WS, on the other hand, seems to allow for "upstream" revision; it allows me to resolve my inconsistency of not intending to board the plane that I take to be a necessary means to my end of going to Paris by revising my instrumental belief that I must board the plane in order to get to Paris. But focusing on a version of the principle of instrumental reasoning that is a manifestation of our instrumental rational powers in the way explained above circumvents this issue. Given that questions of normative assessment are secondary to the purpose of explaining the rational power, we need not settle on one of these formulations. But, more importantly, each possible change of

---

[51] My own view is that a proper understanding of what makes a power a rational power makes questions about the normativity of rationality at best secondary. See Tenenbaum (forthcoming).

[52] There is also a "medium"-scope view of the normative principle in which the instrumental belief clause is outside the scope of the "ought" operator, but the ought operator takes a wide scope with relation to the intention clauses ($B(e \rightarrow m) \rightarrow O(Ie \rightarrow Im)$). To my mind, this is the most plausible version of the principle. See Way (2009) for a defence of a similar medium-scope formulation of an instrumental requirement.

attitude receives a different treatment. Belief revision is never a manifestation of our instrumental rational powers; it is instead a manifestation of our contemplative rational powers. Revising the ends is the manifestation of this rational power in light of the realization that our ends are incompatible (in light of the principle of coherence). The principle of instrumental reasoning is our only principle of derivation and thus it applies only to the derivation of means through ends in the case in which we pursue the means *because* we are pursuing the end.

1.3 Brief Remarks on Evaluating Theories of Instrumental Rationality

This is doubtless a very abstract presentation of what theories of instrumental rationality are supposed to be; the main reason, again, to try to have such rough and abstract characterization is to help us understand how some radically different theories could have the same subject, as well as comparing the relative benefits and costs of various proposals. In this spirit, we can formulate three very general constraints on a theory of instrumental rationality:

(i) *The Dependency Constraint.* A theory of instrumental rationality is only concerned with criticisms of rational agents that depend on the agent's having certain given attitudes—an agent can fail to conform to requirements of instrumental rationality only in light of desires, preferences, ends, etc. that she has.

(ii) *The Toleration Constraint.* A theory of instrumental rationality puts no restriction on the content of given attitudes, except as those that are necessary for meeting the standard of success[53] of these representations as defined by the theory.

(iii) *The Adequacy Constraint.* A theory of instrumental rationality should determine which actions are instrumentally rational.

The two first conditions give us some general orientation on how to evaluate proposed theories of instrumental rationality; it will count against a theory of instrumental rationality if its demands threaten to violate

---

[53] See p. 11.

Dependence and Toleration. But it suggests a broader standard of comparison: a theory of instrumental rationality is interested in the coherence of various attitudes, and on what the attitudes and actions of an agent should be, given the other attitudes she has or the other actions she is undertaking. The more limits on how the basic attitudes can be coherently joined, the heavier the burden of justification that lies on the shoulders of advocates of the theory. If, for instance, a theory of rationality thinks that "trying to do two things at once" is incoherent, this is definitely a strike against the theory. After all, agents often seem to try and succeed to do two things at once (I have many witnesses who would attest to the fact that I can clap and wink at the same time), so this seems to be, if anything, a substantive principle of rationality (though probably a not very plausible one). Part of what I am going to argue is that many theories of rationality impose excessive restrictions on the nature of the given attitudes; their tolerance is significantly lower than the theory I'll put forward. In other words, they can only satisfy Tolerance by leaning heavily on the "except" clause.

Finally, the adequacy constraint might seem trivial but it is important to see that it is not. It is indeed trivially satisfied by the proposal if the theory takes the fundamental exercise of the rational capacity to be an intentional action. In the view I defend here, both the given attitude and the attitude that expresses the fundamental exercise of our rational powers are intentional actions; the fact that the view satisfies the adequacy constraint trivially turns out to be a significant advantage. For if our theory says that we exercise our rational power in *choosing* an option or *intending* an outcome or a state-of-affairs, there is a further question about whether the view can also say that some actions are rational or irrational; but ultimately the point of practical reasoning is to determine our *actions*, so if the theory cannot explain how it does this, then that theory fails in a rather significant way. Of course, one might argue that it is equally trivial for such views to explain the rationality of actions: actions are rational if performed according to a rational choice or if they are the effect of a rational intention or an action that was rationally chosen.

So, for instance, one could argue that if my intention to go to the dentist is a rational intention and my going to the dentist is the execution of this very intention, then the action is rational exactly in virtue of being the execution of a rational intention. However, on this view, the relation between my intention and my action is not a rational relation, or at least a relation of inference; it is nothing like the relation between, say, my intention to have my teeth fixed and my intention to go to the dentist. In the latter case, if I fail to form the intention of going to the dentist (at least if I know that I can only get my teeth fixed if I go to the dentist), then this failure should count as a failure of rationality. On the other hand, if I intend to go to the dentist, but trip on my way and die, or due to my poor sense of direction end up trapped in a spaceship that does not return until it's too late to fix my teeth, my failure to pursue the means to my end of getting my teeth fixed is *not* a rational failure. At a first glance this even seems like a rather plausible way to meet the adequacy constraint. But as we'll soon see, matters are not so simple and not all views that have mental states as basic given attitudes can meet this constraint.

1.4 The Division of Our Practically Rational Powers

Before we finish our presentation of the subject matter, it's worth trying to get a better grip on the distinction between instrumental and substantive rationality in the practical realm. Needless to say, not everyone will accept what I have to say about the nature of rationality and rational powers, but I hope that this way of drawing this distinction will be useful even for those who do not share some of the assumptions here.

The employment of practical rationality has a natural division into two parts. If we think the aim of the employment of this faculty is to act well or perform actions that are good, we can distinguish between what is intrinsically good and what is instrumentally good.[54] Practical reason thus needs to determine each of them, and it is incumbent upon philosophers to develop different theories of substantive and instrumental rationality. The division in these two parts seems natural for various reasons. First, it seems that agreement about what is instrumentally good is often possible despite large disagreements about what is intrinsically good. It is a difficult question whether one should aim to be rich and powerful, but whether or not we are of one mind on this issue there seems to be little room to disagree that *if* one has such an end, then choosing to be an average dogcatcher over an outstanding corporate lawyer is the wrong way to achieve it. Moreover, agents can exhibit different levels of competence in each area. Assuming that practical rationality enjoins us to be morally good, we know that people

---

[54] Although this formulation presupposes a (weak) version of the "guise of the good" thesis, I take it that the plausibility of this division of our rational powers is independent of any version of the "guise of the good" thesis.

who pursue the right ends are often sadly incapable of pursuing them effect-ively, and that those who have the most demonic ends might be extremely adroit in pursuing them.[55] Philosophers since Aristotle have had different words to describe the virtue of those who excel in one or the other employ-ment of practical reason, the virtues that we can call in a somewhat tech-nical language, "cleverness" (or, more fitting with our current philosophical usage, "prudence") and "wisdom".[56] For Aristotle *deinotēs* and *phronēsis* are separate capacities. Kant distinguishes between *Klugheit* and *Weisheit*; Kant does not spend much time on the distinction, but, I take it, simply because it is obvious that the good-willed agent exhibits the latter, not the former, virtue. Lack of prudence is one of these obstacles that stepmotherly nature can put between the good-willed agent and the object of her will without taking away anything from the goodness of the action.[57] In fact, the division in two powers should help us resist the temptation to reduce one to the other, or to try to show that any form of practically rational agency must include moral agency.[58] If these are two separate powers, it seems conceivable that an agent will have one and lack the other—thus a purely instrumentally rational agent must be at least a conceptual possibility. In fact, although a will that is not effective is an absurdity, it seems equally conceptually possible to have substantive rational powers without having instrumental rational powers. The divine intellect would be such an example, but also, perhaps, a race of angels who do nothing other than autonomously contemplate the One. Of course, ideally, we'd also explain why all those things count as rational powers. For the record, my own (Kantian) view is that a rational power is a capacity of self-determination through the representation of necessity. In the theoretical case, what is determined is the mental state of knowledge, in the practical case it is action. For the practical case, if the necessity is unconditioned, then this is a manifestation of our substantive rational powers, and if the necessity is conditioned, it is a manifestation of our instrumental rational powers. But it would take a rather docile reader to

---

[55] There might be limits on how ineffective one can be and still count as fully good or evil. Someone who has "the best intentions" but always does the wrong thing might be less good for that reason. Someone who has evil ends but is extremely incompetent in the pursuit of them might be less evil for that reason. See Setiya (2005) for an interesting discussion.

[56] See Engstrom (1997).

[57] Here too there are limits on how much the virtuous agent can fall short of *Klugheit*. Given that we have a duty to develop our capacities, complete incompetence in the pursuit of moral ends can itself be a sign of a less virtuous disposition.

[58] This is reminiscent of Goodman's claim that we should not be tempted to reduce induc-tion to deduction any more than we are tempted to reduce deduction to induction (Goodman (1983)).

grant me all this without much more detailed argument, so I'll leave the task of explaining the unity of our rational powers to another occasion.

So the problem or the task that the classical conception of instrumental rationality sets up is the quest for an account of what the prudent agent knows, or which principles guide the prudent agent, or which causal powers are manifested by the prudent agent.[59] It is worth mentioning that these points are largely independent from questions about "reason first" or "rationality first", or whether we take "good" or "reasons" or something else to be basic. Whichever way we go with these questions, we still need a distinction between the "instrumental" and the "non-instrumental" (or intrinsic).

A well-known conception of instrumental rationality proposes a single principle for evaluating the instrumental rationality of the agent: the clever agent takes all the necessary and some sufficient means to each of her ends.[60] Even though it is beyond my historical competence to provide significance evidence for this claim, I would hazard a guess that this was a dominant conception of instrumental rationality for most of the history of philosophy. So dominant that it might seem to be a tautological answer to the problem. A theory of instrumental rationality based on the principle of instrumental reasoning seems to be saying that the effective agent pursues her ends effectively.

But it is very important to notice that the view that the principle of instrumental reasoning is the single principle of instrumental rationality is in no way trivial. First, one might think that the principle is not sufficient. Although how we understand this insufficiency claim will depend on the precise formulation of the principle, we might think, for instance, that instrumental rationality depends on rules of resoluteness and steadfastness ("do not change your ends too often") that are at best loosely related to the principle of instrumental reasoning. On the other hand, some might argue that it is not really a principle of rationality; it at best describes an analytical

---

[59] This is a relatively narrow understanding of "prudence". If one thinks that the prudent agent is the one who provides well for her well-being, then "prudence" might include significantly more than our notion, depending on one's understanding of well-being. Although "prudence" often has the connotation of planning for one's future, I'm not making here any commitments on how, or whether, an instrumental agent must care for her future ends (even though the temporally extended nature of our ends and actions is a central topic of the book).

[60] Strictly speaking we need only one of these conditions since among the necessary means to an end E is "taking some sufficient means to E" and any sufficient means to E will include all the necessary means to E.

relation between ends and means: agents cannot fail to follow the principle of instrumental reasoning, at least not without accepting other principles as well, since what their ends are is partly determined by what they are effectively pursuing.[61] On this view, if I am knowingly taking means to go to Timbuktu and knowingly fail to take the necessary means to go to Poughkeepsie, than my end must be to go Timbuktu rather than to Poughkeepsie. Or one might think that the principle of instrumental reasoning is at best a clumsy description of a more precise principle, such as the principle of maximizing expected utility.

In other words, the idea that instrumental rationality is a distinct part of practical rationality is significantly more general than a commitment to the principle of instrumental reasoning as a true principle of practical rationality. We can have a general conception of a part of practical reasoning that determines not what is good (or good for the agent), but what the right steps are in its pursuit. One might then have the view, for instance, that we should not conceive of this part of practical rationality in terms of means and ends at all; one might think that the language of "ends" is too coarse to capture the decisions that rational agents must make, decisions that will often depend on the relative importance that various courses of action might have. In fact, theories of instrumental rationality have distanced themselves from this minimal view in favour of theories of preference maximization, more complex theories of diachronic rationality, and so forth. The aim of this book is, to a large extent, to reverse this trend. My aim, of course, is not to say that there is nothing to these developments, but that they tend to overlook the power and fundamentality of the principle of instrumental reasoning. More generally, I think that impoverished conceptions of actions and ends led us to misconceive many of the important insights in the theory of (instrumental) rationality in the last century. But, more importantly, the book will argue that the principle of maximization of expected utility is a consequence of the principle of instrumental reasoning in certain domains, but it cannot be a general principle of instrumental rationality; an instrumentally rational agent cannot be one that chooses the most preferred outcome whenever exercising her practically rational powers. Further, I'll argue for the plausibility of accepting that the principle of instrumental reasoning

---

[61] Korsgaard (1997) argues at least that a theory in which the principle of instrumental reasoning were the only principle of practical rationality would not be a coherent one because one could not fail to act on the principle on such a theory. I argue against Korsgaard's view in Section 8.4.

is the only principle of instrumental rationality. This is not to say that compliance with the principle exhausts our instrumentally rational power of agency; as I'll argue in Chapter 6, there are aspects of this power that are not reducible to compliance with principles. But, first, in Chapter 2, I'll start explaining the basic tenets of ETR I defend in this book.

2

Extended Theory of Rationality

Basic Tenets and Motivations

2.0 Introduction

This chapter will start the first step in presenting the advantages of the theory of instrumental rationality defended in this book, the extended theory of rationality (ETR). The chapter first presents a number of potential problems for orthodox decision theory as a *fundamental, general* theory of instrumental rationality. The second section starts laying out the basic claims and tenets of ETR as well as explaining some of its advantages. The third section outlines how decision theory could be a *derivate* theory of instrumental rationality for *limited domains* if we accept that ETR is the fundamental theory of instrumental rationality. The final section provides a summary of the main commitments of ETR that the reader might want to come back to throughout the book.

It is important to make it clear from the outset which interpretation of decision theory is being examined in this chapter. For our purposes, there are at least two possible interpretations of utility in terms of what fundamental mental state a utility measure expresses. Classical decision theorists were often "preference-first" theorists.[1] According to preference-first views, utility is just a measure of preference, or a way of representing a weak preference ordering.

Roughly, on this view to say that A, B, and C have utility 0.1, 0.2, and 0.4 is just a way of representing that C is preferred over B, and B over A and that C is preferred over B (0.4–0.2 = **0.2**) to a greater extent than B is preferred

---

[1] My distinction between "preferences-first" vs "utility-first" decision theory tracks, to some extent, the distinction often referred to as "constructivist" vs "realist" views of utility (see Buchak (2016) for the labels "constructivism" (originally in Dreier (1996)) and (psychological) "realism"; see also Bermúdez (2009) and Buchak (2013)). However, since I am not interested in the metaphysical commitments of either view, but what the view takes to be the fundamental basic attitude, I prefer to use these different labels.

over A $(0.2-0.1 = 0.1)$. Preferences are, therefore, neither a response to some independent psychological state nor defined in terms of a more basic psychological state.[2] In fact, for our purposes, preference-first theorists are only committed to the view that preferences are not *rationally grounded* on a more basic mental state, at least not for the purposes of the theory of instrumental rational relations. So it is compatible with this view that, for instance, preferences are *caused* by desires, as long as the relation between the preferences and the desires in question is not a rational relation.

Although there might be some other understanding of preference that fits the preference-first framework, I will assume that, on such views, preferences are comparative (possibly latent)[3] choice dispositions. A preference for A over B is a disposition to choose A over B in choice contexts in which both A and B are options.[4] I'll not try to explain how these dispositions are picked out or individuated.[5] On some versions of the preference-first view, the relevant preferences might be fully informed, considered, or relative to belief. Most likely, not all preferences are basic, some of them are derived from more basic preferences. I will not try to settle any of these issues. I'll just assume that these choice dispositions are picked out in a way that is compatible with the resulting preferences being the basic attitudes for a theory of instrumental rationality. So it is worth noting that a common method used by economists to determine preference, the revealed preference model,[6] will not serve our current purposes. The revealed preference model reads off an agent's preferences from her behaviour, *on the assumption that the agent maximizes utility*. If choice that maximizes utility is the proper exercise of our rational capacities, then the model of revealed preferences determines the agent's preferences by first assuming that the agent is infallibly rational. But our choice of basic attitudes for a theory of instrumental rationality should allow at least for the conceptually possibility that an agent acts irrationally.[7]

---

[2] Classical decision theorists often understood utility as a measure of *revealed* preference—that is, our preferences are determined by our actions on the assumption that we maximize utility. Such theories have no normative implications. For an example of a philosophical view committed to a preference-first understanding of utility, see Gauthier (1986).

[3] See Hausman (2011).

[4] Choice dispositions in risky contexts allow us to make the interval comparisons mentioned in the previous paragraph.

[5] See Gauthier (1986, ch. 2) for one such attempt. See also Hausman (2011).

[6] As far as I know, the first advocate of this method was Samuelson (1938).

[7] For more general problems with the revealed preference model in economics, see Hausman (2011).

A "utility-first" view on the other hand takes utility to represent the degree of an independent mental state (or some aspect of it), and preference between two state-of-affairs or objects to be determined, for the ideal agent, by the comparative degrees of attitudes towards these states-of-affairs or objects. I'll assume that for the utility-first view the relevant mental state is desire and that desire is graded, so that an agent can desire X to degree n, or, more colloquially, that agents have desires with varying strength for different objects. So a utility measure expresses the strength of the desire for a particular object, and A is preferred to B just in case A is more strongly desired (desired to a greater degree) than B. The model of degree of desire parallels the model of degree of belief when we talk about credences rather than outright beliefs. In a nutshell, we can explain the distinction between the preference-first and the utility-first interpretations, as I understand them here, in terms of how they understand the follow biconditional (where "u(X)" stands for x's utility):

(UTILITY) A is weakly preferred[8] to B if and only if u(A) ≥ u(B).

On the preference-first approach, (UTILITY) is true in virtue of the fact that utility is a measure of preference. So the explanatory direction for the preference-first view is from left to right. If we assume that the conditions are true, then the preference-first view will accept the following:

(UTILITY)$_C$ u(A) ≥ u(B) because A is weakly preferred to B.

While for the utility-first view the explanatory direction is from right to left; it would accept instead:

(UTILITY)$_R$ A is weakly preferred to B because u(A) ≥ u(B) (or, equivalently, A is weakly preferred to B because A is at least as strongly desired as B).

So, preference-first and utility-first views differ on what they consider to be the basic given attitude for instrumental rationality, and thus they need to receive separate treatment in our discussion. This chapter will only discuss the preference-first interpretation; the utility-first interpretation is left

---

[8] Weak preference includes also indifference. If an agent weakly prefers A to B and B to A, then she is indifferent between A and B.

to the next chapter. The main reason to start with the preference-first interpretation is that it presents a sharper contrast with ETR, and thus it makes it easier to present the main tenets of ETR as well as its initial advantages. Those who think that preferences, being a comparative state, are poorly suited to be the basic given attitudes will need to wait till the next chapters when I put forward the argument against both the utility-first view and, more generally, against any theory that takes decision theory to provide us with the basic principles of derivation and coherence of a theory of instrumental rationality.

2.1 Shortcomings of Orthodox Decision Theory as a General Theory of Instrumental Rationality

The work on formal decision and game theory pioneered by von Neumann and Morgenstern, and Savage, among others, is certainly one of the most important recent developments in our understanding of instrumental rationality. Unsurprisingly, the power of these theories depends on certain idealizations. Indeed any theory of rational agency will, by its very nature, presuppose certain idealizations. A theory of practical rationality will presuppose that the agent in question is ideally rational; there is no fundamental difference between providing a theory of rationality and explaining how an ideally rational agent would act. Given this feature of a theory of rationality, there might be certain difficulties in applying the theory to normal human agents. Not only are we not perfectly rational, but it is not clear that aiming to approximate this ideal is a desirable end for us. However, these idealizations are *constitutive* idealizations; without them, no theory of rationality is a theory of rational agency as such. On the other hand, some of the idealizations in decision theory are not of this kind, or at least not obviously so. For instance, the von Neumann–Morgenstern axioms of completeness and continuity do not seem constitutive of rational agency as such, as is widely acknowledged. These axioms require that, for every two lotteries L_1 and L_2 involving any combination of outcomes, the agent either prefers L_1 over L_2 or L_2 over L_1, or is indifferent between the two options. The axioms are arguably problematic even for choices under certainty;[9] if

---

[9] Only completeness is relevant for choice under certainty. Completeness (or connectedness) requires that any two possible outcomes A and B are comparable (that is for any A and B, either A is preferred to B, or B is preferred to A, or A is indifferent to B). Continuity requires

we accept that some pairs of outcomes are "incommensurable" or "on a par", then a rational agent might not have any of the specified preference relations to such outcomes.[10] Perhaps I don't prefer joining the resistance to helping my ailing mother or vice versa, but I am also not indifferent between these two outcomes; they are simply non-comparable. But once we introduce risk, continuity requires that our preferences be fine-grained in a way that is clearly not possible for human beings. It might be straightforward enough to determine that I would prefer to eat the banana over the orange, and the orange over the apple. But what would be my choice between a lottery that gives me a .62 chance of getting the banana and a .38 chance of getting the apple compared to a lottery that gives me a .81 chance of getting the orange and a .19 chance of getting the apple? What about other variations of the probability assignments here? No human agent has the fine-grained preference ordering that such axioms require, and it is not clear why an ideal rationality would require that an agent *must* have one of these attitudes for any such possible lottery. As I said above, very few philosophers would insist that these axioms represent real rational demands.[11] But I think there is a more serious problem with taking preferences as the basic given attitudes; such a view would seem to violate adequacy.

What is exactly the object of a preference like "bananas over oranges"? "I prefer bananas over oranges" is really an open formula, and no matter where we stick the quantifiers, we do not get the attitude we're looking for. It is not true that I prefer any banana to any orange, it is true but uninteresting to say that I prefer some bananas to some oranges, and whether there are some bananas such that I prefer them over any orange is something that I am probably in no position to know (and largely irrelevant to my choices). And, of course, we haven't specified how I am getting a hold of the banana or the orange. Will I need to make an appointment? Will I need to step on a stepladder to reach the banana? And if there is a lottery involved, do I need to press a lever to run the lottery and did anyone else touch this lever leaving

that for every outcome A, B, C, such that $u(A) > u(B) > u(C)$, there is a lottery L, $(pu(A), (1-p)u(C))$, such that the agent is indifferent between L and B ($u(L) = u(B)$).

[10] See Raz (1986) and Chang (2002) on these issues.

[11] Most, if not all, advocates only require at most that one's preference ordering be extendible. See Nehring (1997) for a model of extendible preference. See also Weirich (2004) and Joyce (1999). But this assumption itself is problematic. If we do not think that continuity and completeness are constitutive idealizations, why would we require that a preference ordering be extendible? As we'll see in Chapters 3–5, there are seemingly reasonable combinations of attitudes that we encounter in real life that do not satisfy this condition: they cannot generate a set of preferences that are extendible in this manner.

germs behind? The claim must be something like: in most circumstances that I am likely to face, I will prefer the average banana over the average orange, *ceteris paribus*.

Putting the claim this way should already make one feel less comfortable that there is any basis for the claim that one's answer to these betting proposals expresses any significant fruit preference. But irrespective of how we feel here, we learn that no matter how optimistic we are about the ease with which an ideal rational agent will answer questions about such bets, the availability of such procedures cannot show that the actual choices of even the most rational and cooperative agent satisfy continuity. For, after all, most situations are not typical, and no matter what we put in the content of our preference, we cannot go further than this. The objects of preferences are general: states of affairs, propositions, and so forth. But we choose particular actions in particular circumstances.[12] Since I cannot infer from my general preference of bananas over oranges that I would choose the banana over the orange in any specific situation, the preference ordering represented by the outcome of a procedure where we interrogate an agent about her preferences in various hypothetical situations will be at best a rough blueprint of the choices that I make or ought to make when I actually act.[13] We cannot thus infer the properties of the actual choice dispositions from the properties of the blueprints. Thus having preferences as our basic given attitudes violates our adequacy constraint.

One could complain that I have chosen an example of a very general preference, and have unsurprisingly shown that focusing on such very general preferences leaves a number of factors out that might be relevant for choice behaviour. So what we need on this view is to specify the preference further, so that we know we hit the appropriate level of generality. Perhaps the important preference is a preference for ripe premium bananas over top-quality oranges. But one moment of reflection will tell us that this is not enough. The more specific preference is still general in character, but every choice will be for a particular action or object of choice. We still have an open formula here, and, again, no combination of quantifiers will deliver a proposition that is both true and strong enough to pick out the basic attitudes of a theory of instrumental rationality.[14] Of course, we have been

---

[12] This is a generalization of a point I make in Tenenbaum (2007a) defending the idea that the conclusion of practical reason is an action.

[13] This is not quite the same, but it is related to the issue that Richard Bradley calls "option uncertainty" (Bradley (2017), pp. 35–9).

[14] Could we say that I have a *pro tanto* preference for bananas over oranges? Of course, there's nothing wrong with that, but we'd still then need to have a way of determining how the

assuming that preference relations must range over things that are general in character; we have been suggesting that they range over open formulae. Is there any way of specifying the object of preference that would escape this problem?

This is, in important ways, not a new problem. It is roughly, on Jeffrey's framework, the issue of determining the relevant partition of a proposition **p**. In order to calculate the desirability of **p** on Jeffrey's theory, we need to determine the relevant partition of **p** that will include all the different ways in which **p** could turn out to be true that could potentially make a difference to the desirability of **p**. In other words, we need to distinguish different ways in which, for instance, "I eat a pear" can turn out to be true that would differently affect the desirability of "I eat a pear".[15] So presumably whether the pear is a Bosc pear or an Asian pear will make a difference to its desirability. So our partition must include both p_1 = "I eat an Asian pear" and p_2 = "I eat a Bosc pear". On the other hand, whether the pear was picked in the morning or in the evening will probably make no difference to its desirability, so we *don't* need a more fine-grained partition that will include the propositions p_{1a} = "I eat an Asian pear picked in the morning", p_{2a} = "I eat a Bosc pear picked in the morning", p_{1b} = "I eat an Asian pear picked in the evening", and p_{2b} = "I eat a Bosc pear picked in the evening". However, even though this further subdivision is unnecessary, a partition that includes p_1 and p_2 will be obviously too crude; it probably matters whether the Asian pear is overripe and whether the Bosc pear is poisoned.

In fact, as we try to specify the relevant partition, we are pulled in two directions if we try to take "desirability" to be a basic given attitude.[16] On the one hand, if the propositions in the partition are very coarsely grained (such as "I eat a pear when I am hungry"; "I eat a pear when I am not hungry"), we'll be missing ways in which the proposition "I eat a pear" could be true that affect its desirability. If the partition is too fine-grained, it is unlikely that the propositions in questions are the content of the fundamental given attitudes. After all, even if we do represent the content of such

---

pro tanto preferences combine to form an all-things-considered preference. Preferences can only play the role they do in decision theory if they're all-things-considered preferences.

[15] Jeffrey (1990). The desirability of **p** is a weighted sum of the desirability of all the relevant ways in which **p** could be true (weighed by the conditional probability of each of these ways being true on the assumption that **p** is true; formally, $Des(p)=\sum_i Des(p_i).Pr(p_i|p)$ for all p_i that are members of the relevant partition set).

[16] Here again, it's important to emphasize that the pressure is relative to the job that we expect the theory to perform. There are many ways of understanding rational choice theory for which those concerns are irrelevant.

attitudes in anything resembling the detail we'd need for members of a proper partition,[17] it is unlikely that these are the brute primitives for which we employ our instrumental rational powers. Rather it seems that the desirability of, say, "an average sized pear not too ripe while I'm hungry but not in a rush and without any convenient way of washing my hands" is explained in terms of more basic attitudes we have. It seems plausible that the *reason why* I have this preference is that it is rationally derived from the ends (or at least the desires) I have; in other words, the choice dispositions are themselves rational because they are *instrumental* in bringing about some of my ends.[18] To the extent that we can determine the desirability of such a proposition at all, it'll be "precipitated" from my ends of tasting pears or delicious foods more generally, staying healthy, avoiding bodily discomfort, getting in time for a meeting, and so forth.

The very comparative nature of the preference relation suggests that it is not a basic given attitude. That I rank A higher than B would seem to depend on my conative attitudes towards A and towards B. For this reason, a certain utility-first view might seem, well, preferable.[19] If utility is a measure of something like strength of desire, rather than just a "construct" from our choice dispositions, then it seems the right kind of thing to be a given practical attitude. Unlike preferences, neither the content nor the strength of our desires seems to be derivative from anything more basic. The proposal that our (intrinsic) desires that p of strength s are the basic given attitudes is an important one and we'll examine its plausibility in great detail in Chapter 3. But let me briefly state here my main reasons for being sceptical. Once we allow desire to be the basic given attitude, there is no reason to suppose that each desire comes with some extra aspect, such as strength, that can give rise to a standard of comparison among desires; it seems to be an empirical question whether a desire also has this extra component. Moreover, even if we accept such a basic component, given that desires are our basic given attitudes, shouldn't the importance of strength of desire depend on a further desire that my desires be ranked in importance in accordance to their strength (at least from the point of view of our theory of instrumental rationality)? In other words, if this extra feature of desire is

---

[17] See Pollock (2006) for the potential combinatorial explosion as we attempt to specify the relevant partition.

[18] Thoma (2017) argues that many of the arguments for the decision theory axioms require that we presuppose that a different attitude, such as desire, is basic.

[19] For a defence of the "utility-first" (or realist) interpretation, see Bermúdez (2009). See also Buchak (2013).

supposed to have any bite, rather than being trivially conformed to in every action, it will threaten to violate the Toleration constraint; unless we have a further desire to act in accordance with this feature of desire, why should actions that do not conform with it count as failures of rationality? And even if we had such a further desire, wouldn't it be just one more contender[20] for being satisfied, rather than have a privileged role in determining how to rank all our desires for the purposes of our theory of instrumental rationality?

2.2 The Advantages of the Principle of Instrumental Reasoning and the "Classical" View

Let us start with a seemingly trivial advantage of the classical understanding of the theory of instrumental rationality in terms of means and ends. The principle of instrumental reasoning enjoins us to pursue the means to our ends. The means in question might be causal, but they also might be constitutive. "Watching a movie" is a means to "having fun", not because in watching a movie I cause a separate event of my having fun but rather because watching a movie is a way of, or an instance of, having fun. But this entails that the principle of instrumental reasoning allows my rational power to reach all the way to my action: a particular action is a constitutive means of pursuing a general end. More precisely, if my end is, for instance, to ϕ, ϕ-ing in the particular way w is a constitutive means of ϕ-ing and thus a form of taking sufficient means to my end. But there is no rational relation between preferring apples over oranges, and preferring *this* apple to *this* orange, let alone *grabbing* this apple (rather than this orange). In other words, making intentional action our given attitude puts us in a better position to satisfy adequacy.

Now this might seem like a cheat. For it might seem that a similar problem besets a theory of instrumental rationality based on the principle of instrumental reasoning. My end might be to lie in bed after a difficult day but the opportunity to use a bed covered by sheets drenched in apple juice would not count as the realization of my end. But here the problem can be identified by the theory of instrumental rationality as a failure to act in accordance with another end you have; in this case, the end might be "not experiencing physical discomfort", and, more importantly, it is also a failure

---

[20] This is, of course, an instance of the type of worry that Gary Watson raises against Frankfurt's hierarchical conception of freedom of the will. See Watson (1975).

to pursue ends such as "resting" or "sleeping"; that is, a failure to pursue the very ends for the sake of which my end of lying in bed was adopted.

On the other hand, when I move from a general preference to a particular action in light of the preference, the more general preference does not necessarily imply anything about the particular choice among actions that I need to make. My general preference for bananas over oranges need not imply my preferring *this* banana over *this* orange independently of further, more specific, preferences I might have.

It is true, however, that an end is also general, and not any specification of the end counts as satisfying the end I was pursuing. If my friend and I are both arrested, gagged, and sent to the gallows together, this will hardly count as a realization of my end to spend the evening with a good friend. It's not just that I have as an end not to spend time gagged in jail; but rather that *this way* of spending time with a friend does not count at all as an appropriate way of realizing my end. To complicate matters, most of our ends are vague or indeterminate, and so in some cases it is not clear what counts as an acceptable specification of my end.

But there is an important difference here. If instead of facing imprisonment, I spend an evening pleasantly dining with my friend, this counts as the realization of an end of mine *in virtue of* being an acceptable specification of my end of spending an evening with a good friend. The same cannot be said about my preference for eating this banana over this orange. This is not a preferred outcome in virtue of a general preference for bananas over oranges; the preference for bananas over pears is more like a statistical generalization of the more specific preferences. So it is the principle of instrumental reasoning, rather than a principle of preference satisfaction or maximization of utility, that can explain how acting can be the manifestation of a rational power.[21]

One might complain that the principle of instrumental reasoning faces a complementary problem. My ends might not be jointly satisfiable. I might learn that there is no way that I can realize both my end of lying in a bed today and my end of not violating property law; it might turn out that my

---

[21] Again, we're interested in a theory of rationality that is "action-guiding" or one that a rational agent acts on. Some of these claims (or at least similar ones) would be readily granted by many advocates of decision theory as a theory of instrumental rationality understood as having a purely "evaluative" role. See Dreier (1996) and Joyce (1999). See Bermúdez (2009) on the various possible roles of a theory of instrumental rationality; Bermúdez argues that all these roles are connected. If he's right, then my argument will extend to these other understandings of decision theory.

bed has been destroyed, I am penniless, and no one is willing to lend me their bed. Here too, one might argue, the principle of instrumental reasoning gives no guidance, as it does not tell us which among these incompatible ends we should prefer.[22] I fully accept this point; the theory of instrumental rationality here has nothing to say beyond the injunction to revise my ends. Given that the possibility of making the world conform to a given set of representational attitudes does not depend only on the structure of the set of attitudes but also on facts about the world, a set of given attitudes on its own might not be coherent in conjunction with a given piece of information. This is true no matter what our theory of instrumental rationality takes to be the given attitudes. Doubtless, the end of speaking of my mind and the end of being one of the popular kids might turn out not to be jointly realizable in light of the facts about what I think and what my school mates like to hear. Decision theory might appear not to suffer from a similar predicament, but this appearance is illusory; it is just the artefact of a further simplifying idealization of the theory. Orthodox decision theory assumes that the two-place predicate "x is preferred to y" generates a relatively transparent context, but this obviously cannot be true. A preference ordering that ranks the "destruction of the Morning Star" above E and E above the "destruction of the Evening Star" is incoherent, but its incoherence can only be known once we learn that the Morning Star is the Evening Star.

2.3 Decision Theory and Pursuing Ends

It would be a serious strike against a theory of instrumental rationality if it made no room for the impressive achievements of decision theory. In other words, a theory of instrumental rationality in which the intentional actions (or more specifically, the intentional pursuit of ends), rather than preferences, are the basic given attitudes should meet a couple of related desiderata. It should (i) make room for an attitude of preference to play a role in the theory; (ii) explain how the pursuit of ends could in some instances generate a commitment to a preference ranking. In other words, even if preferences are not the basic attitudes, a theory of instrumental rationality should be compatible with some basic insights of decision theory by allowing that *at least in some cases* an agent is (fails to be) rational in virtue of maximizing

---

[22] As we will see in the Chapter 3, this is arguably a motivation to take preferences or degrees of desire (utility) to be the given attitudes.

(failing to maximize) expected utility. Here I'll start explaining how ETR generates partial preference orderings; more detailed discussion will appear in the later chapters.

On the view I propose, the basic given attitudes are conscious pursuits of ends, many of which are indeterminate. For our purposes, an end can be indeterminate in at least three (non-exclusive) ways. First an end can be indeterminate because its content contains vague predicates. So, for instance, if my end is to build a tall tower, there will be some "borderline" towers I might build such that it will be neither determinately true nor determinately false that I built a tall tower.[23] Second, an end can be indeterminate because the content of the end (or any further specification of it) does not fully determine what counts as achieving the end, or what counts as an *acceptable realization* of the end. In other words, an end is indeterminate in this way if it is possible that the content of the end is made actual without the end itself being realized (or made actual): in our example above, the content of the end "spending an evening with my friend" is made true when we're shackled and gagged next to each other, but my end was not realized. My end of writing a book is similarly indeterminate. Suppose one day I accidentally print out my archive of shopping lists, and my cousin, who owns a press, decides to publish the whole thing in book form as a joke. It seems that in this case I did write a book, but the outcome doesn't count as an acceptable realization[24] of my end of writing a book. Arguably, in such a case I did not write the book intentionally (I certainly did not publish it intentionally), but this is not the problem. If I am pursuing the end of making dinner for the children and I realize that my partner has just finished making their dinner in our second kitchen, my end has been acceptably realized, even if not intentionally. There is no point for me to continue to pursue this end; dinner has been made. But in the book writing case, my end was to have written *a different sort of book*, and this end has not yet been acceptably realized.

Of course, one could say that this means that my end wasn't really to write a book, but to write a book about the nature of instrumental rationality, or publish a book with a respectable press, and so forth; the complete representation of my end must have been more specific than "writing a book".

---

[23] Not all theories of vagueness will understand borderline cases as being neither determinately true nor determinately false. Assuming that this is the case makes for ease of presentation in this context, but no substantial point depends on this assumption.

[24] More on the notion of acceptable realization in the next chapters.

But even if this were true here, it is implausible to think that for every end we pursue we represent it in a fully determinate way; I do not know in advance all the ways in which my end could be improperly realized.

Finally an end can be indeterminate if the content of the end does not determine *to which degree* I achieve the end. So, for instance, suppose that I have running a fast marathon as my end. Typically, this will imply that I'll not be indifferent to how fast I run a marathon. *Ceteris paribus*, insofar as I am guided by the pursuit of this end, I'll choose to run it faster than slower even if my slower pace also counts as a fast marathon.[25] But notice that even if there are no gradable predicates in the content of my end, the end might still be indeterminate in this third way. Typically, when I have the end of writing a book, I'm not indifferent to the quality of the book; *ceteris paribus*, I'll choose to write a better book.

Now first it is worth noting that any theory that starts from ends immediately imposes a very basic preference structure. After all, *ceteris paribus*, if I pursue E, I prefer to pursue it successfully over pursuing it unsuccessfully. And given that this is true for every end, we always prefer any Pareto optimal arrangement of successful pursuits; that is, I always prefer the case in which all my ends $E_1, \ldots, E_n$ are actualized over the case in which some of these ends are not.[26] This is, of course, not very informative; there will be many "gaps" in such preference orderings, as they say nothing about trade-offs in cases in which I would have to choose among different ends being realized. In fact, my view is that the theory of instrumental rationality cannot say anything about such cases.

A more interesting preference ordering can be derived if we relativize preferences to an end. First, there is the obvious fact that various different means are more or less likely to promote or contribute to the end in question. If I am writing a book, then typing a page of the book contributes to my end to a greater extent than typing half a page, and either of them is preferable to not typing anything. Going to bed early is preferable to staying up late at night playing video games. Taking a nap might help concentration later, but doing my research right now will raise the odds that I'll finish all the research while leaving myself enough time to do the actual writing. We can even compare these means by their likelihood to realize the writing of my book. I might prefer the nap because I think that it is more likely that I

---

[25] Isn't my end in this case to run the fastest marathon I can? I consider this possibility momentarily.

[26] More on this point in Chapter 3.

will complete my book if I can focus on finding the elusive argument that is supposed to connect my premises to the conclusion.

More importantly, ends that are indeterminate in the third way generate by their very nature an ordering of better and worse realizations of the end. As we said above, my end of writing a book is not indifferent to the kind of book I write and how good it is; it is a better realization of my end if I finish it in a month and if it is nominated for the Man Booker Prize than if it takes me ten years and it is a very slight, awkwardly written contribution to some of the topics it covers. The latter still counts as the realization of my end (unlike, say, my publishing a random assemblage of fortune cookie messages), but it is a worse realization of the end than the former. Of course, there is much that falls between these two extremes, and what is between these two extremes will be the basis for my preference ordering relative to the end of writing a book. We can even try to rank lotteries involving these outcomes using a similar method to that used by classical decision theory for ascribing a determinate preference ordering to an agent: we try to determine an indifference curve by asking how I would choose between various lotteries. Would I choose a .1 chance of getting the Booker (and otherwise not finish writing the book) or the certainty of writing a mediocre book that will be read by 2,121 people and deservedly receive a rating of 3.6 in Goodreads? If I am indifferent between these two options they have the same "utility" relative to the end of writing a book. The resolution of my preference ordering relative to this end is determined by how many of these questions I can (meaningfully) answer. There is no a priori limit on the resolution; it is in principle possible (though obviously unlikely) that some of my ends are such that a preference ordering relative to them satisfies the axioms of orthodox decision theory (or at least a set that is extendible into one that satisfies the axioms).

One could complain that if such ranking is possible then my end is not really to write a book, but perhaps to write the best possible book, and everything else is at best a backup end for cases of failure. But my end is certainly not to write the best possible book I can write or anything like that. I am not sure what I would need to do in order to write the best possible book I can; however, I am quite confident that it would involve spending many more hours researching and thinking about the topics I write about, revising, and so forth. I would have to reduce to a minimum any time spent with family and friends, teaching, watching movies, or engage in such activities only if they would help me write an even better book (or at least did not hinder the quality of my book). I do care about the excellence of my philosophical work, but not *that* much. The problem is that writing the best book possible is not compatible with my other ends; in fact, it is hardly compatible with having any other ends. One might say that, in this case, the end should be "write the best book possible compatible with my other ends", but as I'll be arguing in the next chapters, this won't do. In a nutshell, part of the problem is that the other ends I have would have to be similarly specified, and thus we would not have made much progress in further specifying the end of writing book by understanding it as "writing the best book compatible with my other ends". Since the other ends would only be able to be specified as "X insofar as compatible with my end of writing the best book compatible with…", this path would be trapped in a maze of unresolvable cross-references.

A theory that takes the pursuit of ends to be the primary given attitude is compatible also with a different, and more important, role for preference orderings and utility maximization. Some of my ends are for the sake of other ends; in other words, some of them are means to other ends. I am taking the early bus to Lima because I need to be in Lima before noon. But a reflective rational agent is not only preoccupied with the pursuit of means for *particular* ends, but also with having adequate means to pursue her ends *in general*, and, at least as long as her continued rational agency is among her ends, also with the means to the ends she *might* have. Kant talks about the end of happiness as an "ideal of imagination",[27] as a reflective conception of how life would go according to wish and will. Without needing to accept all details of Kant's conception of happiness, we can accept that a reflective agent forms a general conception of the joint realization of all her ends,[28] and consequently forms a set of instrumental ends that are simply *general means* to the pursuit of many, or all, of her ends (including those that she has not formed yet, given her expectation that she'll have ends in the future whose content she is not yet aware of).

Of course, if each end required completely different means for its realization, reflection on our interest in the general pursuit of our ends would be idle. It would only recommend that we pursue the means to our particular ends, but this adds nothing to what the principle of instrumental reasoning requires in the pursuit of the particular ends themselves. However, there are a number of general means, some more general than others. Possessing a

---

[27] Kant (1996), 4:418. Of course, many plausible conceptions of happiness (arguably even Kant's) will include significantly more than this, as I might turn out to be unhappy even if all my ends were realized (they just weren't the right ends to pursue). The notion of happiness here is a rather narrow and technical one.

[28] If you accept the guise of the good thesis, this will be her general conception of the good.

car is a general means that can serve our ends of enjoying a good meal, going to the movies, and so forth, but it might be of no, or almost no, use to some of our other ends (such as running regularly). Ensuring an adequate stock of food supplies at home has a similar level of generality. The pursuit of wealth, health, and knowledge, and the cultivation of our talents and skills, are probably among some of the most general means. The pursuit of any of these is recommended by our general interest in the adequate pursuit of our ends.[29] In fact, it seems safe to say that many of us spend a great deal of our time in procuring these means for ourselves and for our loved ones; our pursuit of these general means is an important part of our practical life. But general means, considered individually, also naturally generate a preference ordering given that there are often obvious candidates for being "better and worse realizations" of the end of pursuing a certain kind of general means. The pursuit of wealth generates a quite obvious ranking, at least in cases in which no risk or uncertainty is involved; considered as general means, leaving aside some bizarre cases, the more money one has, the better one will be in a position to pursue different kinds of ends.[30] The maintenance of health and bodily integrity is also a general means, but ranking its various actualizations is sometimes more difficult. It is rather easy to determine that losing the tip of one's finger is preferable over kidney failure, but it is less clear how to rank the loss of a leg as compared to the loss of an arm. Moreover, health, knowledge, and so forth are things that people pursue also as ends, and more specific forms of knowledge have a special role to play in the pursuit of particular ends.

Still, the function of these pursuits as general means allows for an ordering, and here too there is no predetermined limit on how fine-grained this ordering can be. And we might have more or less determinate ways in which we can evaluate the fungibility of different type of general means: How do healthy legs compare with owning a car? Or detailed knowledge of public transit with extra money? It seems harsh to ask how much a certain level of health is worth, but this is because we value health not merely as means; qua general means, this is a perfectly sensible question: Can I

---

[29] I will not try here to give a precise definition of "general means". There is a sense in which anything could be the means to any end, but there seems to be a great difference between money and peanuts, even if peanuts could potentially be a means to almost any end (one could need peanuts in order to go to Timbuktu, if the only horse who would take us to Timbuktu will not move unless fed peanuts).

[30] Of course, this is particularly trivial in the case of money given that someone in possession of less money has a subset of the means at the disposal of someone who has more money.

provide for my ends better by avoiding the flu by taking the flu shot, or by keeping the money that I would use to pay for the flu shot? Here too, there is no in-principle limit for the resolution of the rank order of general means considered severally.

In other words, the view that the given attitudes are intentional actions, or more specifically, the intentional pursuit of ends, is compatible with the view that in many contexts we will be engaged in the maximization of utility (as a measure of a preference ordering) envisaged by traditional decision theory. A general theory of instrumental rationality that accepts only the principle of instrumental reasoning as its basic principle of derivation, and intentional actions as the only basic given attitude, can accommodate the insights and the obvious importance of work in this tradition. The only claim that the view defended here must reject is that decision theory is the only, or a foundational, part of the theory of instrumental rationality. In fact, on the view I'll defend here, the complete theory of instrumental rationality is also not extensionally equivalent to any version of decision theory, since our ends do not settle a preference ordering among our possible actions; an end is general, and does not immediately determine how to order all possible actions that we might perform while pursuing this end. So, for instance, if my end is to climb Mount Everest, the end does not determine when I should do it, or how much time I should devote to the climb. But this means that in various choice situations (Should I start climbing right now? Should I take a break right now?), my end will not determine a preference ordering. One might think that there is a simple answer such as, "take the fastest path at the least cost". But "fastest path" already presupposes a more determinate end ("get to the top as fast as possible") and "least cost" a precise ordering (so that you can determine what counts as the *least* cost).

2.4 The Extended Theory of Instrumental Rationality

Here are the central tenets of ETR, the theory of instrumental rationality that'll be defended in the rest of the book.

(1) *ETR BASIC*: The basic given attitude is intentional action, more specifically, the intentional pursuit of an end.

This contrasts with views in which the basic attitudes are mental states. So, it's not an *intention* to write a book, or a *preference* for writing a book over not writing a book, that determines that my, say, writing chapter 2 of the book is an exercise of my instrumentally rational powers. Rather, the basic given attitude in this case is my *writing a book* (intentionally) or my *intentional pursuit* of writing a book (or intentionally pursuing the end of writing a book). Given the nature of intentional pursuits, our basic given attitudes extend through time and we can be engaged in the same intentional pursuit for indefinitely long periods of time (though, arguably our mortality places an upper bound, at least on individual actions). The basic given attitude is the extended action, not its momentary snapshots.

(2) *ETR DERIVATION*: An instrumentally rational agent derives[31] means from ends according to the following principles of derivation:

Principle of Instrumental Reasoning (Sufficient)

Pursuing A[32]

Pursuing B_1 & Pursuing $B_2, \ldots,$ & Pursuing B_n is a (nontrivial) sufficient means to pursuing A

———————————

Pursuing B_i (for any i between 1 and n) (while also pursuing B_j for every j such $1 \geq j \geq n$ and $j \neq i$)

Principle of Instrumental Reasoning (Contributory)

Pursuing A

Pursuing B_1 & Pursuing $B_2, \ldots,$ & Pursuing B_n is a contributory means to pursuing A

———————————

Pursuing B_i (for any i between 1 and n)

Both the conclusion and major premise are intentional actions. The minor premise expresses the content of the agent's relevant knowledge. So, for instance, if I am pursuing the end of cooking dinner tonight, and I know that the ingredients can be bought by going to the store, then my going to the store intentionally is the conclusion of the piece of practical reason. For most of the book we assume that the agent is in possession of relevant knowledge that enables her to pursue her ends efficiently and that no false beliefs interfere in her pursuit of such ends. In Chapter 9, we look at

---

[31] I take "derivation" and "reasoning" here to be not a process, but a grounding relation that holds between two attitudes. This is similar to Valaris's conception of reasoning in Valaris (2018).

[32] A and B are variables for agent's ends.

situations of risk, and cases in which the agent's actions are guided by false beliefs. The principle of derivation explains the action of an agent, when the agent manifests their instrumentally rational power. Or, better, it is a generalization of explanations of instrumentally rational actions. So if I type this sentence *because* I am writing a book, then my knowledge of the instrumental relation between typing this sentence and writing a book (together with my end of writing a book) *explains* my writing this sentence. From the first-person point of view, I infer the action (writing of sentence) from my awareness of my end of my writing the book and the instrumental relation between writing the book and writing this sentence.

> (3) *ETR COHERENCE*: When an instrumentally rational agent realizes that her ends are incompatible (cannot be jointly realized), she abandons at least one of the ends from the smallest subset of her ends that cannot be jointly realized.

So if you're currently pursuing the ends of learning Danish philosophy, travelling to Kathmandu in the summer, and attending the anti-Globalization meeting in Stockholm in July, you might realize that constraints on your time and financial resources do not allow you to go to both Stockholm and Kathmandu in the summer. In such a case, you would have to abandon one of these two ends, given that there is no way of successfully deriving means that will realize all these ends. But of course this conflict puts no pressure on your pursuit of learning Danish philosophy; thus *ETR COHERENCE* requires that you abandon a member of the smallest subset of ends that cannot be jointly realized (in our example {going to Kathmandu, going to Stockholm}).

> (4) *ETR EXERCISE*: The exercise of instrumentally rational agency is an intentional action.

ETR EXERCISE states that the exercise of our instrumentally rational powers is manifested in intentional actions, and thus the conclusion of instrumentally practical reasoning, as presented above by *ETR DERIVATION*, is an intentional action ("pursuing the end of writing chapter 2" in our example above). It contrasts with theories in which the exercise of our instrumental rational powers is manifested in choices or intentions.

> (5) *ETR COMPLETE*: No other basic principles govern the exercise of our instrumentally rational powers.

These central tenets will be developed in more detail (and argued for) in the next chapters of the book, but a couple of quick observations might be helpful. We'll discuss various implications of the principle of instrumental reasoning later on, but for now a few clarifications are in order (further clarifications will be presented as the book progresses). First the principle must work to some extent like a principle of existential instantiation in first-order logic; the agent acts from the principle of instrumental reasoning when she pursues *a* sufficient means to her ends, not, of course, when she pursues *all* sufficient means to her end. But, unlike existential instantiation, the principle is properly followed when the agent acts on a specific instance of sufficient means (it would be, of course, a mistake to infer a specific instance from an existential generalization without further information). In deontic terms, we can say that the agent is *permitted* to take any sufficient means and that she is *required* to take at least some sufficient means (more on this point in the next chapters). In fact, this is a consequence of the nature of sufficient means. Sufficient means are such that if pursuing end A is a sufficient means to pursuing end B, then actualizing end A also actualizes end B. But now if the actualization of my end A guarantees that B is also actualized, then all other pursuits I might engage in are sufficient means, but only in the trivial sense that if actualizing $B_1 \ldots B_n$ is sufficient to actualize A, so is $B_1 \ldots B_{n+1}$.[33]

A contributory means is one that is neither necessary nor sufficient but contributes to a better realization of my end. As we saw above, many of our ends have an internal structure. My end of travelling through Spain will have better or worse actualizations. A visit to Spain in which I go to the Prado is a better actualization of my end than one in which I miss the Prado because I overslept on the day of my scheduled visit. Similarly, learning Spanish will be a contributory means to my travels. It is neither necessary nor sufficient for the actualization of my end, but it'll be a better actualization of the end if I can communicate with the locals. Unlike sufficient means, the pursuit of some contributory means does not make the pursuit of others otiose, so there is no limit, *at least insofar as the pursuit of A is concerned*, to taking further contributory means to the pursuit of A.[34]

---

[33] Assuming, of course, that they do not interfere with each other, in which case not pursuing both would be part of any sufficient means.

[34] Of course, in some cases pursuing some contributory means will make pursuing *some* other potential contributory means otiose. But except for cases in which it is possible to reach an actualization of the end that is the best possible actualization, pursuing some contributory means will not make the pursuit of *any* other contributory means otiose.

Although I have proposed that we focus on instrumental rationality as a power, and rational agency as a manifestation of this power, we still want to know what follows from the principle of instrumental reasoning for evaluating a rational agent in terms of how they measure up to ideal (instrumental) rationality. This question will occupy us for a significant portion of the next chapters. But at the very minimum we can say the following: *an agent is instrumentally irrational if she is knowingly failing to pursue some sufficient means to an end she is pursuing.* Of course, an agent might have not yet specified the particular sufficient means she is pursuing. I might have the end of vacationing in Paris but have made no decisions about hotels. But I am still pursuing the means at least in the general sense that I am preparing for my trip to Paris or planning to do what is needed to vacation in Paris.

ETR COMPLETE tells us that our principles of coherence and derivation exhaust the content of the principles of instrumental rationality, but it is compatible with the possibility of there being other principles of instrumental rationality as long as such principles are consequences of our principle of derivation and/or our principle of coherence.

ETR also relies on a couple of background assumptions; these assumptions were important "auxiliary hypotheses" in the argument above explaining how in certain contexts, our ends will determine a preference ordering, and they'll also play a role in some of the other arguments of the book.

(6) *AUX INTERNAL STRUCTURE*: Certain ends that we pursue have an internal structure such that certain actualizations are better actualizations of the end than others.

(7) *AUX HAPPINESS*: A reflective rational agent can form a conception of the totality of their ends, and this general end (the pursuit of happiness, or the pursuit of a good life) is itself an end that the agent pursues.

(8) *AUX GENERAL MEANS*: Certain objects of pursuits are *general means*; they are means to a wide array of ends that we have (such as wealth, health, and the cultivation of our skills and talents).

And finally a central thesis of ETR that is implicitly or explicitly denied by most, if not all, theories of instrumental rationality:

(9) *NON-SUPERVENIENCE THESIS*: The rationality of an agent through a time interval t_1 to t_n does not supervene on the rationality of the agent at each moment between t_1 and t_n.

In other words, an agent might be rational at each moment t_x such that t_x is within the interval t to t_n, and yet not be rational at interval t_1-t_n. So, for instance, my book contract might require that I finish the book by end of the summer. I might postpone working on my book in a rational manner at each moment during the summer, but by the end of the summer have not finished my book, and thus no longer be able to publish it. Was I irrational during the summer? The answer to this question is "yes", even though I was not irrational at any particular moment in the summer. Or at least I will argue that such a scenario is possible. This type of example will reappear many times in the next chapters, so I'll leave more detailed discussion for later.

This chapter presented an overview at ETR. It also put forward some basic motivations for it, as well some considerations in favour of it—especially trying to pre-empt some of the force of the objection that any view that rejects decision theory as the fundamental theory of instrumental rationality is engaging in some bizarre form of obscurantism. The next chapter starts the more detailed argument for ETR.

3

Pursuing Ends as the Fundamental
Given Attitude

3.0 Introduction

In the next two chapters, I'll try to show some advantages of taking the pursuit of ends, rather than preferences, to be the practical given attitude. The argument will have two stages. This chapter first continues to lay out the basic structure of the view, and argues that the introduction of multiple (and potentially incompatible) ends adds complexity to the view, but it does not give us any reason to favour preferences over the pursuit of ends as our fundamental practical given attitudes. The next chapter presents a more positive argument in favour of ETR: it argues that a number of instrumentally rational choices and actions cannot be represented by orthodox decision theory,[1] but can be represented by a theory that takes pursuit of ends to be the primary given practical attitude. Some of the arguments in this and the next chapter speak in favour of taking extended actions (rather than mental states) as the basic attitude generally; however, the main contrasting views will be the ones that take preferences or degrees of desire as basic. Further argument against taking the *mental states* of intending ends (rather than extended actions of pursuing ends) are put forward in Chapters 5 and 6.

Section 3.1 presents a very general argument against ETR, "The Comparative Argument". According to the Comparative Argument, the fundamental given attitudes must be a comparative (or a graded) attitude, such as preference (or degree of desire). On this view, theories that take non-comparative attitudes as basic cannot provide enough structure to determine what an instrumentally rational agent does when her ends

---

[1] Although, again, I'll focus on orthodox decision theory due to its simplicity and popularity, I hope it'll be clear that the argument extends to other theories that take preferences or desires to be the basic practical attitude.

conflict. In order to answer this challenge, we need to develop ETR further, and explain how, and to what extent, ETR can generate comparative attitudes out of its basic non-comparative attitude (the attitude of pursuing an end). Section 3.2 starts by examining more carefully how the pursuit of different ends will typically conflict. The section argues that a common feature of our ends tends to generate a partial preference ordering relative to each end. However, the same feature makes conflicting ends potentially ubiquitous. The fact that most of our ends have better and worse realizations both determines end-relative preference orderings but also generates conflict between the unrestricted pursuit of almost any two ends. ETR seems to direct us to revise such unrestricted ends, but it is silent on how to revise them. According to ETR we cannot simultaneously engage in the unrestricted pursuit of singing and the unrestricted pursuit of running, but it seems to give no direction in how to balance an agent's competing interests in these activities.

It seems then that the Comparative Argument provides a powerful, intuitive consideration in favour of taking degree of desire as the basic attitude. It might seem rather intuitive that *something* determines how the agent should balance these pursuits. For instance, it seems that it matters *how much* the agent cares for each of these ends: if she cares *more* about running than singing, then running should take priority. Section 3.3 discusses the views in which the basic attitudes are degrees of desire or utility, or, more specifically, utility-first interpretations of decision theory. The section examines the plausibility of these views and raises a number of obstacles for views that take such graded attitudes to be the basic attitudes. Section 3.4 re-examines the resources available to ETR for generating comparative attitudes and providing direction for the revision of conflicting ends. I put forward there a more systematic account of both how ETR can generate preference orderings and how the principle of instrumental reasoning and the principle of coherence (which prevents us from having incompatible ends) determine the revision and pursuit of our indeterminate ends through actions that are extended through time. An important consequence of the view is that ETR, unlike nearly all extant views of practical rationality, accepts the *NON-SUPERVENIENCE THESIS*—the view that the rationality of an agent in an interval t_0-t_n does not supervene on the rationality of the agent at each moment in the interval. Section 3.5 puts forward a related implication of the view that also puts ETR at odds with many extant theories of practical rationality. An instrumentally rational agent will often not be in a position where she can "maximize"; according to ETR, in many circumstances a rational agent must "satisfice". On ETR, unlike the views of many advocates of various satisficing rules, this is not a consequence of our bounded rationality. The nature of our basic given attitudes makes maximization impossible even when we restrict our attention to ideal rationality. With this structure of the view in place, we can propose our final view about how ETR deals with conflicting ends. In a nutshell, ETR is in principle compatible with almost any revision of conflicting ends. However, ETR not only allows for further ends which might, and likely will, significantly restrict the range of possible revisions for a rational agent, but also specifies a default minimal revision for typical cases of incompatible ends. This turns out to be a compelling understanding of the exercise of our instrumentally rational powers in revising ends, or so I will argue. Finally, Section 3.6 formulates two derivative principles of derivation regarding preferences that will play an important role in the Chapter 4.

3.1 The Comparative Argument

Let us look at a very general argument in favour of having comparative attitudes as basic attitudes. I don't know anyone who explicitly defends a version of this argument in print, but I think it presents, in very rough form, a broad motivation to reject a conception of instrumental rationality that does not appeal to preferences, degrees of desires, or some kind of attitude that orders the objects we pursue in terms of their relative importance to us. I'll call this "The Comparative Argument":[2]

(1) Rational agents may (and typically do) have multiple, potentially conflicting ends.

(2) Instrumental principles that are sensitive only to the content of an agent's ends (as opposed to the degree to which they are desired, or the

---

[2] The Comparative Argument here resembles in interesting ways, the arguments that Maguire and Lord (2016) present in favour of having "weighted notions" in a normative theory. And some of the responses here parallel Horty's use of a priority ordering in his default logic. However, the arguments are significantly different here, since Maguire and Lord are not focusing on the theory of instrumental rationality, or even on practical rationality. But it is worth noting that many of the considerations here will extend to a substantive theory of practical rationality, given that such a theory will be a theory of how an ideally (practically) rational, human agent acts, and thus it will be a theory about which indeterminate, extended ends such an agent pursues.

weight the agent assigns to the end) do not provide any guidance when ends conflict.

(3) Instrumentally rational agents are guided by principles that determine their choices in cases in which their ends conflict.

Therefore,

(4) Instrumentally rational agents must be guided by principles that are sensitive not only to the content of their ends, but also to the comparative weight or strength of the ends they pursue (from 2 and 3).

(5) Comparison between the relative weight or strength of each end an agent pursues (or each instance of a basic attitude) is best represented as a preference ordering.

Therefore,

(6) The principles of a theory of instrumental rationality, insofar as they are the principles that guide an instrumentally rational agent, must be sensitive to the agent's preference ordering (from 4 and 5).

(7) The principle of instrumental reasoning is insensitive to the agent's preferences among the content of their various ends.

Therefore,

(8) The principle of instrumental reasoning cannot be the only fundamental principle of a theory of instrumental rationality (from 6 and 7).

Of course, this is not a very precise form of the argument. We need to know more about what "providing guidance"[3] means in (2) and how we move from these premises to our conclusions. At any rate, the basic idea behind this argument is straightforward: there are many things I want and that I would pursue if they were not in conflict with other things I want. Moreover, it seems intuitive that practical reasoning is essentially comparative: practical rationality concerns itself with choice *among available alternatives*. Thus if we do not take into account how strongly I want such things, and if our principles of derivation are not sensitive to the strength of our conative attitudes, we will miss an important aspect of the agent's instrumental rationality. I will argue for the rejection of (3)–(8). The weight or strength of attitudes need not play any role in the theory of instrumental

---

[3] In fact, it is commonplace that decision theory aims to provide evaluation rather than direct guidance (see Joyce (1999), p. 80, among others), but to some extent these questions are related. Arguably, an ideally rational agent would be guided by the same principles that we use to evaluate rationality.

rationality (practical rationality is, I will argue, not essentially comparative), and the principle of instrumental reasoning does make room for at least some partial preference orderings. In contrast I will defend, among other things, a view according to which a form of "satisficing" is the minimal way in which one revises conflicting ends; rather than engaging in the incompatible pursuit of two unrestricted ends, the agent pursues good enough actualizations of each end that are mutually compatible. Again this form of satisficing is not a concession to our bounded rationality; rather, it is a consequence of the fact that the nature of our ends does not allow for a maximizing rule.

But let us first examine the intuitive appeal of the Comparative Argument. Suppose, for instance, I have reading novels and playing basketball as my ends. As I am about to open my book, a friend of mine calls and asks me whether I would like to replace an injured player on his team. What should I do now, given my attitudes? If a theory of instrumental rationality says that the only principle of derivation is the principle of instrumental reasoning, it is not clear how it could settle between playing basketball and reading my novel. In fact, it seems to imply that I got myself into a dilemma. The necessary means for playing basketball is walking in the direction of the court; the necessary means (at least given my limited ambulatory skills) for reading my novel is staying put. Whatever I do, I violate the principle of instrumental reasoning.

Obviously, this is not an intractable dilemma. An ideally rational agent would not pursue incompatible ends, and thus, insofar as I am rational, I revise at least one of these ends once I recognize the conflict; this is what *ETR COHERENCE* prescribes. Similarly, an agent who recognizes that her preference ordering is incoherent (for instance, she strictly prefers visiting the birthplace of Mark Twain over visiting the birthplace of Karl Marx, but strictly prefers visiting Karl Marx's birthplace over Samuel Clemens's birthplace), must revise her preference ordering.

However, this response does not seem to register all that matters in the situation. After all, I might *strongly* desire to read my novel and only be mildly interested in basketball. And, if this is the case, if I choose to play basketball instead of reading, it might seem that I have failed in the coherent pursuit of my ends. In other words, the principle of instrumental reasoning seems to rely only on whether or not the agent possesses the relevant given attitude, but gives no relevance to the *degree* to which one has the relevant given attitude. The complaint here seems to be analogous to a complaint one could make to an epistemological theory that relies only on outright beliefs but ignores credences.[4] If we take into account only a subject's belief and ignore degrees of confidence, we seem to be ignoring an important aspect of the agent's epistemic rationality. Similarly, ignoring degrees of desire would overlook a central component in our understanding of the agent's practical rationality. Thus it appears that unless we add the relative strength of my conative attitudes towards reading novels (or this particular novel) and playing basketball games (or this basketball game), we cannot determine what is instrumentally rational for me to do.

I think the appearances are misleading here. This chapter provides an understanding of instrumental rationality in the pursuit of multiple extended ends that does not rely on a given strength of attitudes or on comparative attitudes.[5] I will argue both that (a) the theory can explain what counts as the rational pursuit of these ends in particular actions, and (in Chapter 4) (b) the explanation provided by the theory makes fewer substantive assumptions about the range of permissible given practical attitudes than orthodox decision theory, and thus can classify as rational seemingly unproblematic pursuits that orthodox decision theory must deem irrational. In other words, Toleration favours ETR over a theory that takes preferences as the basic given attitude. But before I can make good on these claims, we need to develop ETR in a bit more detail. In particular, we need to examine how ETR can generate preference orderings out of its basic non-comparative, non-graded attitudes and some of the ways these attitudes conflict.

3.2 Conflict of Ends and Preference Orderings

Orthodox decision theory assumes that a rational preference ordering is fully determinate so that for any lotteries L_1 and L_2, either $L_1 \geq L_2$ or $L_2 \geq L_1$. As we argued above, this requirement is probably better seen as a simplifying idealization than a requirement of rationality. Moreover, orthodox decision theory assumes that the rationality of an extended, continuous action

---

[4] In Savage (1972), the agent's credences and utility are simultaneously ascribed; in von Neuman and Morgenstern (2007), on the other hand, do not rely on subjective probabilities.

[5] For a recent interesting formal account of practical reasoning without the assumption of weighing, see Horty (2012). Of course, my aims here are quite different from Horty's, but Horty's framework is compatible with the views presented here.

can be understood and evaluated in terms of a series of momentary choices.[6] Of course, whether these assumptions can serve as a complete, or nearly complete, theory of rationality depends on whether the resulting theories leave out important aspects of rational agency. If not much is lost by representing rational agents as having a fully determinate preference ordering, and if the rationality of extended action supervenes on the rationality of momentary choices, none of this represents any serious problem.

Yet all, or at least nearly all, our ends are indeterminate and need to be pursued through actions that extend through time. Even rather simple actions such as baking a cake cannot be completed in a single momentary action. Given my lack of divine powers, I must bake a cake through a series of actions. Moreover, my end of baking a cake will be in various ways indeterminate or vague: what counts as an edible cake (or a cake at all), how long it should take to bake it, how large it should be, and so forth, is not precisely determined.

Suppose, for instance, that Mary has the end of running a marathon. There is a great deal that is indeterminate about her end. First, of course, there are many opportunities to run a marathon. Perhaps, if it takes too long for Mary to run a marathon, she would not count as achieving her end. Suppose, for instance, she trains a great deal, starts running a marathon, and then quits. But then without even thinking about it again, she runs a marathon the next day and completes it. In such a case, Mary has clearly achieved her end. On the other hand, if, after not giving any thought to it for fifty years, one day she sees a sign saying "Marathon here", runs it and completes it, she has, one would suppose, not taken necessary means to her original end; in such a case, Mary arguably had given up her earlier end and engaged later in a different pursuit of an end of the same type. However, there is a range of time with vague (or at least unknown precise) boundaries in which any marathon she completes within that time would count as reaching her goal. She also does not necessarily set on a particular time in which she wants to complete a marathon, even if there are obvious scenarios in which she would not have achieved her goal of running a marathon simply because it took her too long to cover 26.2 miles (most of us have covered 26.2 miles on foot in the course of our lives, but relatively few of us have run a marathon). Moreover, in such cases, how to achieve the goal is also vague

---

[6] This is a straightforward consequence of the axiom of Reduction of Compound Lotteries. McClennen (1990), among others, rejects this axiom. But, as will be clear later, even his defence of resolute choice is still committed to the denial of the NON-SUPERVENIENCE THESIS.

and indeterminate. It is not clear how many minutes of training Mary needs to be ready to run a marathon, and when her training will happen; she needs a balanced diet, but she can sometimes eat cake; as she is running the marathon, she might start very fast, or somewhat fast; and so forth.

In fact, we might notice something important about Mary's momentary decisions as she is pursuing this end. Let us assume she also has the end of singing, but unfortunately she cannot sing while running or training for the marathon. Now suppose she needs to decide whether she is going to go out right now for a run or if she'll keep singing. Given the indeterminacy and vagueness of the situation, it seems that at any time, she might, say, spend one more second singing instead of going out for her run. Of course, if she does this continuously, at some time, it will be too late to go for a run on this day. But since one missed day of running is unlikely to make a difference to her chances of being ready to run a marathon, these choices will not be incompatible with successfully running a marathon. Surely, if she does this every day, at the end she will no longer be in a position to run a marathon in a way that would count as successfully fulfilling her goal. But looking back at her decisions, there might be no (knowable) point in time for which we can say that at this point either Mary would have started training at this very instant or she would have no longer been able to fulfil her end. Mary's ends put her in a sort of predicament: she does not need to train at any particular moment to be successful in her pursuit of her ends, but she must train enough to be able to run a marathon.

Mary has two basic ends: singing and running a marathon (and, consequently, a derivative end of training to run the marathon). At this level of abstraction, these ends are fully compatible. However, as we suggested in Chapter 2, most of our ends have an internal structure: there are better and worse realizations of these ends. Most obviously, a faster marathon is better than a slower one. If no other ends were relevant to one's life, one would train as much as one could without risking injury, would eat only those foods that would not interfere with one's training, and so forth. And at any moment in which she starts training or running, she needs to stop singing; the ends are, in fact, in constant conflict.

There is an important difference between the end of running a marathon and the end of singing. If my only final end is to run a marathon, then my life's purpose ends as soon as I cross the finish line. Unlike the end of running a marathon, singing has an internal structure that never fails to give purpose to one's life. There is no point at which singing reaches its natural stopping point; moreover it is always "complete" at any point when one would stop singing. If I stop my marathon training too early, I'll have failed to achieve the end for which I was training for a marathon (namely, completing a marathon). But no matter when I stop singing, I'll not have failed to realize the end of singing. And if I keep training for a marathon after I ran it, I'll just be wasting time (unless I aim to run another one); but if I keep singing, I'll keep realizing the end of singing. "Singing" is one of the verbs that fall under the category that Vendler calls "activity terms"; roughly, those terms that refer to activities which are complete in themselves and do not have an end outside of themselves.[7] To simplify our exposition, I'll leave aside our ephemeral end of running a marathon and focus on the slightly different end of being a marathon runner. Having this end is enough to prevent my having nothing to do once I run a marathon; completing my first marathon would not necessarily be my last activity in pursuit of this end.

With this further structure in place, we can see why the principle of instrumental reasoning seems to run out of prescriptions rather quickly. Once an agent has these two ends, the principle of instrumental reasoning will fail to provide determinate guidance to an agent. On this understanding of the end of singing, there is nothing about it that dictates that its pursuit should ever terminate, and thus the pursuit of any end that cannot coexist in time with singing conflicts with my unrestricted end of singing. Of course, most of us get tired or bored of singing. So for most human singers the end of singing is significantly more limited: we only aim at singing in certain suitable occasions, and possibly for most us, the pursuit should be better characterized as "enjoyable singing" such that it does not count as a realization of this particular end if I sing to sooth the child even when my vocal chords are too tired or the song is an annoying Disney theme song that the child loves. But, in principle, I could have the end of singing such that, the longer I spent singing, the better the realization of the end.[8] There used to be bumper stickers that said "I'd rather be fishing" or "I'd rather be dancing". Although these are arguably hyperbolic, the implication is that these car owners *always* saw something good in dancing or fishing; were it not for other demands on their time (and leaving aside various limitations of the human body), they'd be, respectively, fishing or dancing at any time that it was in their power to fish or dance. The end of singing, understood in

---

[7] See Vendler (1957) and see also Mourelatos (1978). My usage slightly departs from theirs.
[8] The same could be said of the end of "enjoyable singing" and any end that is an activity rather than an accomplishment.

this way, is thus in potential conflict with any end whose pursuit would take away time that could have been spent singing.

Moreover, as we know all too well, singing can be done better or worse. Back to Mary, as long as she cannot run and sing at the same time, or even cannot do both just as well concomitantly as in isolation, she cannot, insofar as she is rational, adopt the (unrestricted) end of singing and the (unrestricted) end of being a marathon runner. However, the principle of instrumental reasoning says nothing about how she should proceed to revise her ends in such cases; our principle of coherence determines that I revise at least one of these ends, but there are no principles of derivation determining *how* to revise them.

This same structure that generates conflicts also generates an end-relative partial preference ordering. The nature of my end in building a house, combined with the instrumental principle, suffice to determine a certain partial ordering internal to this pursuit. For instance, insofar as a rational agent aims to build a house she will prefer, *ceteris paribus*, to use bricks over papier mâché, given the empirical facts about construction. This partial preference ordering comes not from the degree of the attitude, but from the nature of the end. It is worth distinguishing the claim I am making here with a similar claim made by Korsgaard (2008, 2009). Korsgaard says that because a house has constitutive standards, in adopting the end of building a house we are also committed to building a good house. Even a shoddy builder, if he is building a house at all, must be bound by the norms of good house building.[9] I agree with Korsgaard that there is a characteristic function of building a house that determines to some extent that some houses are better than others. Moreover, typically when one adopts the end of building a house, one adopts the end of building something precisely because it has this function. In such cases, abstracting from competing ends, adopting such an end requires that one choose the better house over the worse house, *ceteris paribus*. However, nothing we say here commits us to the view that *everyone* who builds a house must adopt precisely this end. Someone might be building a historically accurate house or a highly profitable house; it might be of no practical significance to these builders that polyethylene ground-cover insulation provides for a more comfortable living. If this type of cover was not available at the right period, or if it cuts into the profits, they'll not consider it an option.[10]

---

[9] Korsgaard (2008), p. 113. See also Korsgaard (2009).

[10] See Tenenbaum (2011) for more on this issue.

But even suitably restricted in this way, where does this structure come from? Why would my end have such an internal structure? Given my other views, the answer to this question is rather straightforward. Since I endorse the "guise of the good" thesis, by my lights, in pursuing an end an agent conceives the end as good, and the good that the agent sees in the end determines that some versions of the end better exemplify such a good. If I am writing a fiction book, I see, for instance, having written a book as good, and given the nature of this good, there will be better and worse instances of such a good—there is better and worse fiction. If you do not accept the guise of the good thesis, you'll not be happy with this is explanation. But in that case, you'll need a different explanation of the phenomenon; for my purposes, I just need the recognition of the phenomenon. In other words, I just need to recognize that for most, if not all, of the ends we pursue, both these statements hold true:

(a) Some possible actions are such that if they occur my end is actualized and some possible actions are such that if they occur my end is not actualized.[11]

(b) Among the possible actions that actualize my end, some are better actualizations of my end than others.

For instance, suppose I do write and publish a book, an indisputably brilliant book. There is no question that I have achieved or actualized my end. The book contains a particularly beautiful description of how my eating a certain sweet brought up memories of my childhood. But now that the book is done, I decide to try to write an even better version of this passage. Suppose I end up writing a version of the passage that is incontestably superior. There is also no question that had I originally used this version of the passage, the book would have been a better actualization of my end. Of course, one way to express the point is to say that I am not indifferent to how good the book that I write is, which might seem to concede that preferences have a better title to be the fundamental given practical attitudes. However, my preference for writing the better version of the passage is not "brute"; it is not that I just have this basic preference for the better passage that is not explained by anything else. It is explained exactly by *what I am trying to do* and the (apparent) good I'm trying to achieve.

---

[11] I am assuming that I have sufficient knowledge of necessary means in my power such that it is possible for me to actualize my end.

However, we should not expect that such comparative judgments would always yield a complete ordering; although some houses are clearly better than others, there are probably many houses such that neither is clearly better than the other nor are they clearly equally good. More importantly, once we compare different ends, it is not clear whether we can avail ourselves of anything to determine a ranking of options. There is no end of singing-while-marathon-racing that generates an internal ordering (or if there were, we would be looking at an altogether different case).

In sum, the same structure of our ends seems to both alleviate and amplify the impact of the Comparative Argument. The end-relative preferences do give us guidance in choosing among alternatives. As far as only running is concerned, I can choose among alternatives in a way that is determined by the nature of my end. But this structure also seems to leave me in a predicament for almost any two ends I pursue unrestrictedly: after all, there seems to be nothing in the nature of either the end of marathon running or singing that determines how the conflict should be resolved. However, there is an important sense in which this predicament is not really a problem for the theory: on ETR, *in the absence of any further ends*, any way in which I revise my ends so that they can be jointly realized is compatible with my being fully instrumentally rational. Since there is no further principle of derivation than the principle of instrumental reasoning, ETR is maximally permissive with respect to resolving conflicts *between* ends,[12] as long as the conflict is resolved. So, for instance, if I revise my ends so that I am just training to complete one marathon and to sing a few hours per week, I can coherently pursue the means to each of these ends, and this fact suffices to make the revision permissible.

3.3 Degrees of Desire and Comparative Attitudes

This outcome might seem counterintuitive. There seems to be something in the nature of the attitudes that determines the comparative importance of each end. If I care *more* about running than about singing, then not all coherent revisions are equally rational; the fact that it matters how I care about the different ends I have explains the plausibility of the Comparative Argument. On this opposing view, there is something in the nature of the

---

[12] As long as we are not pursuing any second-order ends that bear on this issue. More on this possibility in the next section.

agent's attitudes towards these ends (how *much* she cares about each end) that determines the relative importance of each, and consequently a preference ordering. In other words, desires are not distinguished from each other simply by their content; they are also held with different degrees of intensity or strength. My desire to sing might be very strong, while my desire to run a marathon might be very weak. And these facts seem relevant to the exercise of the agent's instrumental rational powers.

I cannot claim to have conclusive arguments against such a popular view,[13] but I do think it faces serious obstacles. More importantly, it is not clear that such a view has any advantages over ETR when we examine more carefully how our ends can give rise to preferences without appealing to their strength. Let us start by examining more precisely what "strong" and "weak" stand for here. One possible answer is that they denote different degrees to which I *care* about the end. But how exactly is the extent of my care being measured? The most obvious proposal is that we simply read it off from the agent's behaviour. The simplest way to "read off" a preference ordering from the agent's behaviour is not going to work here. We could simply take the agent's choices to fully determine her preferences on the assumption that she is maximally rational; this is what is usually called the agent's "revealed preferences". But, as we said in the last chapter, the agent's revealed preferences cannot be the basis of a theory of rationality; it is conceptually true that an agent never fails to act on her revealed preferences.

With this clarification in mind, we can pose the following dilemma for this view. On the one hand, we need to avoid defining "strength of desire" in ways that would obviously trivialize the view. For instance, if we define "*x* is a stronger desire than *y*" as "there is a stronger instrumental reason to pursue the object of *x* than the object of *y*", there is doubtless nothing wrong with the view that instrumental rationality requires that you pursue your desires in proportion to their strength. But we have not made much progress in understanding how we determine that a desire is stronger or

---

[13] Mark Schroeder (2007) defends a version of a Humean theory of reasons, but rejects the view that he calls "Proportionalism"; namely, that the weight of reasons to φ is proportional to the strength of the desires that φ-ing would promote. Although Schroeder's arguments against proportionalism are unrelated to considerations of instrumental rationality, insofar as one accepts the Humean theory of reasons and Schroeder's arguments, it would be strange to also accept that *when it comes to the theory of instrumental rationality*, the strength of desires plays a significant role in determining what we have reason to do. Schroeder presents an alternative view of the weight of reason, but since the weak notion of "weight" advanced there is not clearly incompatible with anything I argue for here, I'll not try to adapt his proposal to a theory of instrumental rationality.

weaker; we still lack independent criteria for determining what makes an instrumental reason the stronger one. But if "strong" and "weak" are being used in a non-question-begging way, it is unclear why instrumental rationality would recommend that preferences track strength of desire. Suppose there is some kind of psychological reality that we are tracking in our measurement of strength of desire. Couldn't an instrumentally rational agent be unconcerned about this bit of psychological reality? Would it not be a violation of the purported "neutrality" of the theory with respect to ends if we were to assume that an agent is committed to the end of bringing about, or realizing, the psychological states that possessed this property to the greatest extent? Wouldn't such a theory fail to satisfy the Toleration Constraint?

If someone proposed, for instance, normative hedonism as a theory of practical rationality, one would certainly not be proposing a theory of *instrumental* rationality. After all, the theory proposes that only one possible end is a legitimate end, only the pursuit of one object can be rational: the maximization of a certain psychological state (pleasure combined with the absence of pain). Of course, a utility-first interpretation of decision theory is not committed to the claim that the object of your pursuits should be the maximization of a certain psychological state. The theory does not tell us that the maximization of a psychological state is the *object* of our basic attitudes; rather, it says that the degree of strength of the attitude is relevant in determining rational choice. Still, the theory would be co-extensive with the theory that calls for such a maximization. In fact, this would not be different from a sophisticated form of normative hedonism. According to at least one version of hedonism, an agent should always pursue *the objects she takes pleasure in,* rather than pleasure itself.[14] So on this version of hedonism, someone who takes pleasure in snowboarding should not be pursuing pleasure as an end and snowboarding as a means to gain pleasure; rather, such a person should have snowboarding as her end because she takes pleasure in it. It is interesting to ask how different sophisticated and classical hedonism are. But moving from classical to sophisticated hedonism does not change the status of the theory as a theory of *substantive* rationality.

Doubtless we give higher priority to some ends over others; my end of providing a good education for my children takes considerable precedence over my end of growing sunflowers in my garden. It is undeniable that

---

[14] The difference here is basically the difference between whether the theory determines a substantive end or whether the theory determines what makes something a rational end (see Schroeder (2005) for similar distinctions).

certain ends are more important than others for the agent. The question is, however, whether this fact is true simply in virtue of the attitudes the agents have in holding each end, or whether they depend on further attitudes. For instance, it is true that I take my end of providing for my children to be more important than my end of keeping my car clean. But the question is whether such differences, insofar as they pertain to the theory of instrumental rationality, are explained by *the way in which* I desire each object of my ends or by *other, possibly higher-order, attitudes* that we have towards those ends. The strength-of-desire view is committed to the first alternative.

In other words, the degree of desire view claims that *simply in virtue of having each of these ends or desires* (or at least of having them in a certain manner), the agent will also have preferences that express the relative importance of each of these ends or desires (possibly to an arbitrary degree of precision). There are indeed some attitudes whose degree is intrinsic to the nature of the attitude. If I am angry at Larry and at Mary, perhaps it is the way in which I am angry that determines whether I am angrier at Larry than Mary. If I can barely concentrate when I think about Larry, foam at the mouth when I see him, and can barely stop myself from hitting him, while having no difficulty in interacting with Mary, it would seem hard to deny that I am angrier at Larry. And the same seems to be true of desire: it often makes sense to talk about the intensity of a desire, and thus we can think of the intensity with which the agent cares about an end. However, it is not clear what such an intensity of desire could be and how it could be legitimately incorporated as a constituent of the given attitude for a theory of instrumental rationality. One version of intensity of desire is relatively straightforward; it is some kind of introspectable quality of my experience. There is no doubt that I experience a different dimension of intensity when I desire to drink water after a long walk in the desert than when I desire to finish a paper by the appointed deadline. We might even be able to devise a rough ranking of intensity that approximates a partial order. But as Hume has pointed out in his distinction between "calm" and "violent" passions, such a ranking does not correspond to actual motivation.[15] More importantly, without arguing about the intrinsic choiceworthiness of the object intensely desired, it is unclear why there is any rational pressure on an agent to give preference to what's more intensely desired. Even if there is

---

[15] How exactly to interpret Hume's distinction between "calm" and "violent" passions is a difficult matter, but I do think Hume notes that a relatively intuitive notion of intensity of desire does not correspond to motivational strength.

a dimension of intensity to the way we hold an end, there is no reason to think that this dimension corresponds to the comparative importance of the end for the agent.

We could also understand strength of desire in terms of its downstream relation to various emotions and attitudes associated with the satisfaction or frustration of certain desires, such as regret or contentment.[16] But it will be implausible to think that these emotions can determine the antecedent rationality of the agent, unless we stipulate that these emotions themselves are rationally felt.[17] It does not follow from the fact that I experience regret whenever I fail to live up to my mother's expectations that it is instrumentally rational for me to meet these expectations. The regret here is not rational, but once we restrict the relevant regret to cases of "rational regret", it is no longer clear, again, that this is giving us any independent purchase on the question of what it is instrumentally rational to choose; we hit against the trivializing horn of our dilemma.

One might complain that I am demanding too much from the degree-of-desire, or utility-first, view. I have been essentially arguing that such a view violates the Toleration constraint. No matter how we try to capture the idea of degree or strength of desire, it will impose substantive restrictions on what counts as instrumentally rational agency. However, the advocate of the degree of desire might insist that this is not correct: the theory poses no restrictions on the *objects* of the attitude. It simply argues that there is one more dimension of the attitude that determines how a rational agent acts: not just the object, but also the degree of the attitude is relevant for the choices and actions of an ideally rational agent.

But there is, in fact, a restriction here on the objects of attitudes. This becomes apparent when we move to second-order desires: among those desires I might have desires to give priority to some desires over others. So I might have a desire to give priority to my desire to visit cousin Helen over my desire to visit cousin Allen. These desires might even be grounded on my substantive judgments about what I have reason, or what is good, to do. I might want to give priority to my desire to visit cousin Helen because I think it is more *important* to visit cousin Helen; however, this will turn out to be potentially in conflict with the degree of my respective desires to visit each cousin.

---

[16] See Bratman (1999) for the use of a regret condition as way of adjudicating between competing agential perspectives at the time of the choice.

[17] See Holton (2004) for a similar criticism of Bratman's no-regret condition.

Any theory of instrumental rationality will have to rule out contents of the basic attitude that are incoherent or have liar-like structure (I cannot pursue the end of failing in this very pursuit). One might object that these second-order desires are merely introducing liar-like structure to my set of desires; there is no special problem here for the utility-first view. But this is not correct. Let us propose a possible theory of rational desire: a rational agent desires only what she correctly believes to be good (in some way), and desires to rationally prefer x over y (or desires to give priority to x over y) only when x is better than y. One might not be sympathetic to this view, but it seems to be a view that cannot be ruled out by a theory of *instrumental* rationality. A degree-of-desire or utility-first view, in particular, should be silent about what is rational to desire; after all, it takes desires to be the given attitudes. Now, a substantive theory of rational (or correct) desire might also make claims about the right intensity for each desire—or, as one might prefer, a theory about the fittingness of varying degrees or strength of desires. Assuming our theory of rational desire and preference, the utility-first view now requires that it is fitting to desire x more than desiring y only when I should choose x over y. After all, if fitness of intensity and "choice-worthiness" did not dovetail in this way, the utility-first view would put us in a rational dilemma: we could not at the same time be instrumentally rational and have only fitting and rational desires. If the substantive theory does not require that they dovetail, then there will be cases in which the strength of my desires are fitting and my evaluative judgments are correct, such that the theory of instrumental rationality prescribes that I choose x over y even though I correctly judge that I should choose y over x[18] (since *ex hypothesi*, there are cases in which this judgment is compatible with my fittingly desiring y more strongly than x). We would in such a case be caught in a dilemma, in which we (knowingly) could not be both substantively and instrumentally rational.

But this "dovetailing" view has implausible consequences. I strongly desire the welfare of my children, and much less strongly desire that positions in my university be divided according to merit. These seem to be fitting responses: I would be a cold parent or an overly enthusiastic meritocrat if this were not true of me. Yet, when I need to decide between candidates in

---

[18] For simplicity, I am assuming that the substantive theory allows also that it is fitting that you desire x more than y also when y is worse than x (rather than just when x is not better than y). The example of a plausible theory that allows this kind of divergence accepts this stronger claim.

appointing new Associate Deans, I certainly judge it to be better that the position be given to the more meritorious candidate than to one of my children, even if such appointments would greatly contribute to their welfare; I might even be happy to be outvoted even if I think that my colleagues are making a mistake in appointing one of my offspring.[19] Of course, one can insist that in this specific case I must desire more strongly that the Associate Dean's position be filled by the most competent candidate than I desire the welfare of my children, but this now seems to be just a different way to express, rather than the explanation of, my rational preference of the former over the latter; we are back to the trivializing horn of our dilemma. We could also argue that the mistake is to think that the fundamental basic attitude is degree of desire or utility rather than the preference itself. But in such a case we have abandoned the utility-first view in favour of the preference-first view criticized in the previous chapter.

One might also be tempted by an analogy with degrees of belief. If degrees of beliefs are relevant for the (epistemic) rationality of the agent, shouldn't degrees of some conative attitude also be relevant for the agent's practical rationality? But first, there is no particular reason for these two things to go together; in fact, it would be incumbent on the proponent of such a view to argue for the parallel. More importantly, there is an important disanalogy between degrees of belief and degrees of desire. A plausible view about the relation between evidence and belief pressures us to accept a view in which degrees of belief are important in assessing our rationality. Evidence does not always speak univocally in favour of one among many incompatible beliefs. The fact that the murderer used a knife is evidence that Mary, who is so fond of knives, is the murderer, but also that Larry, who had easy access to the knife, is the murderer. It seems plausible to say that in such cases we spread our credences over these incompatible hypotheses. And if we accept anything like the Principal Principle, these degrees of belief will also have coherence conditions dictated by the probability calculus.

However, there is no similar phenomenon that leads us to postulate degrees of desire in the realm of practical rationality. At least insofar as we are considering basic, rather than instrumental, desires, there is nothing

---

[19] See Tenenbaum (2014) for a similar argument in another context. Note that it might be fitting that I desire more that I *choose* the welfare of my child in this case (it might be fine, for instance, to welcome the news that I will be under the effect of a drug that will make me choose my child for the job).

that determines that a rational agent must have a certain strength of desire with regard to basic desires; in fact, desires could not be the basic given attitudes if their rationality was determined by some other attitudes. And, obviously, no similar coherence principle applies to strength of desire: I can have arbitrarily high strength of desire to each of two incompatible propositions. In fact, this is often our predicament. I very strongly desire to go to the theatre tonight and I very strongly desire to go to the opera, but I can only engage in at most one of these activities.

An alternative way of accounting for the fact that we obviously care more about some of our ends than others is significantly friendlier to ETR. On this proposal, we take the relative importance that the agent attaches to each end to be a further attitude of the agent—a reflective take on the comparative merits or attractions of the options.[20] Suppose I have an end of φ-ing and an end of ψ-ing, and when I reflect on the possible choice of φ-ing or ψ-ing in certain circumstances, or φ-ing or ψ-ing *hic et nunc*, I form a further attitude of giving priority to my end of φ-ing. My preference for the welfare of my children over the appearance of my car is grounded in a *further* second-order comparative attitude. Once we accept that these preferences are grounded in further second-order attitudes, we can simply identify such preferences with second-order ends; in other words, we do not need a further type of basic attitude. In our example, I simply have a second-order end to give priority to the pursuit of my children's welfare when the pursuit of their welfare and the pursuit of a better appearance for my car come into conflict.

It is worth distinguishing two cases in which this second-order end could be relevant. In the first case, we can think of a conflict between two (parts of a) sufficient, but not necessary, means for an acceptable realization of each end. So perhaps I can spend some money on an especially fantastic detailing job for my car, or send my children to an enrichment program that will significantly improve their lives. In this case, the pursuit of each of the first-order ends (the welfare of my children; the appearance of my car) is fully compatible with the realization of each end, though of course, spending the money on the car will result in a better actualization of the end of preserving the appearance of the car, and vice versa. However, at least under a certain version of the second-order end, not choosing to invest the money in the welfare of my children is a necessary means; using the money for the

---

[20] See Tenenbaum (2007a, 2018b) for more details on my view on these comparative attitudes.

car is not compatible with any acceptable realization of my end of giving priority to my children. A different case would be a conflict in which it would be impossible to realize both of my first-order ends. In such case, we would need to give up one of the ends, and the higher-order end would guide the *revision* of the ends; I give priority to the welfare of my children by revising my ends in such a way that I do not abandon it when it is in conflict with the end of my car's appearance.[21]

But have we fully answered the Comparative Argument? Does instrumental rationality have something to say about our conflicting ends only when there are second-order ends to give priority one of these ends? In order to fully answer the Comparative Argument, we need to look into more detail about how our basic attitudes combined with the principle of instrumental reasoning can generate partial preference orderings, and, more broadly, how the principle of instrumental reasoning determines us to act in situations in which our ends seem to conflict. I'll argue that the principle of instrumental reasoning not only has enough to say, but it says exactly enough about the exercise of our rational agency in such situations.

3.4 Conflicting and Competing Ends and the Principle of Instrumental Reasoning

In order to take stock of how broadly ETR can generate comparative attitudes, let us pull together the discussion of preferences so far in a systematic manner. We can distinguish four different ways in which preferences can play a role in our exercise of our instrumental rational powers:

(1) *Preferences Internal to Ends.*[22] As we argued in the previous chapter, various ends I pursue have better or worse realizations and thus they entail a partial preference ranking among the possible ways of pursuing an end. *Ceteris paribus*, a rational agent pursuing an end will pursue a better realization of the end.

(2) *Preferences as Dispositions to Pursue Ends in Certain Contexts.* We can ascribe preferences to an agent also on the basis of her dispositions to pursue certain ends in certain circumstances. If Mary

---

[21] More on these issues below.

[22] For some related ideas (though very differently pursued and with different aims), see Andreou (2015).

typically abandons her travel plans when she realizes that she will face no risks to her life and limb, we can ascribe to Mary a preference for adventurous travel. These preferences bear on the agent's rational powers only indirectly in a way that can inform her general pursuit of happiness (as defined in the previous chapter). So Mary may buy expensive travel insurance, as she knows that she is likely to have a serious accident in her trip, and one of her ends is not to go bankrupt. I will often call these preferences just *behavioural preferences*.

(3) *Preferences as Higher Order Reflective Ends*. We can also ascribe to an agent a preference in cases in which the agent has the reflective end of giving priority to one end over another in her pursuits. As such, it is simply one more end that the agent pursues. I will often call these preferences just *reflective preferences*.

We now introduce one more way in which preferences are relevant in understanding the exercise of our rational powers:

(4) *Preferences as Pareto Optimal Potential Pursuits*. Suppose right now I am pursuing three ends: I am building a house, I am preparing my trip to Kathmandu, and I am trying to prove the Goldbach conjecture. Now I am offered $1,000, no strings attached. Should I take it? Money is a general means and thus many of our ends are well served by our having more money. In our case, two of my ends can be better pursued if I have more money (having a house built, travelling to Kathmandu), and it is, we stipulate, irrelevant to my actualization of my third end (a proof of the theorem). In cases in which the pursuit of x contributes to a greater extent to the pursuit of some of the agent's ends than the pursuit of y without it being the case that the pursuit of y contributes to a greater extent than the pursuit x to any of her ends, then, *ceteris paribus*, an instrumentally rational agent pursues x when she can pursue x or y but not both. In such a case I'll say that the agent, insofar as she manifests instrumental rationality, prefers x over y on *Pareto Grounds*. I will often call these just *Pareto Preferences*.

Note that I am not saying that these are four different meanings of "preference"; "preference" is being used here univocally. In all such cases preferences are dispositions to choose among alternatives, or, in other words, dispositions to engage in a certain pursuit over another when pursuing both is incompatible. The dispositions in (1) and (4) are themselves manifestations of our rational power. In (3), the disposition is grounded in our adoption of the end of giving priority to one end over another. In (2), the disposition is "brute": it is simply a disposition we *have* to abandon certain ends in certain contexts.

It might seem that we could get rid of the *ceteris paribus* clause in (4) by specifying either that pursuing x and pursuing y are the only relevant alternatives, or, with greater generality, by adding a clause that there is no option that is preferred over both pursuing x and pursuing y. But, in fact, even with such addenda, we would still need the *ceteris paribus* clause. Sometimes a rational agent may choose an option m, even when she knows that she prefers option n to option m and nothing prevents her from choosing n over m. Or so I'll now proceed to argue. But first we need to bring out some important aspects of the pursuit of indeterminate ends and the nature of what I will call "gappy actions".

Let us distinguish the general pursuit of singing (or being a marathon runner) from the more specific end of actively singing (training for/running the marathon) *hic et nunc*. The general activities of singing and being a marathon runner extend over long periods of time, and within these long periods of time, there'll be many moments in which we're not actively engaged in any part of this activity. Mary's general activity of singing does not require that she sings at every moment; her being engaged in this activity is compatible with her stopping here and there while training for the marathon; the same holds *mutatis mutandis* for being a marathon runner. Mary might also be a committed runner, and thus give greater priority to her pursuit of being a marathon runner than to her pursuit of singing. Thus Mary has, according to (3), a general preference for being a marathon runner over singing. Given the priority she gives to the first end, if these turn out to be incompatible pursuits, she would give up singing but not being a marathon runner.

Let us add one more end to Mary's modest list of pursuits. She also has the end of engaging in the enjoyment of pleasant activities. Now suppose Mary takes pleasure in singing but not in training for marathons.[23] At a particular moment in time, singing will represent a better actualization of her

---

[23] Ed Whitlock, the late over-70, over-75, over-80, and over-85 marathon record holder, would describe his training runs as "a chore" (http://www.cbc.ca/sports/olympics/trackand-field/world-marathon-record-holder-ed-whitlock-1.4023053).

ends of singing and enjoying pleasures without, arguably, making any difference to how she actualizes her end of being a marathon runner. One more second of training will not make a difference to how good a marathon runner she is. By (4) then, at each moment, she has a *Pareto Preference* for singing over training.

Now one might think that an instrumentally rational and coherent agent can't prefer singing at every particular moment while holding on to the end of being a marathon runner (let alone to the end of giving priority to marathon running). At some point, Mary *must* prefer to train. If she never abandons her end of being a marathon runner, there must have been some point in time at which she does not prefer to sing over training; for instance, at the very last moment that she could still have run a marathon if she would only train.

This reaction, however, underestimates the vague or indeterminate nature of the end. In Chapter 4, I'll provide a more detailed argument for the claim that rational (and rather mundane) ends cannot be "precisified" in this manner. But for now, let's just assume that this is the case in virtue of the fact that there is no precise date by which Mary needs to run her marathon and no precise pace below which it would not count as running a marathon, and so forth. If this is true, there might be no moment at which she must have the preference for training over singing *hic et nunc*.[24]

ETR takes actions to be the basic given attitudes. Actions extend through different intervals and can overlap partially or in their entirety. Even if one cannot, at least in a sense, sing and train for a marathon at the same time, in a broader sense of "singing" and "training" both these activities *can* be pursued at the same time.[25] Most long-term actions are what we might call "gappy". As a first approximation, we can call a (token) action A "gappy", if it extends through an interval of time t_0–t_n such that at some intervals contained in the t_0–t_n interval, the agent is not doing anything that is a (constitutive or instrumental) means to A. This is just an approximation since some gappy actions would fail to qualify under this definition if their means are themselves gappy. For instance, a means to training for a marathon is stretching regularly. However, stretching regularly is itself gappy; I am still engaged in the activity of stretching regularly even on my days off stretching (say, Wednesday). But now if we follow our current definition, it comes out

---

[24] More on this issue in the next chapters.
[25] This is what is often called the "broad" sense of the progressive. On these issues, see Falvey (2000) and Thompson (2008).

that training for a marathon is not gappy and no intervals within t_0-t_n are gaps. After all, at any moment in the interval I am pursuing a means to training for the marathon: given that stretching regularly is itself gappy, at any moment I am engaged in pursuing these means. We therefore need a more precise definition of gappy actions.

Suppose I perform an action A (the pursuit of some end) extended through an interval of time t_0-t_n. Let us call the interval t_0-t_n "A's range". I perform A by performing other actions whose range will be a proper subset of A's range; such actions are either instrumental or constitutive means. But I also perform other actions whose ranges are proper subsets of A, but are neither instrumental nor constitutive means to A. Let us call any action that I perform within a proper subset of A's action a "momentary action relative to A". This might sound like strange terminology as some of these "momentary" actions might extend for quite some time, but this terminology is useful for our purposes; in evaluating the agent's instrumental rationality relative to A, the momentary actions relative to A demarcate exactly the minimal intervals that are relevant to this evaluation.[26] Let us say that A is a "basic action" if there is no action B such that B is momentary relative to A. If there are basic actions,[27] then these will be "absolutely" momentary actions; that is, they are momentary relative to any other action with which they overlap in time.

We are now in a position to give a more precise definition of "gaps" and "gappy" actions, but the definition will vary whether or not we assume that there are basic actions. The definition is much simpler on the assumption that they exist, so I'll start with this one. Let us start with the idea of a "fully active" part of an action. Basically we want to understand a "fully active" part of an action in contrast with a gap—a part of the action in which the agent is fully engaged in taking the means (constitutive or instrumental) for performing the action. We can give a kind of recursive definition of "fully active part" by starting from basic actions. We say that all parts of a basic action are fully active. Next, you define fully active parts of a non-basic action A that extends through an interval i that overlaps with A as follows:[28]

---

[26] Often when discussing actions that overlap, I'll simply talk about "momentary actions" and drop the relativization clause.

[27] Not everyone accepts that there are basic actions. See Lavin (2013). For earlier scepticism about the existence of basic actions, see Baier (1971).

[28] These definitions assume that the agent has knowledge of all the relevant facts. Introducing the possibility of false beliefs (or even accidentally true beliefs) will complicate matters. I leave the discussion of the rationality of these actions for Chapter 9.

(1) If throughout an interval i an agent is doing B in order to do (for the sake of doing) A and doing B is a basic action, then the part of the action contained in i is a fully active part of doing A.

(2) If throughout an interval i an agent is doing B in order to do (for the sake of doing) A and all parts of doing B in i are fully active, then the part of the action contained in i is a fully active part of doing A.

(3) No other parts of A are fully active (they are "gaps" if they do not contain any subparts that are fully active).

Of course, we can now define a "gappy" action as one where some of their parts are gaps. If you assume instead that there are no basic actions, we need to define a different notion of "basic* action" that can serve our purposes. Let us start by looking at a rather rough version of a central argument against the existence of basic actions. The argument starts from the premise that if I am walking from A to B, I am also walking from A to the halfway point, and from A to the quarter-point, and so forth. We then argue that any such "segment actions" must be knowingly done for the sake of the larger action of walking from A to B. Since each of these segment actions are constituted by other segment actions to which we can reapply our argument, we never reach a basic action.

Now this certainly does not do full justice to the arguments against basic actions.[29] But what matters for our purposes is that even those who deny the existence of basic actions do not deny that some actions are continual such that *each* part in the continuum is being done in order to do (for the sake of) the larger action. As I walk from A to B, I might stop, sit down and rest, and so forth. But there'll be at least some segments, say C–D, such that the subparts of C and D are teleologically ordered in such a way that for each interval shorter than the C–D range in which I am acting at all,[30] there is always an action that I complete such that I complete it for the sake of walking from C to D. If this is true, then we say that walking from C to D is a basic* action. We can now replace "basic action" with "basic* action" in our definitions of "fully active parts", "gaps", and "gappy action".

It is worth noting a couple of things about how we define these terms. First, the parts that are fully active will equally include constitutive and

---

[29] For the proper version of the argument, see Lavin (2013).

[30] This clause is just intended to rule out very short intervals which are arguably too short to count as an interval in which I act. I take no position on the question of whether there are such intervals.

instrumental means. But we ordinarily balk at classifying instrumental means as part of the action. Suppose I am buying a pair of new running shoes. This is something I am doing for the sake of training for my marathon. By our definition when I am in the store choosing the shoes I am doing something that is a fully active part of training for a marathon. But suppose someone phones me while I am paying for my shoes and asks, "What are you doing at this moment?" It would be at the very least misleading to say, "I am training for a marathon"; this answer would be appropriate only if right now I were engaged in a fully active part training for a marathon that is a constitutive part of training. Now we could try to devise definitions that would distinguish between constitutive and instrumental means that would explain these differences in usage. However, since this distinction is not relevant for our purposes, I'll not try to capture this bit of ordinary language.

My practical rationality in pursuit of an end depends both on how I manage the pursuit of the end throughout the whole interval of my action—how I engage in the fully active parts of the action—and how I manage the gaps. If I am baking a cake I must make sure first that *at some point* I put the cake in the oven, even if I can let my action stretch so that I am checking my email when I could have already put the cake in the oven. Second, while checking my email is a fine activity to engage in through at least some of the gaps of my action, taking hallucinogenic drugs or boarding transatlantic ships would possibly jeopardize my cake baking; even during the gap parts of my cake baking I need to monitor that I am not undermining this pursuit. An instrumentally rational agent engages in the fully active parts *in order to do* (or *for the sake of*) the larger action and she ensures that the actions performed in the gaps are *compatible with* the acceptable[31] completion or maintenance of the larger action. I will frequently use a chart like Figure 3.1 representing training for a marathon to represent the rational relations between the larger action and its parts.

Figure 3.1 Training for a marathon

---

[31] More on "acceptable" later.

The shaded box represents actions that are not done for the sake of the larger action but are nonetheless within its range. Actions to the left happen at an earlier time than actions to the right. Note that we could represent also the pursuit of being a marathon runner as a larger action in the same way. And, of course, the actions that are part of the larger actions are themselves extended and could have their parts represented as in Figure 3.2.

The lower actions in our diagrams are momentary relative to the upper actions as long as the former are in the range of the latter, and, again, actions to the left are earlier than actions to the right. In Mary's case, we have assumed that training for a marathon is not pursued for the sake of anything else, so there is nothing "higher up" in our representation of Mary's action than "running a marathon". For our purposes we can stop here and not ask whether this is a coherent possibility. In fact, some might find it unnecessarily tentative to warn readers that my views do not require such inquiry; isn't it clearly possible that Mary does not run for the sake of anything else? But in some views of the nature of agency, there *must* be something higher up. If agency has a constitutive end or aim, then everything we do is for the sake of this end,[32] so everything we do, we do in the pursuit of the good, or autonomy, or self-understanding, or eudaimonia, and so forth. For our purposes it will not matter whether there is a "highest" end at which all actions aim.

The diagrams so far only represent the pursuit of one end at a time. Since singing is also one of Mary's ends, we can add singing to our diagram; singing will have the opposite relation to the momentary actions that running the marathon had (see Figure. 3.3). Particular acts of singing will be done for the sake of singing, while episodes of training will be merely in the range of the end of singing. Once we have multiple higher actions, we can

Figure 3.2 Marathon running

---

[32] Of course, any plausible version of such a view would take some of our other ends to be constitutive means or expressions of the pursuit of this end, rather than instrumental means. And such views will have to be able to say, like Aristotle, that some things are pursued for their own sake and at the same time for the sake of the noble (or for the sake of eudaimonia).

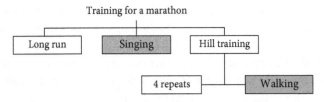

Figure 3.3 Training for a marathon

Figure 3.4 Marathon running and singing

represent the relation of '*x* is done for the sake of *y*' by matching fonts to the ends (Figure. 3.4).[33]

We can now go back to the structure of Mary's ends and try an alternative description of Mary's predicament. Let's take a choice of momentary action. Let's say at t_1, Mary chooses to sing because it is her preferred choice; this can now be captured as the fact that singing right now is preferred on Pareto Grounds; after all, singing for one more second does not affect her realization of her end of being a marathon runner. But this will still hold for the next momentary action, and the next, and the next, and so forth. If there is no (epistemically accessible) precise point in time in which Mary's singing at that moment makes it impossible for her to run a marathon, then her singing *hic et nunc* is known to never (or at least not ever known to) undermine her end of being a marathon runner. So even though Mary prefers, in general, being a marathon runner over singing, she never chooses counterpreferentially when she chooses to sing at each particular moment. In other words, no particular choice of singing is incompatible with any of the ends she is pursuing. Of course, at some point Mary will no longer be able to train for the marathon, so her holding the end of training for the marathon at that point would no longer be rational.

---

[33] We're assuming that each momentary action is pursued only for the sake of one immediately higher action. This assumption, of course, is not true, as we have already seen in the case of general means. But for now there is no reason to complicate our notation to allow for the possibility of actions done for the sake of multiple immediately higher ends.

Suppose Mary has been singing at each particular moment and at t_n she realizes that she is no longer able to run a marathon. Since she held on to the end of running a marathon from t_0 to t_n but she did not pursue adequate means to these ends (without the interference of any unexpected, unknown, or even "risky" circumstances), she was instrumentally irrational in the pursuit of this end through this interval. But the "shorter" actions that she performs during this interval individually manifest no irrationality, as each of them is pursued for the sake of an end that she does have, and none of them is incompatible with any one of her ends. Given that Mary was irrational relative to the larger action, but none of her shorter actions were irrational, we can say that her ends allow for the possibility of *top-down irrationality*.[34] ETR introduces the possibility of top-down irrationality, or, in other words the possibility that the rationality of an agent in a t_0–t_n interval does not supervene on the rationality of the momentary actions contained within the interval (what we called in the previous chapter *THE NON-SUPERVENIENCE THESIS*). Since Mary's end does not *require* that she runs at any particular moment, but if she fails to do this at all moments she will not have pursued efficient means to her end, it seems that what instrumental rationality demands with respect to such ends is that she be rationally permitted to run even if running is not her preferred momentary action, since the cumulative effect of always choosing her preferred action leads to the choice of a less preferred option. In other words, Mary exercises her instrumental rational powers with respect to the end of training for the marathon by engaging in training activities even at times when she has a Pareto Preference to sing instead.

I propose that in evaluating actions in the pursuit of long-term, indeterminate ends, we need to evaluate the action from two distinct (but compatible) perspectives; a perfectly (instrumentally) rational agent is never deemed irrational by either perspective, and an agent acted rationally through a period of time if (and only if) during that time the agent didn't fail to act rationally at any interval or moment that is a (not necessarily proper) subset of the interval in question. A *punctate* perspective evaluates whether a momentary choice or action was rational, given the agent's various preferences and ends. For our purposes, all that matters is that a punctate perspective will permit the agent to choose her (Pareto) preferred momentary action but will also permit the agent to forego her preferred action in favour of pursuing actions that are constitutive of the pursuit of

---

[34] A more formal presentation of top-down irrationality and the conditions under which it obtains is presented in Chapter 4.

the agent's long-term, indeterminate ends. Were it not for such permissions, the agent in the above example would be required to sing at every moment, and thus would not be able to run a marathon (an option that is in tension with her end of giving priority to being a marathon runner).

The *extended* perspective evaluates whether enough of these permissions have been exercised and thus whether the end has been achieved. If our agent does not train on enough occasions, she will be unable to run the marathon. Although at each point she will have chosen something that from the punctate perspective she was permitted to choose, she will have violated a requirement from the extended perspective: the requirement to take the means to an end that she held stably through the whole extent of the time interval in question. Although we cannot locate her irrationality at any particular moment in time, the extended perspective deems that she has acted irrationally by failing to take the necessary means to one of her long-term ends. On the other hand, an agent who stops singing from time to time in order to properly train for a marathon is rational (assuming no other failures) even if either (or both) of the following is true:

(1) The agent preferred to sing at times in which she was training for the marathon.
(2) Had the agent trained a little bit less, she would have still trained enough.

For all we said Mary could also train for the marathon non-stop and never spend any time singing. The punctate perspective allows an agent to exercise permissions not to choose a preferred action. But since we imposed no limits on how often those permissions can be exercised, Mary could *always* choose to go running rather than singing. Given what we know of human nature, this is rather unlikely, but nothing we said so far would make it irrational for Mary to choose this alternative, even if she would not have acted irrationally at any particular point. But assuming that Mary does have singing as one of her ends, always exercising such permissions would also be a violation of instrumental rationality, which is revealed from the extended perspective.

In sum, an extended agent exercises her rational power over time. The exercise of these powers cannot be understood as simply the sum of its exercises moment by moment. This is obviously just a rough sketch of how principles of instrumental reasoning apply to long-term, indeterminate ends, but we will refine these ideas as the book progresses.

3.5 Satisficing and Conflict Resolution

The principle of instrumental reasoning issues a quite robust set of permissions and requirements[35] with respect to *competing* ends, even if it cannot give us much guidance on how to revise *conflicting* ends. But this might seem not quite enough. First, it does not tell us exactly when to exercise such permissions. More importantly, it does not seem to answer our original question: What should a rational agent do when they realize that their ends conflict? We still seem to be stuck with the view that every revision is possible when faced with actually conflicting ends, as in the case of the pursuit of the *unrestricted* ends of singing and marathon running.

However, the ideal of having a determinate answer to these conflicts imposes requirements on our pursuits that violate the Toleration Constraint,[36] or so I'll argue in the next chapter. It is true that, in principle, every revision is rationally permissible, but this is a desirable result; Mary's original situation is compatible with her having any reflective preference between pursuing singing to any extent and running a marathon to any extent. But in an important sense, ETR is not completely silent on how to revise conflicting ends. If Mary does not have or form a reflective preference, there is a default *minimal* revision that she could make to her ends. She could simply adopt restricted ends of "enough singing (given that I am also a marathon runner)" and "enough training (given that I am also a singer)". At least insofar as we assume that the agent will make the minimal possible revision to her ends, we can determine that she will make this revision. "Enough training" and "enough singing" are vague or indeterminate ends, but there seems to be nothing intrinsically irrational about having ends with this kind of structure. In fact, it seems to be a violation of Toleration to rule them out a priori.

This minimal revision leaves us with two vague or indeterminate ends, which still have the same internal structure as the unrestricted ends (that is, the same things will count as better or worse realizations of singing or marathon running). Due to this structure, there will be no point at which it will be the *maximum* amount of singing I could have done while still being able to train for the marathon. At each point, singing for a millisecond longer would not affect my marathon running, or at the very least, I would

---

[35] In Chapter 4, we will examine more carefully how these permissions and requirements work.

[36] See Chapter 1.

never be in a position to know that it would. If at each millisecond, I had the thought "one millisecond longer will make no difference" and kept on singing, at some point I would realize that it was too late to train for a marathon. Thus when evaluating over a period of time whether I was successful in my pursuit of the ends of singing and training for a marathon, the criterion for success could not be whether I reached the greatest amount of singing or training or a maximum point in some function that combines both. I will be successful in my pursuits instead if I have done *enough* singing and training. And since non-accidental success in the achievement of an end should suffice for determining that an agent did not run afoul of the principle of instrumental reasoning, instrumental rationality requires no more than that I satisfice. That is, I should pursue singing in such a way that the actualization of my end of singing is good enough, and I should train in such a way that the actualization of my end of being a marathon runner is good enough. We exercise our rational agency by reaching an *acceptable*[37] realization of each end, not (or at least not necessarily) by reaching its maximal point.

It is important to note that this kind of satisficing requirement is not a requirement imposed by our bounded rationality[38] such that a more idealized version of ourselves would maximize rather than satisfice. There is no level in the theory in which any kind of maximization is taken to be an ideal. In fact, maximization is not possible in the context of these two ends.

I would hazard a guess that as we look at human actions in the wild, we rarely see the kind of decisions that lie at the focus of the Comparative Argument. Most of the time, we move from the pursuit of one end to the next, without much thought about the relative importance of competing ends, let alone any kind of reasoning that even approximates maximization. In our book-opening example of a subway ride, once I leave the subway, I would probably continue on my way to the office without paying much attention to all the alternative actions I could take. And on arriving at my office, I would prepare for my meeting with a student, then chat with a colleague, then start working on a paper, and so forth. These activities themselves, as well as my moving from one to the other, involve no more comparative deliberation among ends than my subway ride. Of course, within the pursuit of our ends, we often make choices that involve comparing alternatives (would it be better to make this paragraph a footnote, or should I leave it in place?). There are also times in our lives when we need to

---

[37] More on "acceptable" in Chapter 4.

[38] This is obviously what motivates the initial proponents of a "satisficing rule", such as Simon (1972). For a more detailed discussion of how this conception of satisficing differs from others, see my Tenenbaum (2015).

make decisions among competing ends, where these decisions may be momentous or trivial (should I betray my commitment to the workers in order to accept a lucrative job? Should I spend the evening working or just watch a movie?). But these are relatively special moments in a practical life of generally engaging in pursuing the means to our ends, without engaging, implicitly or explicitly, in fundamentally comparative reasoning. Within ETR's framework, this comes as no surprise: comparative assessment of competing ends is an interruption, a kind of reasoning we need to deploy only when we notice that our ends are in conflict and thus in need of revision.

However, it seems plausible that a life of missed opportunities to do better must be, almost by conceptual necessity, a life that falls short of ideal. Given the time it takes to deliberate, our modest computational powers, our susceptibility to mistakes and biases, and so forth, this more "laid back" existence is probably the best we can hope for, where ideal agents would always choose the best possible action. In other words, a maximising conception of rationality seems to have nearly irresistible appeal. But if maximization is not even possible in light of the nature of our ends, this supposed ideal is not a coherent one as far as human agency is concerned. And without such an ideal guiding our understanding of practical rationality, we might lack any reason to hold on to the picture that practical rationality is essentially comparative, or that agents in these mundane scenarios are in any way falling short of rational ideals.

3.6 Preferences and Rational Agency

Yet, there seems to be something to the thought that an agent who acts according to her preferences displays a virtue of practical rationality. Although behavioural preferences are not directly relevant to our understanding of the agent's rational powers, the other type of preferences certainly are. Indeed, there would be something strange with an agent to whom we could attribute a preference ordering in many choice situations, but who would always act counterpreferentially without any particular reason to do so. It is not even clear that sustained counterpreferential agency is a coherent form of agency. Although I'll say more on this topic in the last chapter, here is what we can already accept without further ado:

> [PREF1] Acting in accordance with one's preferences is always permissible.
>
> [PREF2] We may act counterpreferentially only for the sake of an end that requires acting counterpreferentially.

The defence of the coherence of the first claim with the general theory will come in Chapter 4, as well as a clearer explanation of the second principle.

I have given very general reasons to accept that competing or conflicting ends do not pose a problem for ETR. In Chapter 4, I'll argue more systematically that in fact cases of competing or conflicting ends with the structure of Mary's predicament are better accounted by ETR principles than by the principles proposed by other theories of instrumental rationality. The philosophical treatment of this issue is most clearly presented in attempts to answer to Quinn's puzzle of the self-torturer, which has a very similar structure to Mary's choices. In Chapter 4 I'll look at the puzzle and examine various ways in which philosophers have tried to respond to the puzzle within the framework of decision theory, as well as attempts to deal with the puzzle by introducing other given attitudes. I argue that only ETR gives a satisfactory answer to the puzzle. Moreover the structure of the puzzle is present in almost all our pursuits. Thus, only ETR can provide an adequate account of instrumental rationality insofar as normal human pursuits are concerned.

4

Indeterminate Ends and the Puzzle of the Self-Torturer

4.0 Introduction

In Chapter 3, I explained why ETR was committed to the possibility of top-down independence, and consequently the non-supervenience of the instrumental rationality[1] of an agent through an extended period of time on the rationality of the agent moment by moment. This possibility, I argued, was a consequence of the nature of the pursuit of indeterminate ends that extend through time. In this chapter, I argue that these features of ETR explain common patterns of instrumentally rational human agency that other theories of instrumental rationality cannot explain. Theories of rationality that take preference or utility as basic, and especially theories of rationality committed to decision theory, will classify as irrational large swaths of perfectly intelligible manifestations of human agency and thus will result in a massive failure to conform to the Toleration Constraint.

The central case for ETR will be Warren Quinn's notorious puzzle of the self-torturer.[2] Although the puzzle puts a forward a highly fictionalized case, it manifests a structure that is common to almost every extended pursuit of an indeterminate end. So the problem is not a local problem for orthodox theory at the fringes of the phenomena we're trying to account for; the failure is a failure to account for the rationality of almost any action that we engage in.

The main advantages of focusing on the puzzle of the self-torturer is that, first, the puzzle presents the issue in a very sharp manner: the self-torturer has only two fairly ordinary ends (roughly avoiding pain and making money) whose better and worse actualizations are quite clear (more money

---

[1] Namely to the *NON-SUPERVENIENCE THESIS*: The rationality of an agent through a time interval t_1 to t_n does not supervene on the rationality of the agent at each moment between t_1 and t_n.

[2] Quinn (1990).

is better than less, less pain is better than more), and, as we will see, will generate a very clear (though not well-behaved) preference ordering. Moreover, the puzzle has received a significant amount of attention from philosophers sympathetic to orthodox decision theory; since I argue that decision theory cannot provide a good understanding of instrumental rationality in such contexts, we should look at how decision theorists try to approach such contexts. Finally, the puzzle of the self-torturer presents a relatively "well-behaved" type of extended action: it consists of a series of discrete choices; the actions that the self-torturer takes in these discrete choices are neither gappy nor problematic in some other way; the scenario does not stipulate in advance that the agent has indeterminate ends; the conative attitudes of the self-torturer seem to be quite ordinary and not essentially different from other attitudes that decision theory routinely ascribes to agents. So the structure of the choices faced by the self-torturer makes it a particularly favourable case of extended action for decision theory; if decision theory cannot provide a good account for instrumental rational agency in such a case, it will certainly not be in position to provide a good account in cases of continuous action with more radically indeterminate ends.

I will be mostly contrasting ETR with decision theory. Some of the problems I raise for decision theory will apply to theories that take the mental state of intention to be the basic given attitude as well. However, my main argument against having a mental state of intention (more particularly future-directed intention)[3] as the basic given attitude is that it is otiose: it does not replace (intentional) action as a basic given attitude, and insofar as it adds anything to the theory of instrumental rationality, it is either redundant or unsound. I argue in this chapter that this applies to the case of the puzzle of the self-torturer. We cannot explain the rationality of the agent who makes the right choices in such a scenario[4] by looking at the future-directed intentions of such an agent. But, of course, this is only one way in

---

[3] Future-direction intention contrasts with intention in action. If one thinks that intention in action is inseparable from intentional action then a view that takes intention in action as basic is not significantly different from the view presented here. If the intention in action is a separable mental state that causes or accompanies intentional action, then it seems that the state is not essentially different from future-directed intention. Thus, I'll focus on future-directed intentions when discussing a view that is supposedly an *alternative to* ETR, since any view that takes intention as the basic given attitude that is significantly different from ETR will also take future-directed intentions as a basic given attitude. More on this issue in Section 4.7 and Chapter 5.

[4] Or the irrationality of the agent who makes the wrong choices.

which one might think future-directed intentions are relevant for the instrumental rationality of the agent. The full case against the view that future-directed intentions are among the basic given attitudes is made primarily in the next two chapters.

If orthodox decision theory fails, I argue that ETR shows how a solution to the puzzle can fall directly out of an application of the principle of instrumental reasoning to indeterminate ends. This solution preserves all of the intuitive assumptions that seemed to generate the puzzle, yet it employs only a minimal set of rational principles. If the argument of this chapter is sound, two important tenets of ETR are vindicated: *ETR BASIC* and the *NON-SUPERVENIENCE THESIS*.[5] Moreover, the principle of instrumental reasoning turns out to explain the exercise of our rational powers where other principles fail. Finally, taking the pursuit of an end to be a basic attitude turns out to be essential to our understanding of rational agency in these contexts.[6]

4.1 The Puzzle

A person has agreed to wear a device that delivers a constant but imperceptible electric shock. She, the self-torturer (ST), is then offered the following trade-off: she will receive a large sum of money—say, $100,000—if she agrees to raise the voltage on the device by a marginal, that is, imperceptible or nearly imperceptible, amount. She knows that she will be offered this same trade-off again each time she agrees to raise the voltage. It seems that, at each step of the way, the agent should and would raise the voltage; after all, each rise in voltage makes at most a marginal difference in pain, well worth a gain of $100,000. But in so doing, she would eventually find herself in unbearable pain, and would gladly return all of the money, even pay some in addition, to be restored to the initial setting, at which she was poor but pain-free. Thus the ST appears to face a dilemma: no matter which choice she makes—continue indefinitely or stop at some point—her action seems irrational, or leads quickly to a state of affairs that no rational agent would accept: If she continues indefinitely she continually loses money for no gain, while if she stops she fails to act on her preferences.

---

[5] *ETR BASIC*: The basic given attitude is the intentional action, more specifically, the intentional pursuit of an end.

[6] Once again, the full argument against the claim that future-directed intentions are basic given attitudes depends also on the next two chapters.

Let us suppose that the shocking device is worn on a strap around the wrist, like a watch. Instead of a watch face, it has a dial with a large number of ordered settings $a_0 \ldots a_n$, on which higher settings correspond to higher voltages; and we assume that severity of pain varies with voltage level. ST can raise the voltage by turning the dial. The difference in voltage between adjacent settings of the dial is very small. Again, Quinn assumes it is so small that ST cannot discriminate between the pain levels she experiences at adjacent settings. Nevertheless, she experiences significant differences in pain between some settings that are farther apart. In particular, she feels no pain at the initial setting a_0, when the device is turned off, but feels unbearable pain at some higher setting a_n.

Initially the device is set at a_0 and ST is presented with the following choice:

(1) Stay at a_0 and be paid nothing.
(2) Raise the voltage to the next setting (a_1) and receive $100,000.

If she decides to raise the voltage, ST is then presented with the same choice *mutatis mutandis*. These are the only choices available to her; in particular, ST never has the option to return to a previous, lower setting. Moreover, the device will remain on her wrist forever, or at least for a very long time. She knows this, and knows also that each choice situation in which she turns the dial will be followed by another just like it.

Let us assume the following about ST's preferences:

(a) ST prefers more money over less money and less pain over more pain.
(b) There is some setting of the voltage level a_j such that for any setting a_k where $k \geq j$, and for any monetary reward, ST prefers a_0 over the conjunction of (i) remaining for a long period of time at setting a_k, and (ii) getting the associated monetary reward.
(c) No other preferences of ST are relevant for these choice situations.

We can easily see how these are natural preferences to have; in fact, preferences that would be shared by most, if not all, of us. (a) is just a Pareto Preference: in situations in which our end of earning money is better actualized, but no other end is threatened, we prefer to earn money. (b) is a reflective preference to give priority to the avoidance of debilitating pain over the pursuit of riches.

We are now in a position to generate the puzzle. Given that adjacent voltage levels feel the same to ST, the only relevant preference in each case is a preference for more money. Hence, since she is paid $100,000 to move to the next setting, she should do so in each case. It follows that insofar as ST is rational, she will accept the monetary payoffs all the way up to the last, highest setting. At the same time, according to (b), she will eventually reach a stage so painful that she would prefer to return to a_0. ST's preferences are thus non-transitive (and cyclical), even though they seem entirely ordinary: most people prefer more money over less, and most people would not accept *any* amount of money to be tortured for a long period of time. The result is that seemingly ordinary preferences fail to meet a seemingly fundamental constraint on rational choice—namely that one's preferences be transitively ordered.[7] We can interpret the puzzle of the ST in either of two ways: (1) as a challenge to orthodox rational choice theory,[8] or (2) as arising simply from certain intuitive judgments. Let's begin by considering these two interpretations in turn.

It is important to understand exactly how the case of ST is supposed to challenge orthodox decision theory. Orthodox decision theory says that *ST* is irrational: since her preferences are non-transitive, we cannot match them to a utility function. But this charge of irrationality is counterintuitive: ST does not seem irrational. What could be irrational about forming preferences so that one accepts monetary trade-offs for all imperceptible increases in voltage, but not for at least some larger increases? More precisely, the challenge appears to come from the conjunction of three plausible claims:

(1) Were ST confronted with any of the choices in the series in isolation, that is, with any single pair of adjacent settings, she would always choose to accept more money. (Thus she exhibits a behavioural preference for more money at each choice situation.)

---

[7] As will emerge, the puzzle does not depend on the axiom of transitivity in its full generality. Readers familiar with the sorites paradox may wonder whether the ST puzzle is just an especially picturesque instance of it: perhaps ST is proceeding along a sorites series of pains from a clearly bearable one to a clearly unbearable one, attempting to decide where the bearable ones end and the unbearable begin. However, this way of thinking about ST overlooks a crucial element of her situation: at each step of the way she is also trying to decide whether a certain incremental difference in pain can be compensated by $100,000 at that point in the "spectrum" of her pain. The latter task is what appears to put pressure on her rationality and is, at bottom, the source of the puzzle. More on this later.

[8] This is how Quinn sees the puzzle.

(2) At least one stage in the series, a_k, is such that ST would prefer the initial stage of the series, a_0, over a_k. In fact, she would willingly pay a premium in order to return from a_k to a_0. (Thus she exhibits a behavioural preference for relief from the pain experienced at a_k over retaining her financial gains all the way up to a_k.)

(3) Considered either singly or jointly, the behavioural preferences described above are not irrational.

Orthodox decision theory cannot accept all of (1)–(3); taken together, these assumptions amount, or at least seem to amount, to endorsing the rationality of a non-transitive set of preferences. (1) and (2) seem non-negotiable, since we can simply stipulate that some agent behaves in this manner. In general, solutions that are sympathetic to decision theory will reject (3). But they need to reject (3) without violating Toleration. The challenge to decision theory will be to explain how to reject (3) without imposing substantive constraints on which basic attitudes we are permitted to have.

4.2 Orthodox Attempts at a Solution (I)

Let's look more closely at an orthodox solution, and see the sorts of difficulties it faces. An especially interesting approach within the decision theory framework is proposed by Arntzenius and McCarthy (1997). According to their view, the assumption that adjacent settings of the device are indiscriminable is incorrect, and once we notice this we can see that ST's preferences are indeed irrational. Arntzenius and McCarthy propose the following modified version of the thought experiment:[9]

Self-Torture 2
The setup is the same as Quinn's, except that ST has a trial period in which she experiments with various settings of the device in different orders. Each time she experiences a given setting, she describes it with terms like "not painful", "slightly painful", "moderately painful", etc. At the end of the trial period ST gets a report of the frequencies with which she uses each description at each setting.

---

[9] This is a slightly modified version of their proposal.

Arntzenius and McCarthy point out that since the first and last voltage settings are clearly discriminable, there must be some adjacent settings that differ in the frequencies with which ST uses the various descriptions. For instance, two adjacent settings a_n and a_{n+1} might be such that the first is described as "slightly painful" 96.3 per cent of the time and "moderately painful" 3.7 per cent of the time, while the second is described as "slightly painful" 96 per cent of the time and "moderately painful" 4 per cent of the time. Arntzenius and McCarthy argue that given everything ST knows, she would be unreasonable not to treat this difference in the frequencies of the different descriptions as evidence of a difference in pain levels; hence ST should take the expected level of pain to be higher at a_{n+1} than at a_n. As a result, since *ex hypothesi* ST cares about differences in levels of pain, she should assign different utilities to the two settings. But since the assumption that adjacent voltage settings would feel the same was essential to the argument that it was rational always to choose the monetary reward, we no longer have reason to think that ST's non-transitive preference ordering is rational. Given that ST prefers a_0 over a_k irrespective of the monetary reward at a_k, she should conclude that the increase in monetary reward will eventually stop compensating the increase in expected pain.[10]

---

[10] Quinn thinks that a version of the ST puzzle can be constructed in which adjacent voltage settings are absolutely indiscriminable, i.e., not discriminable even by (e.g.) triangulation with other settings. Quinn says, "Surely it ought to be an open empirical question whether such triangulations are possible; if there are increments of voltage just small enough to be directly undetectable, it seems there might be even smaller increments that cannot be detected by triangulation. And I want such a case" (Quinn (1990), p. 201). Tempting though the idea may be, such absolute indiscriminability is not in fact logically possible (see Carlson (1996), for a similar claim). The puzzle stipulates the following:

(1) Pairwise Indiscriminability
For every two adjacent settings a_j and a_{j+1}, the Self-Torturer cannot discriminate between a_k and a_{k+1} in pairwise comparisons.

Quinn is proposing to add the following:

(2) No Triangulation
For any settings a_j and a_k, a_j and a_k are pairwise indiscriminable if and only if a_k and a_{j+1} are also pairwise indiscriminable.

However, (1) and (2) entail that *all* settings of the dial are indiscriminable, contradicting the stipulation that the first and last settings are discriminably different. Consider for example the first three dial settings a_1, a_2, and a_3. *Ex hypothesi* a_1 and a_2 are indiscriminable, and likewise a_2 and a_3. Given the No Triangulation rule, a_1 and a_3 are indiscriminable (otherwise a_1 would be discriminable from a_3 but a_2 would not, contradicting the stipulation that a_1 and a_2 are indiscriminable). Given Pairwise Indiscriminability, a_3 and a_4 are also indiscriminable. But then given No Triangulation, a_1 and a_4 too are indiscriminable; and so forth. Hence at least some adjacent settings must be discriminable by triangulation.

One might have doubts about whether the described probability distribution somehow tracks what ST cares about. In particular, at each stage ST might care only about the character of her current subjective experiences, the way she feels right now. The fact that in other circumstances, or even simply at other times, she would apply different descriptions to her experiences of adjacent voltage levels does not imply that there is now a felt difference between them. Nevertheless, let us grant that the probability distribution reflects what ST cares about. Still, the Arntzenius–McCarthy solution works only if we assume that ST's situation involves some hidden uncertainty—in this case, uncertainty about the location of the tipping point, namely, the first point in the series at which the increased monetary reward is less valuable (or has lower utility) than avoiding greater expected pain. (The uncertainty is contingent because it can be removed by showing ST the statistical record of her descriptions.) But a parallel puzzle can be generated even in the absence of such uncertainty. Consider a pattern of preferences often exhibited by smokers.[11] Many people think that the pleasures of smoking, no matter how many times repeated, do not compensate for the disease and premature death often caused by heavy smoking. On the other hand, for each next cigarette, these same people prefer smoking it (and perhaps quitting immediately afterward) over not smoking it (what difference could one cigarette make?). Like ST, they have a non-transitive preference ordering that seems to result from ordinary, not obviously irrational, preferences.

Now consider two hypotheses as to how smoking causes cancer. On the first hypothesis, smoke causes cumulative damage to one's lungs, so that although one cigarette will not cause cancer, and any single extra cigarette will cause only incremental damage, repeated smoking of single cigarettes will eventually result in lung cancer. (Assume for the moment that no single cigarette ever puts a smoker over the threshold for lung cancer.[12]) Call this the "incremental hypothesis". On the second hypothesis, each cigarette has a low probability of causing a relevant cell mutation. Although smoking one cigarette is unlikely to result in lung cancer, repeated smoking over many years raises the probability of developing lung cancer near to 1.[13] Call this the "stochastic hypothesis".

---

[11] For simplicity, I will ignore the complication that smoking is addictive.

[12] If lung cancer is an on/off condition with no vague threshold, we can change the case to a fatal condition that is gradually or incrementally debilitating. Since the main point of the example is the contrast with the stochastic hypothesis, this will not affect the argument.

[13] I am making no claims about the scientific plausibility of either hypothesis. Note that some debates about body scanners vs "pat downs" at US airports had a similar structure.

The Arntzenius–McCarthy solution might work if the incremental hypothesis is correct. One might think that a person who *always* prefers to smoke the next cigarette is not properly taking into account its expected harm; a rational agent who appreciated the expected harm would find a point at which the trade-off between the pleasure of a cigarette and the prevention of cancer shifts in favour of the latter. However, their solution makes no sense on the stochastic hypothesis. Assuming that the pleasure of smoking each cigarette is independent of the pleasure of smoking any others (that is, pleasure neither increases nor decreases the more one smokes), and that the smoker's preference ordering does not change, each choice situation the smoker faces is identical. The probabilities are independent, so the trade-off at each choice situation is the same: a very small chance of developing cancer against the pleasure of smoking a single cigarette.[14]

On the incremental hypothesis, the Arntzenius–McCarthy solution allows some latitude in one's choice of cigarettes over health consistent with the hypothesis that one's preferences are stable; one could locate one's tipping point at any total number of cigarettes. But given that their solution does not work on the stochastic hypothesis, assuming stable preferences, orthodox rational choice theory appears to allow only two rational sets of choices: never choosing to smoke, and always choosing to smoke.[15]

One might question whether the choice situations would differ so radically depending on which hypothesis is correct. But leaving that worry aside, the idea that a rational agent in such a situation is confined to these two sets of preferences is badly in need of justification. Surely a person whose stable preferences dictate that she'll smoke only a few cigarettes and then quit so as

Experts often said that frequent fliers and flight crews would perhaps prefer the "pat down" even though the choices they faced on each occasion were identical: there was no chance of cumulative harm, only a small risk of harm in each exposure. See, for instance, www.npr.org/2010/11/19/131447056/are-airport-scanners-safe.

[14] Of course, at some point one might have already developed cancer, and past choices might raise one's credence that that is so. But assuming that smoking does not introduce further risks to those who already have lung cancer, the expected utility of smoking only goes up for later choices (provided the agent has the usual smokers' preferences).

[15] Of course, orthodox decision theory doesn't say that the utility of smoking n cigarettes is a function of the utility of smoking one cigarette, or anything like that. That's why we need to assume that the utility of smoking the next cigarette does not vary given that one has smoked a cigarette in the past, and that the preference ordering is stable through time. We assume also that the agent is not indifferent between the pleasure of smoking and the relevant probability of developing cancer (otherwise any combinations of choices would be consistent with decision theory). The same caveats apply to the other cases discussed below.

not to endanger her life unduly is rational in light of her ends. If one's theory of rationality implies otherwise, some independent justification is needed. It's worth noting that orthodox decision theory is committed to the same verdict in many analogous cases. For example, one can coherently avoid the inconvenience of strapping a child into a car seat for a short trip only if one would make the same choice in every similar situation, thereby putting the child at unacceptable risk; and one can slightly exceed the speed limit to avoid being late for a meeting only if one is always willing to speed in similar circumstances, despite knowing that in the long run such a policy would almost surely be disastrous; and so forth.[16]

Moreover the puzzle doesn't require adjacent settings of the dial to be indiscriminable. It seems equally rational to prefer large sums of money over *nearly* imperceptible, or even just slight, differences in pain, and yet prefer poverty over sustained agony; again, these seem to be the preferences of most ordinary agents. Arntzenius and McCarthy anticipate this version of the puzzle and question whether such preferences would in fact be rational. They reason that, given the diminishing marginal utility of money, avoiding even very slight differences in pain will eventually be preferred to gaining \$100,000. However, there is no guarantee that ST will arrive at her tipping point before she arrives at the point at which she would pay back all of the money to return to a_0. Whether she arrives at her tipping point first depends on the rate at which slight increases in pain add up to the unacceptable level of pain, on the one hand, and the rate at which the marginal utility of money declines, on the other. Moreover, as long as the number of increases needed to reach unacceptable pain is not extremely large, one can solve this problem by increasing the monetary reward at each choice node, slowing the decline to a crawl.[17]

---

[16] See caveats at note 15 above.

[17] Voorhoeve and Binmore (2006) suggests that we fall victim to well-known heuristic biases when we judge that small differences in pain are always compensated by monetary rewards. This seems implausible. First, many of the biases they discuss are not recalcitrant; subjects recognize their mistake once they understand how their choices result in a non-transitive preference ordering. In contrast, in ST's predicament we do not revise (or at least don't know how to revise) our general preferences once we are aware of the difficulty. Moreover, it is not clear how our intuitive reasoning about ST could count as a case of (mis)using certain heuristics. After all, the preferences in question are not supposed to be a method used to discover the truth about *something else*; they are supposed to *determine* our basic attitudes regarding acceptable trade-offs between money and pain. Of course one could deny this last point, and say that our preferences reveal only the heuristics we are using in trying to conform to some deeper attitudes regarding acceptable trade-offs between money and pain. But then the claim that these heuristics are (mis)used would need to be supplemented by some account of what determines the correct trade-offs between money and pain.

Arntzenius and McCarthy's solution also faces a related problem that will afflict any orthodox solution to the puzzle. On their view, there is a certain point in the series at which ST's preference function changes from choosing the higher monetary value between two adjacent options to being indifferent between two adjacent options, and then a subsequent point at which ST now prefers the lower monetary value between two adjacent options. More precisely, given ST's series of possible outcomes $[o_1, ..., o_n]$, if her choice situations always involve two adjacent outcomes, then there will be either a precise point at which she now strictly prefers not to accept the money, or there will be at least some triad of adjacent outcomes o_{m-1}, o_m, and o_{m+1} such that $o_m P o_{m-1}$ but $o_m I o_{m+1}$, and a certain later triad of adjacent outcomes such that $o_{m+k-1} I o_{m+k}$ but $o_{m+k} P o_{m+k+1}$, where "xPy" stands for "x is strictly preferred over y" and "xIy" as x and y are indifferent (neither is strictly preferred over the other).[18] And the trouble is that since each of these choices is independent, a rational agent must have the same preferences even when she is not threatened with the continuation of the series. But this seems highly implausible.[19] Surely if an agent with ordinary preferences were to face only one of the choices ST faces, in isolation, she would be permitted, and likely required, to choose the option that increases her wealth significantly rather than avoid an insignificant increase in pain. On Arntzenius and McCarthy's view, indeed on any view according to which the choice situations are independent, if the choices happen to be between o_{m+k} and o_{m+k+1}, the agent cannot secure the outcome with the higher monetary value (viz., o_{m+k+1}) in the one shot case.[20]

This discussion brings to light two desiderata for an acceptable solution to the puzzle of the ST. First, an acceptable solution must explain the rational requirements on ST's decisions in light of the fact that she cares only about financial gain and freedom from pain; an acceptable solution should not postulate preferences other than those two. In particular, it must accommodate the fact that ST's preferences are, or at least appear to be, *discontinuous*: her preferences are such that an increase in pain can be compensated by certain financial benefits—*but not indefinitely*. Her pain can be compensated by money up to a certain vague threshold of pain.[21]

---

[18] It is compatible with Arntzenius and McCarthy's solution that ST go directly from $o_m P o_{m-1}$ to $o_m P o_{m+1}$ for some setting a_m, with no indifference point. But this would make the present problem worse, if anything.

[19] This implausible result violates the Non-Segmentation requirement below.

[20] More on this issue in the discussion of Non-Segmentation below.

[21] For simplicity, I assume that no amount of money can compensate ST above this vague threshold; but all we need to generate the puzzle is a discontinuous function.

The second desideratum says that an adequate solution to the puzzle must respect the following principle:

NON-SEGMENTATION
When faced with a certain series of choices, the rational ST must choose to stop turning the dial before the last setting; whereas in any isolated choice, she must (or at least may) choose to turn the dial.[22]

Consider Barry, whose preferences at t_0 require him to stop no later than the setting a_n. As time goes by, Barry develops chronic back pain (but his preferences remain unchanged). Right now, at t_1, he is at the same level of pain he would be at were he to perform the ST's sequence of choices and stop at setting a_m. Barry is invited to participate in an experiment to determine whether a certain drug enhances the absorption of vitamin A. The experiment involves injecting a single dose of the drug VitA. Barry neither suffers from vitamin A deficiency nor is at risk of "overdosing" on vitamin A, so the effects of the drug on his vitamin A levels are irrelevant to his choice situation. However, for reasons unknown, the VitA injection will slightly exacerbate the condition causing his back pain. Barry cannot discern the difference in pain caused by a single dose of VitA, but we can assume that if the scientists were to inject more and more of the drug, the pain would become progressively worse and, eventually, be so much worse than his initial pain that he would gladly return all of the money to go back to his initial state before he had taken any of the drug. (We assume also that Barry knows all of this.) However, the experimenters, who are trustworthy, want to inject only a single dose; and they offer Barry $100,000 to take the drug. It seems that whatever you want to say about the rationality of stopping before or at setting a_m, if Barry were offered the $100,000 at t_1, he would be rationally permitted (arguably required) to accept it and take the single injection of VitA. Non-Segmentation demands that a solution allow (perhaps require) the ST to accept the monetary offer in any one-shot version of the puzzle.

4.3 Orthodox Attempt at a Solution (II)

In a more recent interesting attempt to defend orthodox decision theory, Luke Elson argues that the puzzle is in fact a sorites argument, but not for

---

[22] Although NON-SEGMENTATION is defined here only for the case of the ST, it can obviously be generalized to any other case that shares the same structure.

the predicate "x is bearable (pain)", but for the predicate "x maximizes utility".[23]

Elson's argument rests principally on two claims:

(1) Orthodox rational choice theory can represent ST's preferences as determined by two functions: one with a positive, less sharp slope (the function from increases in money to positive marginal utility) and another with a negative, sharper slope (the function from increases in voltage to negative marginal utility).[24] ST's net utility at a given voltage setting is the sum of the utilities of these two functions at that setting.

(2) The ST puzzle can be represented as a sorites paradox whose major premise is the following: "If setting k does not maximize utility then setting $k + 1$ does not maximize utility" (Elson (2016), p. 484).

(Elson describes (2) as expressing "Torture Tolerance", signifying that the predicate "does not maximize utility" tolerates incremental differences in pain–payoff combinations.)

The soritical predicate at issue, Elson claims, is "x does not maximize utility". He contends that the utility function of the ST is such that the increased disutility of pain will eventually outweigh the increased utility of the added money, but it's vague just where in the series this shift takes place. So Elson claims,

If the puzzle is simply an instance of the sorites, then the challenge to orthodox rational choice theory is liable to dissolve. If claims such as that…[raising the voltage] is always required on utility-maximizing grounds and that ST has "clear and repeatable reason" to [raise the voltage]…are equivalent to a tolerance principle,…[then the principle is] false.   (Elson (2016), p. 477)

However both Elson's (1) and (2) are false, and so his defence of the orthodoxy fails. Or so I'll argue.

---

[23] The discussion of Elson is largely based on an unpublished manuscript co-authored with Diana Raffman.

[24] In some places I will follow Elson in calling the second function the "pain function", but it's worth pointing out that the proper representation of such a function is a matter of controversy.

4.4 The Structure of the Self-Torturer's Preferences

Elson proposes that the utility function in Figure 4.1[25] represents ST's preferences, except that the point at which the increase in money no longer compensates for the increase in voltage has been arbitrarily precisified. For argument's sake, let us grant that if Figure 4.1 accurately represents (a precisified version of) ST's preferences and ends, Quinn's puzzle does not seriously challenge orthodoxy: rather, it just isn't clear, it's vague, where in the series the utility of increased money is first outweighed by the disutility of increased pain.[26] Thus at worst, Elson supposes, decision theory must make the innocuous, simplifying assumption that we can determine the precise voltage level at which ST should first reject the deal.

Figure 4.1 does not merely precisify the vague predicates at issue, however; it alters the essential features of the case. The point emerges more clearly if we look at a slightly modified version of Tuck's example of the cairn discussed by Elson:

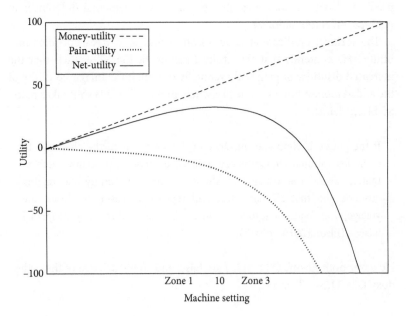

Figure 4.1

[25] Figure. 4.1 is taken from Elson (2016), p. 484.

[26] If Figure. 4.1 accurately represents ST's preferences, then her situation is not significantly different from, say, not knowing exactly how much to pay for a house; there may be no fact of the matter.

Beauty vs Effort (BvsE)
Larry wants to build a beautiful monument of stones, the prettier the
better. Each stone he adds makes the monument prettier, but it also makes
his arms very tired. The more tired his arms are, the more painful it is to
add a stone to the monument (because muscle fatigue increases more
sharply the more fatigued you are), and the pain increases at greater and
greater rates. On the other hand, each stone added makes a smaller marginal difference to the beauty of the monument than the previous one
(because the more beautiful the monument is, the less of a difference a
single stone makes).   (Elson (2016), pp. 478–80)

In *BvsE*, once Larry crosses the (possibly vague) threshold where the
increase in beauty is no longer worth the increase in pain, adding each new
stone is irrational, and increasingly so. After that border crossing, each
added stone represents a greater loss in utility. Now Elson seems to think
that ST's predicament is analogous to Larry's:

> We would not say that once ST "has gone too far" and regrets [raising the
> voltage] so many times, she ought to keep taking the deal. That would just
> make things worse. Even once ST has passed the optimum trade-off of
> pain and money, there are many settings that are clearly worse, with
> respect to her essentially comparative desire for less pain.
>
> (Elson (2016), p. 482)

This remark wrongly suggests that once ST has gone too far, she must reject
all further deals—including, in particular, the very next one.

We need to distinguish two claims. Suppose that s_b is an arbitrary voltage
setting such that, in a pairwise comparison with the initial setting s_0, ST prefers s_0 over s_b. And consider the following two claims:

(A) There is a setting s_m such that for every setting s_n such that $n > m$, ST
       prefers s_b over s_n.
(B) For every setting s_n such that $n > b$, ST prefers s_b over s_n.

(A) says that ST prefers s_b over settings that are much further in the series;
that is, if she keeps choosing to raise the voltage, there will come a point at
which the added money will again not compensate for the significant
increase in pain. (B) makes the stronger claim that ST prefers s_b over *every
setting later than s_b*. If s_b is early enough and ST keeps accepting the deal,

she'll likely end up at a setting (s_n) such that she would gladly give up all the money she accumulated from s_b to s_n just to go back to s_b. So (A) is probably true if s_b comes early enough in the series. But (B) is certainly false. Intuitively, and as Quinn stipulates, in *any* pairwise comparison of consecutive settings, ST prefers the later setting over any earlier one. The falsity of (B) is just a consequence of *NON-SEGMENTATION*. In fact, as we saw above, *NON-SEGMENTATION* is bound to be a problem for any purported solution to the puzzle that is compatible with decision theory. From the viewpoint of orthodox decision theory, there can be no difference between the serial and one-shot choice situations.

One might protest that *NON-SEGMENTATION* appears plausible only because ST is faced with a practical sorites case as described by Elson; the apparent plausibility of *NON-SEGMENTATION* could be a consequence of the apparent plausibility of *Torture Tolerance*,[27] which states that if a setting fails to maximize utility, so does the next setting. But why think that? If Elson's description is correct, ST would eventually reach "an optimum trade-off" point at which she should reject the deal even in an isolated choice. In fact, this is what happens in *BvsE*. If Larry were to come across an already extremely beautiful monument after a day of exhausting manual labour, he might be facing a one-shot version of the same choice he faces in the original *BvsE* scenario after lifting too many stones. Given Larry's preferences, he would always choose not to add a stone to the beautiful monument because the negative utility of the marginal increase of pain would outweigh the positive utility of the marginal increase in beauty (and this would be very clear to Larry). But the falsity of (2) shows that this kind of optimum trade-off point does not exist in the self-torture case; there is no point after which it's always better to choose the lower setting. Even if we were to reject *Non-Segmentation*, accepting this kind of optimum trade-off point would completely misrepresent the structure of ST's preferences.

Perhaps we can save the spirit of Elson's proposal by replacing the utility function in Figure 4.1 with the one in Figure 4.2, which has greater claim to be a precisification of ST's preferences. The precisification in Figure 4.2 has the advantage of departing from Quinn's stipulations only at the points of discontinuity; that is, only at the sudden drops in utility at s_{d1}, s_{d2}, and so forth. But arguably these drops are exactly the points where we introduce sharp boundaries in precisifying the vague predicates that were generating phenomena incompatible with standard decision theory. However, once we accept that Figure 4.2 would represent ST's preference more accurately,

---

[27] See below.

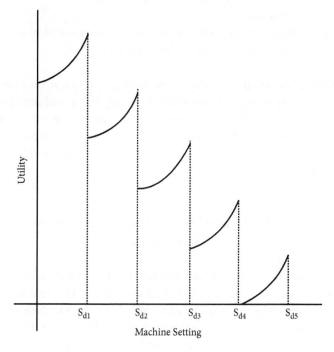

Figure 4.2

there is no hope for interpreting the puzzle as a sorites series as proposed by Elson.

There are also independent reasons to reject Elson's proposal that the ST faces a sorites series with Torture Tolerance as its major premise:

Torture Tolerance
If setting k does not maximize utility, then setting $k + 1$ does not maximize utility.

Torture Tolerance is an implausible major premise for a sorites argument. "Maximizes utility" is a superlative adjective; "maximize utility" just means "is most preferred / has the greatest utility among the alternatives available". But superlative adjectives are not typically tolerant. So, for instance, "x is tall" generates a sorites, but "x is the tallest student in the classroom" does not. (1) below is plausible; (2) is not:

(1) Tall Tolerance
If an **n** millimetres tall person is not tall, then an **n + 1** millimetres tall person is not tall.

(2) Tallest Tolerance*

If an **n** millimetres tall person is not the tallest in the room, then an **n + 1** millimetres tall person is not the tallest in the room.

Obviously if the n millimetre tall person is the second tallest, then the **n + 1** millimetres tall person will be the tallest. Relatedly, in a typical sorites series, we classify early members of the series as *Fx* and late ones as *not Fx*, leaving in-between a penumbral area in which members of the series don't clearly belong to either category. In the ST case, though, both early and late members fail to maximize utility.

4.5 The Rational Structure of Indeterminate Projects and Ends

ST's predicament is not an isolated anomaly to be accommodated by minor revisions or exceptions to a theory of rational choice. On the contrary, as Quinn himself notes, the structure of the puzzle is present in many ordinary actions; Mary's predicament in Chapter 3 also had this same structure. In particular, any instance of vague or indeterminate ends can generate the same puzzle. Orthodox decision theory imposes a substantive restriction on our pursuits: they cannot include indeterminate ends. The puzzle vindicates the idea that such restriction is indefensible: ST's ends are perfectly innocent from the point of view of instrumental rationality. And, again, the same structure is present in the pursuit of nearly all other indeterminate ends. Pursuits that range from writing a book to baking a cake are indeterminate in the relevant sense.

Let us further specify the relevant sense in which an end or pursuit is "indeterminate" here. Suppose you are writing a book. The success of your project is indeterminate or vague along many dimensions. What counts as a sufficiently good book is vague, what counts as an acceptable length of time to complete it is vague, and so forth. In particular, the following assertions seem true of this project:

(i) Its completion requires the successful execution of many momentary actions.

(ii) For each momentary action in which you execute the project, failure to execute that action would not have prevented you from writing the book.

(iii) On many occasions when you execute the project, there is something else that you would prefer to be doing, given how unlikely it is
that executing the project at this time would make a difference to
the success of your writing the book.

(iv) Had you failed to execute the project every time you would have
preferred to be doing something else, you would not have written
the book.

(v) You prefer executing the project at every momentary choice situation in which you could work on the project over not writing the
book at all.[28]

Now suppose that you have completed your book. Looking back, you
recall a certain Sunday afternoon on which you sat on the porch reading
The New York Times. Around 4 o'clock you toyed with the idea of reading
one more article in the newspaper, but decided instead that you had better
get back to work. You didn't find the prospect of going back to writing
intrinsically rewarding; in fact your sole reason for setting the newspaper
aside was the need to complete your book. Looking back, you now realize
that, had you read another article instead of getting back to work, this would
have not prevented you from completing your book. But you are unlikely to
regret your decision, and your lack of regret would not be irrational. The
fact that you could have read one more article and still finished your book
doesn't show that the decision to work was irrational, since there is no precise set of momentary actions that are strictly necessary and sufficient for
the realization of the end, that is, no set of momentary actions such that if
even one had been subtracted from the set, the end would not have been
realized (or, if there is such a set, it is not epistemically accessible to you).

Success in the pursuit of an indeterminate end depends upon a series of
momentary actions and is measured in terms of patterns of activity extending through time; in the case of an indeterminate end, there is no measure
of the rationality or success of any particular momentary action with respect
to the end. Moreover, there are no obvious or systematic consequences of
your adoption of indeterminate ends for the evaluation of the momentary
actions concerned. Consider for instance the following preferences internal

---

[28] (v) is stronger than needed and perhaps implausible in this strong form. Life might be
very unpleasant if at every moment at which I could be writing my book, I was writing it. All
we need is that (v) be true for a large set of momentary choice situations. But the stronger version makes for simpler presentation.

to, respectively, your ends to write a book, run a marathon, and visit Aunt Mary regularly:

(1) You prefer to write the book than not to write it.
(2) You prefer to write the book and visit Auntie Mary regularly than to write the book not visit Auntie Mary regularly.
(3) You prefer to write the book and train enough to complete the NYC marathon than to write the book and not complete the NYC marathon.

None of these preferences dictates what you should do at any given moment.[29] You could work on your book, go for a run, call Auntie Mary to schedule a visit; all of these actions are compatible with the above preferences. Ideally, you would end up writing a book, seeing Auntie Mary regularly, and recording a personal best in the marathon. And insofar as these things are within your rational control and do not conflict with your other ends, you are rational if you accomplish all of them. More to the point, there seems to be nothing *else* that rationality requires of you; as long as you actualize all these ends, and as long as your success in these undertakings is non-accidental, you are perfectly rational.[30] However, since actualizing these ends is compatible with failing to pursue any particular momentary action considered in isolation,[31] there can be no rational requirement stemming from these ends to undertake any particular momentary action.

If the preceding line of thought is correct, then the puzzle of ST shows us that these indeterminate ends do indeed exhibit top-down irrationality and thus that the *NON-SUPERVENIENCE THESIS* is true. The puzzle of the ST shows that many of our pursuits are such that the agent's pattern of activity through time could turn out to be irrational without any of the momentary actions that compose those patterns being irrational. On the other hand, given that *never* taking the means to execute these ends would be irrational, an adequate account of rational agency must imply that the rational agent realizes such ends, which requires that the pursuit of such ends must also be relevant to how a rational agent engages in momentary actions.

---

[29] This claim obviously simplifies matters somewhat; see the preceding note.
[30] Non-accidental success is a sufficient, but not necessary, condition for rationality with respect to these ends. More on this issue in Chapter 5.
[31] With some notable exceptions such as avoiding an oncoming bus etc.

An indeterminate end issues a requirement and a set of permissions. The requirement is just a direct implication of the principle of instrumental reasoning: insofar as one is rational one adopts the means (including constitutive means) one knows to be necessary to realize one's end.[32] The permissions are permissions to choose to pursue an indeterminate end on some occasions instead of always choosing the most preferred momentary action. Indeterminate pursuits are temporally extended actions and their proper execution can be assessed only in light of the entire period during which they were, or ought to have been, executed.

Let us return to the two perspectives we introduced in the last chapter, the extended and the punctate perspective. The extended perspective issues the requirement mentioned above; in this case, the requirement that, roughly, your actions overall can be expected to bring about the writing of your book, or that your actions constitute your writing the book in an acceptable way, that is, in such a way that you end up (or should end up) satisfied that this is the kind of book that you were aiming to write. Obviously, many (perhaps indefinitely many) possible sequences of momentary actions would satisfy the requirement imposed by the extended perspective. If you did go on to finish writing the book in an acceptable manner, the possibility that you could have written a slightly better book had you spent less time reading the newspaper, or the possibility that you would have written the same book had you read an additional article, does not show that you violated the extended requirement. If you wrote an acceptable book without unduly compromising your other ends for the sake of the book, then you satisfied the requirement of the extended perspective.

The punctate perspective determines which momentary actions are open for you at a given moment, as well as how each action on its own can contribute to the satisfaction of your ends. But what counts as an acceptable realization of an end? At the very least, your actualization of writing a book should result in a book that is good enough, in the sense of "good enough" discussed in the last chapter. More generally, what counts as "acceptable" is determined by the nature of your end. Roughly, we can say that if your book project has been completed in a way that you (correctly) recognize to have achieved the end of your pursuit, then the realization of the end is acceptable. "Acceptable" thus just reiterates that your actions do count as a proper realization of the end. Having my friend who owns Vanity Press, Inc. decide

---

[32] Recall that we are assuming that the agent knows how to take the means necessary to actualize her ends. The assumption is dropped in Chapter 9.

to publish my collected Facebook posts as a book won't count, since my end was not to write a book *in this way*. Given that the end is indeterminate, there might be cases in which it is not clear whether my completion of the project is acceptable.

Let us say that your pursuit of writing a book is *implicated* at a certain momentary choice point if a momentary action open to you is to take (constitutive or instrumental) means to writing a book. That is to say, at those moments, one rational action open to you is to exercise the permission to engage in means to writing the book.[33] Here we require a notion of means to an end that is broader than the traditional view according to which a means is either necessary or sufficient (or both) for the attainment of the end. The momentary actions of executing an indeterminate extended pursuit are neither necessary nor sufficient; rather, they are merely *constituents* of a means that is necessary and/or sufficient to bring about the actualization of the end. We can say that token actions of the relevant type are *generic*, as opposed to necessary or sufficient, means to their ends.

It is worth distinguishing between generic means and what can loosely be called sets of "indifferent" means. Suppose my end is to buy milk on my way home, and that between my office and home are seven grocery stores that sell milk. Prior to my leaving the office, none of the stores is such that buying milk there is a necessary means to buying milk on my way home. Although buying milk on my way home will require that I visit at least one of the stores, any store is as good as any other. At the same time, if I don't stop at any of the first six stores, then when I arrive at the seventh store, the only rational action is to stop at the store. This is because the end of buying milk on the way home is not, at least as far as we are concerned here, indeterminate: it can be accomplished by a momentary action.[34] Although no *particular* action of stopping at the store is a necessary means, performing at least one these actions is a necessary and sufficient condition of achieving the end. On the other hand, when my end is indeterminate, like writing my book, no particular moment is such that, given my previous choices, typing at that moment is necessary for the acceptable realization of my end. If I do not write enough, the book will not be completed, or will not be completed

---

[33] Of course, in certain situations this permission might be cancelled. Working on your book might not be rational if one of your options at the time is to keep your dialysis appointment.

[34] It is worth noting that even this case is an approximation. In buying milk, I need to go to the store, grab the milk, pay for it, etc. None of these actions must happen at a precise moment; for instance, I could always take a few more seconds texting between grabbing the milk and paying for it.

acceptably, but no particular momentary action is such that choosing it is necessary for the completion of my project. Momentary actions of writing are *generic means* to the execution of the project.

In analogous fashion we can distinguish between a pursuit being *implicated* and its being *generically implicated*, at the time of a certain momentary action:

(1)   A pursuit of yours is ***implicated*** at a time t if and only if one of the momentary actions open to you at t is to take means to that pursuit, where a means is a necessary and sufficient condition, or at least an INUS (insufficient but a necessary part of an unnecessary but sufficient) condition,[35] of achieving the end of such a pursuit.

(2)   A pursuit of yours is ***generically implicated*** at a time t if and only if one of the momentary actions open to you at t is to perform a token of an action type T such that:
   (i)   In the time interval (that includes t) in which you are pursuing your end, there will be several choice situations in which one of your options is to perform a token of action type T.
  (ii)   Were you never to perform tokens of T, the end you're pursuing would not be realized or brought about.
 (iii)   No particular token of T is (or could be known to be) necessary (or sufficient, or an INUS condition) for the successful pursuit of the end.[36]
 (iv)   You know that (i)–(iii) obtain.

The fact that an end or project is generically implicated is relevant to the rational options open to an agent in virtue of the structure of that kind of end, as delineated above. You need to be engaged in typing on your computer multiple times while you are writing your book, but not at any *particular* time. More specifically, tokens of the relevant action type T, considered singly, are neither necessary nor sufficient to bring about one's end. It is necessary and (in conjunction with other actions or means) sufficient that we perform enough tokens of the relevant action types to achieve the

---

[35] For the notion of an INUS condition, see Mackie (1980).

[36] Here again condition (ii) is stronger than necessary (since *some* of the tokens of T might be necessary), but the stronger condition makes the presentation much simpler. A full account of these conditions would require an account of individuation of actions that singles out the right action types, but this is a difficult issue on its own and trying to settle it would lead us away from the main purposes of this chapter.

end. However, suppose I complete my project of writing a book partly by choosing often enough to type on my computer. Given the indeterminacy of the end, I would never be in a position to say that any of these choices was necessary to realize it. Had I chosen to type for one less second, I would also have completed my project of writing a book.

The extended perspective issues only a requirement to perform sufficiently many momentary actions of the relevant type. However, an agent can satisfy the requirement of the extended perspective only if the punctate perspective permits performance of actions that are generic means to a project that is generically implicated at a certain moment, even when they are neither necessary nor sufficient for the achievement of the relevant end. Of course, that permission will not extend to all actions in which the pursuit is generically implicated; if you must act now to save your beloved from a burning building, there is probably no rational permission to type a few more pages of your book instead. Also, the permission does not apply where your pursuit is *not* implicated because you can no longer successfully realize your end. If you are lying on your deathbed having written only a few pages of your book with no hope of finishing it, the project of writing it cannot generate a permission to spend your last hours typing away.

Note that no new basic principle was introduced; each perspective is generated by the demands of the principle of instrumental reasoning. Given the extended nature of indeterminate pursuits, certain violations of (and instances of compliance with) the principle of instrumental reasoning cannot be located at particular moments but only in extended periods. Moreover, where indeterminate ends are concerned, no particular actions considered in isolation would constitute a violation of the principle of instrumental reasoning.[37] A *requirement* of particular momentary actions would be stronger than what follows directly from the principle of instrumental reasoning. On the other hand, lacking permissions to carry out long-term pursuits would guarantee that the principle is violated.

---

[37] More precisely, certain sets of momentary actions are such that none of the actions considered in isolation would violate the instrumental requirement, but the set of all taken together does violate it. Certainly *some* possible momentary actions are violations of the instrumental requirements considered in isolation.

4.6 Back to the Self-Torturer

What indeterminate, extended pursuits, if any, are implicated when ST makes her successive choices in the original version of the puzzle? First ST has the indeterminate end of leading a life relatively free of pain, as one might characterize it: if the ST continues to accept the monetary offers, she will fail in this project. Her end of living a pain-free life is generically implicated insofar as there is an action such that repeated performance of that type of action (viz., refraining from taking the money) under the same circumstances would normally be necessary for its realization. This pain-free life project does not require that the ST always perform tokens of this type of action; it can be realized as long as the ST does not go too far. Accordingly, the end of a pain-free life issues permission to stop turning the dial, independently of what maximizes utility in light of ST's momentary preferences.

Considered in isolation, the project of leading a pain-free life permits ST to refuse every monetary offer from the experimenters. However, exercising the latter permission would violate the extended requirement generated by ST's other end of making enough money; hence the requirement of the money-making end confines the permission generated by the pain-free life project to the later stages of the series of choices. ST acts rationally just in case she exercises the permissions issuing from the extended perspective in such a way that she realizes both ends in an acceptable manner (which is also *required* by the extended perspective).

If it is right to attribute these ends to ST, ETR's solution satisfies the first desideratum expressed above: it explains the rational requirements faced by the ST given that she cares solely about financial gain and avoidance of pain and without postulating new ends or preferences. This solution also satisfies the second desideratum, namely to comply with NON-SEGMENTATION. To see how, suppose that someone who has the same ordinary preferences as ST is presented with a single choice from ST's series. Is he rationally required to accept the money and turn the dial to the next setting? The answer seems to be "yes". Recall the case of Barry, who suffers from mild chronic back pain and is offered $100,000 to take the vitamin A drug just once. Since his choice is a one-shot deal, the project of leading a pain-free life is not generically implicated. Hence no permission is generated by the latter project; the only end implicated in this choice is the project of making enough money. Thus, Barry is rationally required to accept the $100,000. We may now formulate [*PREF2*][38] more precisely:

> [*PREF2**] We may act against Pareto preferences only when exercising permissions generated by an end that is generically implicated at the time of our action.

4.7 Plan Solutions—Future-Directed Intention as a Given Attitude

I would like to introduce a different type of possible solution, what I'll call a "plan solution" to prefigure the central topic of the next chapter: namely, whether future-directed intentions should be considered one of the given attitudes in a theory of instrumental rationality. There is a trivial sense in which ETR already accepts that intention plays an important role in the theory of instrumental rationality. According to ETR, the pursuit of an end is the basic given attitude, but the end in question is, of course, an intended end. Insofar as there are ends that we can be pursuing that we are unaware of, or are in other ways unintended, they cannot be relevant to the agent's exercise of her rational powers. But plan solutions rely on the claim that *future-directed* intentions give rise to instrumental requirements. According to the plan solution, ST should form an intention to stop at a certain setting; once this intention is formed ST is *rationally required* to act on this intention (*ceteris paribus*). In other words, plan solutions require that the agent make a plan and then stick to it. Arbitrary revisions of the plan are disallowed even if the revision would not take ST to a combination of pain and money that she would have otherwise judged unacceptable.

Plan solutions seem to entail that an agent who stops at an acceptable but unplanned point is irrational, even if the stopping point is preferred over the planned one. For instance, suppose ST plans to stop turning the dial at setting a_{25}, but then when she arrives at a_{25} she decides to go one step further and stop at a_{26}. Also, suppose a_{26} is a setting that ST prefers over the initial setting a_0. Arguably, according to planning solutions, ST has acted irrationally despite the fact that she ends up with more money and an acceptable level of pain— indeed a level of pain that is pairwise indistinguishable from the planned one. Clearly, a charge of irrationality here stands in need of defence.

---

[38] See Section 3.6 in the previous chapter.

Michael Bratman's planning solution works in essentially this way.[39] In a nutshell, Bratman imposes a "no regret" condition on plan revision: it is rational for an agent not to revise a plan even in light of her preference to do so, just in case she reasonably judges that she will regret her choice if and only if she chooses to revise her plan. So suppose that, before she straps the device to her wrist, ST plans to stop at setting a_{25}. As she gets there, she realizes she would prefer to go farther, and wonders whether she should revise her plan. According to the no-regret condition, ST needs to figure out whether she now believes that were she to revise her plan according to her current preference, she would later regret it. Bratman thinks that ST can reasonably expect to regret revising her plan: "She can ask: 'If I abandon my prior intention to stop at $[a_{25}]$, what will then transpire?' And it seems she may reasonably answer: 'I would then follow the slippery slope all the way down to $[a_{1,000}]$[the last setting]' (Bratman (1999), p. 95). According to Bratman, ST would now realize that were she to revise her plan, she would later regret having done so. Thus, revising her plan would violate the no-regret condition.

Granted, if ST has reason to believe that she will either stick to her plan or continue to the end of the slippery slope, that is, that these are her only options, then she shouldn't revise her plan. But why should she believe that? By hypothesis, some of the settings above a_{25} are acceptable but the final setting is not; so a rational agent could certainly stop at a point between a_{25} and the final setting if she didn't stop at a_{25}. Of course someone's *psychology* might be such that he can stop at a setting short of the final setting only if he stops at a planned setting (e.g., a_{25}), but why think this is true of rational agents as such? Bratman writes, "His prior decision to stop at $[a_{25}]$ was his best shot at playing the game without going all the way; if he does not stick to that decision, there is little reason he would stick with any other decision short of the bottom of the slippery slope" (Bratman (1999), p. 95). On the contrary, if ST is rational, she has good reason to believe that she *will* stop short of the end, since the end point is plainly unacceptable. So why must she make a prior decision and stick to it? Surely she could abandon her initial plan and later exercise a permission to stop without forming any plan to do so.

---

[39] Bratman (1999). Bratman revises some aspects of this view in Bratman (2007), but the criticisms below will extend to any planning solution. For another interesting planning solution, see Andreou (2006b).

Naturally, if one rejects the possibility of top-down irrationality, it may seem that if ST doesn't stop at the planned setting, she will have no reason to stop later, since whatever reasons she would have at a later point would also be reasons to stop at the planned setting; and if those reasons were inadequate at the planned setting, they would be inadequate at any other point. I already argued that we should not reject top-down independence, but the implausibility of rejecting it is evident in the ST case itself. Suppose again that ST plans to stop at a_{25}, but at a_{25} decides it's worth going a little further, and then stops at a_{26}. Assuming that a_{26} is still an acceptable stopping point, how could it have been irrational for her to continue to a setting that is acceptable and that she prefers over the planned setting? Perhaps someone will object that ST would stop at a_{26} by sheer luck; she certainly couldn't have counted on that. But ST makes her decision under certainty; she fully controls the outcome. It is hard to see how her choice of stopping point could be merely lucky. In other words, stopping at a_{26} is an unimpeachable exercise of her rational powers.

Of course, here I just tried to show that positing future-directed intentions as a given attitude does not provide a better solution to the puzzle. But since the publication of Bratman's *Intention, Plans, and Practical Reason* (Bratman, 1987), future-directed intentions have been at the forefront of theories of instrumental rationality, especially theories of instrumental rationality that try to do justice to the extended nature of our agency. We need to examine in more detail whether we need to add them to our list of given attitudes, or formulate principles of derivation or coherence that govern future-directed intending rather than the intentional pursuit of an end. Perhaps other, or even similar, contexts provide us reasons to accept that future-directed intentions are an essential component of a theory of instrumental rationality. Thus the task of the next two chapters is to continue to show that postulating future-directed intentions is at best redundant in a theory of instrumental rationality.[40]

---

[40] This chapter is largely based on work co-authored with Diana Raffman (Tenenbaum and Raffman (2012) and an unpublished ms). Many thanks to Raffman for letting me use this work as a chapter here. Of course, she bears no responsibility for the changes and the new material in this chapter.

5

Future-Directed Intentions and the Theory of Instrumental Rationality

5.0 Introduction

If classical decision theory mostly focuses on momentary choices and mental states of an agent at a particular point in time, the same cannot be said about the literature on the role of intentions in practical reason. When Michael Bratman first introduces his arguments for the relevance of future-directed intentions (Bratman 1983, 1999) for human rational agency, his focus is exactly on extended agency. I think it is fair to represent Bratman's views in our terms as follows: given our nature as planning rational agents,[1] future-directed intentions (FDIs) must figure in the fundamental principles of coherence or derivation. They are needed to explain the rationality of agents whose limited resources require that they deliberate at different times than they act. The central claim here, that FDIs must have a central role to play in the theory of rationality due to the fact that we are capable of acting on deliberation that is not contemporaneous with the action, pervades the literature on practical rationality. Different philosophers give different rationales for why certain principles or norms governing intentions are required by the character of extended agency: they might be grounded, for instance, on the need to preserve or promote our diachronic autonomy (Velleman (1997)) or self-governance (Bratman (2018)), or to coordinate with our changing selves (McClennan (1990)), or the need to overcome temptation or preference reversal (Gauthier (1997), Holton (2009), Paul (2014a)). But they all focus on problems that arise from the fact that our agency extends over time.

However, even if these philosophers are interested in the rational structure of extended agency, the principles they propose are principles connecting

---

[1] And in later work, agents who have the end of self-governance. I discuss the later work in Chapter 6.

different momentary states of the agent at different times. For instance, Bratman proposes the following principle:

> (D) The following is locally irrational: Intending at t_1 to X at t_2; throughout t_1–t_2 confidently taking one's relevant grounds adequately to support this very intention; and yet at t_2 newly abandoning this intention to X at t_2.[2]

Principle (D) is defined in terms of a required relation between two momentary states at two different points in time (t_1 and t_2).[3] Similarly, Edward McClennen proposes a diachronic principle "Dynamic Consistency" that relates choice points across different times in an agent's plans; again, this is in fact a requirement on momentary *decisions* at different points in time.[4]

These principles are contrasted with the way that ETR understands the principle of instrumental reasoning. Since intentional actions themselves are the basic given attitudes, the principles of instrumental rationality apply primarily to actions that extend through time. We can characterize the difference as follows: ETR conceives of the given attitudes themselves as extended, while these alternative views impose a diachronic rational structure on momentary attitudes in order to capture the extended nature of our agency. Thus, it is important to examine whether ETR or these alternative views present a better understanding of the nature of rational agency that extends through time: I argue in this chapter (and the next) that ETR is the superior view.

In particular, I argue that FDIs do not play any essential role in the instrumental requirements that apply to our agency over time. FDIs, as Bratman (and many other philosophers afterwards) understands them, come in many flavours; they can be specific intentions, plans, policies, or projects. I argue in this chapter that ETR naturally classifies some of these "flavours" as instances of extended actions, and therefore they are structurally identical and subject to the exact same basic instrumental requirements as other instances of extended actions. Once we see this point, it turns out that norms and principles governing FDIs are either superfluous (they are just restricted versions of the more general requirements that apply to extended actions) or invalid (their demands are false demands; the permissions they

---

[2] Bratman (2012), p. 79.

[3] The principle does make mention of an interval, but the interval simply guarantees the absence of other mental states that might undermine the rational relation between the mental states at these two different moments.

[4] See McClennen (1990). For related principles, see Gauthier (1997).

add over those entailed by ETR are irrational excesses). This will also help develop ETR further, especially by extending its scope of application.

Section 5.1 examines some of the motivations and commitments of a view that takes FDIs to be among the basic given attitudes. More particularly, such views are committed to what I call "intentional autonomy"; namely, the claim that there are non-derivative norms or principles of rationality governing FDIs. I argue that norms or principles of non-reconsideration are central to any view committed to intentional autonomy and thus the focus of this chapter is on norms or requirements directly governing (non-)reconsideration of intentions. In Section 5.2, I consider whether some functions of FDIs, such as coordinating extended actions or closing deliberation and settling a practical question, can generate non-derivative principles or norms governing FDIs. I argue that these considerations fail to ground the purported norms or principles. Section 5.3 puts forward the most plausible way of grounding principles of (non-)reconsideration governing FDIs; namely, grounding these principles in the role that FDIs play in ensuring the successful pursuit of our long-term ends through the consistent performance of momentary actions that are means to it. Section 5.4 examines the resources available to ETR to explain the phenomena described in Section 5.3. I argue that ETR treats some instances of what Bratman calls "general intentions", such as policies, as instances of ordinary action to which the principle of instrumental rationality applies. Sections 5.5 and 5.6 compare ETR's account of the phenomena with the account proposed by various theories committed to intentional autonomy. The conclusion is, as the astute reader would have expected, that ETR's understanding is superior and that the norms and principles proposed by views committed to Intentional Autonomy are either trivial or spurious. In Chapter 6 we look at other possible ways of adding FDIs to the set of basic given attitudes.

5.1 Intentional Autonomy

The role that FDIs play in a theory of instrumental rationality is often thought to fall out from the function that FDIs play in the life of an extended agent. It is thus worth distinguishing three different functions that FDIs might have:

[SETTLE] An FDI can settle an issue in order to avoid reconsideration costs.

Example: I must decide between investing in bonds or mutual funds. I could spend an unlimited amount of time considering the benefits of one option over the other; however, this is not a very fruitful use of my time. So I form a firm intention to invest in bonds.

[LONG] An FDI can allow us to execute long-term plans that require coordination between actions at different points in time.

Example: if I want to go to Machu Picchu, I need to have tickets ready in time, learn some Spanish, and so forth. Unless I now form the intention to go to Machu Picchu next summer, I will (at least typically) have no reason to undertake any of these actions.

[RESOLVE] An FDI can make sure that we do not change our minds in the face of temptation or temporary preference shifts.

Example: If I intend to quit smoking, my intention can see me through those difficult moments when someone offers me a much-craved cigarette.

The rationality of forming and carrying out intentions that serve functions [SETTLE] and [LONG] is quite obvious. If we can count on carrying out these intentions, it will be rational for us to form them. Given that we are beings of limited rationality, it would be prohibitively costly for us to reconsider the wisdom of our intentions at every opportunity. Similarly, in the absence of planning and coordination, our menu of options would be severely limited. Since these benefits are still present when I carry out the intention, insofar as I am rational, I expect I'll carry out these intentions if I form them; it is rational for me to form the intentions if I expect I'll carry them out. So it is easy to see how it would be rational for me to form and carry out these intentions. But this does not show that there are reasons or requirements to act on our past FDIs, or that our current FDIs place any independent rational pressure on our behaviour.

Whatever reasons we had to form the intentions in question are also reasons to carry them out. This is most obviously in the case of [LONG], but not much less clear in the case of [SETTLE]. For, after all, whatever reasons I had to settle on a certain investment will be good reasons to make the investment at a later date. Let us assume that intentions express, or are formed on the basis of, evaluative or normative judgments, such as "I should invest in bonds".[5] If I was justified in forming this judgment and I had no

---

[5] This assumption is not necessary for my argument; all we need to assume is that the intention is based on reasons. But it'll make for a simpler presentation to keep the stronger assumption in place.

reason to update, I am justified in retaining this judgment and thus in carrying out my intention.[6]

[RESOLVE] is a more difficult case, as it is not clear that the justification that I had in forming the intention is preserved at a later time, in particular at the time of carrying out the intention (at least from the point of view of instrumental rationality). But it is in fact much harder to justify the rationality of forming and carrying out intentions that serve the function of [RESOLVE]. [RESOLVE], unlike [LONG] and [SETTLE], raises the suspicion that forming intentions in these cases is either irrational, ineffective, or even impossible. Let us distinguish three different, but similar, kinds of predicaments that might befall an agent:

(A) Cases in which I predict a shift in my reflective preferences due to an overall change in my evaluative judgments.

Example: I am confident that my start-up company is going to make a lot of money in a few years' time. I now prefer that, when my start-up company goes public, I donate half of my money to charity. However, I know that I'll be unwilling to give up half my money when I am wealthy. I form now an intention to donate the money to charity when I become rich.[7]

(B) Cases in which I expect temporary reversal of my reflective preferences.

Example: It is always true that I prefer always to floss over never to floss; that is, if my only options were to floss every single day or to never floss, I would pick the first (though I do not mind skipping flossing occasionally). This general preference never changes. However, as it comes close to flossing time, I find myself preferring not to floss today over flossing today. Since I know that the result of following these immediate preferences would result in my never flossing, I form an intention to floss every day.

(C) Cases in which, even in accordance with my current preferences, I will prefer not to carry out my intention when it comes time to carry out the intention.

---

[6] I am largely in agreement with Luca Ferrero's view that what he calls "the division of deliberative labour" does not threaten the autonomy of my future self. See Ferrero (2010). However, as will be clear later, I do not think that the authority of my past intentions should be understood in terms of exclusionary or protected reasons. For a more detailed criticism of Ferrero's understanding of the authority of my past intentions, see Nefsky and Tenenbaum (forthcoming).

[7] This example is adapted, of course, from Parfit (1984).

Example: Forming an intention to drink the toxin in Gregory Kavka's renowned toxin puzzle case.[8]

Now, theorists disagree about which of these cases are to be handled by norms governing reconsideration. Richard Holton, for instance, thinks that such norms extend to all cases under (B) and possibly some cases that fall under (C).[9] He is also sympathetic to Edward McClennen's account of resolute choice, and McClennen's account, if taken to validate extending the norms generated by the cases under [LONG] and [SETTLE], would certainly apply to at least some cases like (A).[10] McClennen himself, like David Gauthier, would extend stability requirements on intentions to (C).[11] Bratman, on the other hand, thinks that one can build an argument that will make similar norms apply to cases like (B), but certainly not to (A) or (C); sticking to one's intentions in such cases would be what Bratman describes as "plan worship".[12]

But there are problems with extending any norms arising from cases that fall under [LONG] and [SETTLE] to any of these types of cases. Let us start with (A). [LONG] and [SETTLE] are supposed to be cases that display the importance of FDI in ensuring that agents can continue to carry out projects that they deem important. However, cases under (A) are cases in which I consider a certain project to be important now, but I will not consider it important when it comes time to carry out my intention.[13] It is not clear that the fact that coordination and planning are necessary to achieve an end that I will then consider worthless should have any normative pull on me, at least as far as we are concerned only with instrumental rationality. Similar problems apply to (C). (B) seems essentially different since it involves a

---

[8] Kavka (1983).   [9] Holton (2004, 2009).

[10] More specifically, in order for it to apply to cases like (A), the choice in (A) must be optimal given the preferences of my earlier and later self. We'd need to modify the case slightly by, for instance, assuming that I'd think it is worth selling my company earlier and making less money if I know that I would not donate half my money to charity if I were to become a millionaire.

[11] Gauthier (1997); McClennen (1990). In fairness to Gauthier and McClennen, their concerns for optimality are not necessarily best understood as an "extension" of the consideration in [SETTLE] and [LONG].

[12] Bratman (2007). Bratman (2018) argues that the role of intentions in self-governance is to underwrite norms against shifting in (B) (or similar type) cases. I discuss these arguments in Chapter 6.

[13] Gauthier gives the example of a boy who finds girls "yucky", and forms the intention now not to date them later as he suspects that he'll not have the same attitudes in the future. It seems absurd to think that this earlier intention should require anything from his later self. See Gauthier (1997).

preference that I will continue to have through time; namely the preference to always floss over never flossing. However, it seems that my choice situation now is essentially different from my choice situation when I formed the intention to floss always, since now I do have the preference not to floss today. It is important to avoid a possible misunderstanding here. Obviously, when I formed the intention I could have anticipated that my preferences would shift in this manner. So it is true even later, when it comes time to floss, that there are no unanticipated circumstances relevant to reconsidering my intention. I did indeed anticipate that my evaluation of the various courses of action would change. But then I should have anticipated that I would at a later time be required to reconsider the intention; the fact that my intention was formed on the basis of evaluations or preferences that I now reject, or that new relevant preferences have arisen, seems to be a paradigmatic case of a circumstance in which reconsideration is called for.

None of these arguments is decisive; one could argue that these are not important disanalogies after all and that [RESOLVE] cases are relevantly similar to [LONG] and [SETTLE] cases. So we can distinguish two theses that one might defend:

Intentional Autonomy: Forming FDIs generates, directly or indirectly, rational requirements (or rational principles) that do not reduce to non-intention-based requirements or principles.

The Extension View: The new principles or requirements also apply to [RESOLVE] and explain the rationality of sticking to our resolutions in these cases.

The intentional autonomy thesis denies that principles of derivation and coherence that make no reference to intention could exhaust the principles of instrumental rationality. The *Extension View* is just a stronger version of *Intentional Autonomy*. Obviously, if *Intentional Autonomy* is false, so is the *Extension View*, so I will set aside the *Extension View*.[14] Nonetheless, I agree with the proponents of the *Extension View* that there is something wrong with the irresolute agent. But I think that the view is wrong in trying to capture irresolution as a failure conform to a principle rather than being a case of an *instrumental vice*. Thus hopefully we will be in a better position to

---

[14] For further discussion of Holton's view, see Sarah Paul's review of Holton (2009) (Paul (2011)).

appreciate what kind of failure of rationality irresolution is at the end of Chapter 7.[15]

Bratman's original argument for the importance of FDIs for rational agents like us relied on what he called a "two-tier" model of rationality, and this model is endorsed by others.[16] A two-tier theory is modelled on rule-utilitarianism, in which the act is indirectly evaluated by the aim presupposed by the theory. So on a two-tier model we have a first tier that evaluates certain stable states such as habits or dispositions. Such stable states are evaluated, in the case of the theory of instrumental rationality, by their tendency to promote the ends of the agent. The second tier then evaluates the manifestations of the stable state in light of the evaluation of the stable state itself, rather than being evaluated directly by the tendency of each manifestation to promote the agents' ends in isolation. This is similar to the manner in which in (very simple) rule-utilitarianism, compliance with a rule is right if and only if the rule is right, and the rule is evaluated by its tendency to maximize utility. In (a simple version of) the two-tier model of rationality, the manifestation of a habit or disposition is rational if (and only if?) the habit or disposition is rational, and the habit of disposition is rational if and only if it in general or overall tends to promote the ends of the agent. We need to observe two things about our discussion of the two-tier model of rationality:

(a) Since we are focusing on reconsideration requirements, the first tier is, in our central case, not a case of dispositions to form or carry out intentions, but dispositions to (not) reconsider FDIs in certain contexts.[17] As we'll see later, in the case of *general* intentions or policies, habits of (non-)reconsideration will be indistinguishable, for our purposes, from habits of executing or failing to execute the intention in different contexts.

(b) Any view that postulates principles of derivation or coherence governing FDIs can be represented as a two-tier model. We can always

---

[15] Of course, a plausible view is that resolutions are like "promises to oneself" and that one has non-instrumental reasons to keep such promises. Nothing I say here (or elsewhere in the book) speaks against the possibility of there being a *substantive* norm of keeping our resolutions (that is, that the *fully* rational agent always keeps her resolutions).

[16] For instance, see Holton (2004, 2009).

[17] There are complications that can be introduced here. For instance, someone might have poor habits of (non-)reconsideration, but this would not necessarily mean that she is never rational when she reconsiders, or fails to reconsider, an intention. Some of these complications will be important later when I distinguish various versions of the two-tier model, but for now this simplified formulation is good enough for our purposes.

make the first tier redundant; the first tier can simply evaluate as good dispositions all and only the dispositions to comply with the proposed principle of rationality. So the focus on a two-tier model strictly expands the range of theories under discussion.

It is common ground that non-reconsideration is sometimes rational; for instance, since it is rational at times not to reconsider one's evaluative or normative judgments, it is also rational not to reconsider the intentions that are based upon or express these judgments. However, given the coordinating functions of FDIs, one might think that there are reasons unique to the activity of intention formation that provide us with special criteria of when it is rational to revise an intention. When asking ourselves whether we need to revise a judgment, we are concerned only with whether we have reason to think that it is defective, and, perhaps, with whether our resources are better spent elsewhere. On the other hand, were I to reconsider my decision to invest in stocks, I would be undermining the very point of having formed the intention in the first place. And were I to constantly reconsider my intentions for long-term projects, it would make it unfeasible for me to engage in them. So it seems plausible that the norms of (non-)reconsideration and revision for intention are independent of the norms of (non-)reconsideration and revision that apply to judgments about how we should act; these norms of (non-)reconsideration are not mere consequences of these judgments. Moreover philosophers who think that FDIs are determinant of our self-governance or diachronic autonomy, or even those who think that they play a central role in the coordination between past and future selves more generally, must take the stability of FDIs to be of crucial importance. Thus to the extent that they defend such views, they must also defend principles requiring us not to reconsider, or at least not to revise, such intentions in particular contexts.[18] These are thus the norms at the core of the intentional autonomist view.[19]

5.2 Norms of (Non-)Reconsideration

How do planning and coordination give rise to rational norms of reconsideration? The function of intentions we found in [LONG] and [SETTLE]

---

[18] See, for instance, Bratman's Principle D above.
[19] I'll discuss the validity of other norms against intention revision in Chapter 6.

seem to result in the following considerations in favour of special norms governing intention reconsideration:[20]

> [STABILITY] We need stable intentions so that (i) we can engage in long-term projects and so that (ii) we are predictable and can coordinate with ourselves and others. Thus we ought not to reconsider FDIs at every opportunity.
>
> and
>
> [DECISION] We need to be able to decide without constant deliberation. Thus we ought not to reconsider FDIs at every opportunity.

These seem like quite intuitive reasons to accept that it would be rational to have limits on reconsideration. But what exactly are these limits? Let us look first at what sorts of demands [DECISION] makes on us. Of course, sometimes in exigent circumstances deliberation is certainly a bad idea. If I know that my banker will come at 9:00 a.m. to write down my decisions about how to invest the money I have inherited, and she'll leave at 9:01 a.m. and invest my money however I have instructed her (or she'll simply put it under her mattress if I have not instructed her to invest it in any particular way), I'd better do most of my deliberation before 9:00 a.m. And once I come up with a decision, I'd better stick to it during the minute-long meeting, so that my money does not end up at the bottom of my banker's mattress. If I decided that I should put all my money in index funds, reconsidering this intention at 9:00 a.m., insofar as it involves deliberation, would obviously be a bad idea. Sticking to my intention to put all my money in index funds seems to be a better action than deliberation at 9:00 a.m.

But why is it better? Presumably because I have good grounds to think that my previous decision is likely to have been a good one; at least, I expect it to be better than a random guess. Suppose we have a similar setup except that I am not aware that I'll only have one minute to make up my mind; I actually think that my banker will sit with me and talk to me about all my options, give me a further opportunity to think about my options, and be there with me for as long as I want. I spend the day before thinking about the options and, so far, I think the best option is to go for bonds. However,

---

[20] Bratman has lately defended the view that diachronic requirements on intention can be grounded on considerations of self-governance (see, for instance, the papers collected in Bratman (2018)). I discuss these arguments in the final section of Chapter 6. For further discussion of Bratman's arguments in these papers, see (Nefsky and Tenenbaum (forthcoming); Paul (2014a)).

I do not form any intentions; I decide it is better to "sleep on it", and share my views with the banker. I arrive at the bank at 9:00 a.m. without having put any more thought into the issue, and as I step into the bank, my banker suddenly announces that I will have only one minute to make my decision. I have here just as much reason to follow my earlier assessment as I had not to reconsider my intention in the case where I did form an intention.

On the other hand, suppose that I form an intention, and there are no exigent circumstances which prevent me from deliberating, or which make deliberation too costly. Suppose I am facing the same issue of how to invest the money I inherited. The day before the meeting, I form the intention to buy into an index fund. Now I am waiting for my banker, and I expect that I'll have at least half an hour before she can see me. Would it be irrational for me to reopen the issue? There's really no new information, no unexpected circumstances (suppose I know that I generally have to wait about half an hour before I meet my banker), but I am bored, I don't know what to do, and reconsidering my intention seems to be a perfectly good way to spend this half hour.[21] It couldn't possibly be a failure of rationality to reconsider my intention in these circumstances.

Of course, it would be a horrible fate to spend most of one's life reconsidering one's decisions; it would be absurd if a theory of rationality required us to use all our leisure time, let alone all our time, in the service of better deliberation. Since the completion of many of our ends would be hampered if we were to deliberate too much, we are all already under a requirement not to reconsider too much. Given that I also have other extended ends with overlapping ranges, such as exercising, spending time with the children, or watching cartoons, I cannot coherently also engage, at the same time, in endless deliberation. As we saw in the previous chapter, the various ends we are currently pursuing issue permissions not to deliberate at a certain point in time, even if at that time we would (Pareto) prefer deliberating. Doubtless, a theory of rationality must allow that, in most circumstances, we are *permitted* not to reconsider an intention even if we expect that our decision might improve and nothing of much value will be lost if we do. However, the same kind of consideration cannot ground a *requirement* not to reconsider intentions in non-exigent circumstances; after all, reconsidering in any such particular occasion will not prevent me from having enough time left for a quite a bit of exercising, spending time with the children, and watching cartoons.

---

[21] For a similar point, see Parfit (2011).

It is worth noting that similar permissive norms govern any attitude that it makes sense to "reconsider". Take belief, for instance. It would also be a sad kind of life spent reconsidering our beliefs all the time. There is thus no rational requirement to reconsider our beliefs at every opportunity, or to always look for further evidence; we are often permitted to settle on a belief, and once we settle, there is no requirement to keep reassessing the belief. But there is also no general requirement not to reconsider a belief[22] unless there is enough change in information and so forth.[23] In fact, one can hardly imagine that an attitude that one can form in response to reasons would not entail a general (defeasible) permission not to reconsider whether the attitude is warranted. Arguably, a rational agent would, in reconsidering, suspend judgment on whether there are reasons to form the attitude and thus no longer have the attitude in question. So rational attitudes that required constant reassessment would be no more than momentary, self-extinguishing ephemera. If, in forming a belief that **p**, I were *required* to immediately reconsider whether there were good reasons to believe that **p**, I would have to suspend judgment on whether there were good reasons to believe that **p**, and thus, insofar as I am rational, withhold judgment on **p**. I would thus give up my belief as soon as I formed it.[24]

Bratman claims that intention is a kind of mental state that involves a disposition to "resist reconsideration". A natural way of understanding this claim is to take "disposition" here to refer to a normative disposition; insofar as we are rational, our "default position" should be not to reconsider an intention we have.[25] If I am correct then this claim is misleading; at most we can say that intentions typically don't *demand* reconsideration. Cases that fall under [SETTLE] can ground *permissions* not to reconsider FDIs in certain situations; yet, even this turns out to be superfluous. It is in the nature of forming rational attitudes that there is no general requirement to reconsider whether my reasons for forming the attitude were good ones.

---

[22] Of course, there might be requirements not to revise your justified doxastic states without any change in evidence (at least under certain conditions), but a requirement *not to reconsider any belief* without a change in evidence would be too strong (if, for instance, I think that my current belief that **p** might not be justified in light of the evidence I have, it would be, *ceteris paribus*, permissible to reconsider it even if I have no new evidence).

[23] And if one's conceptions of desire, hope, trust, etc. allow for reconsidering one's desire, hope, trust, etc., then similar norms will apply to reconsideration of such attitudes.

[24] Friedman (2018) argues for a norm of inquiry against believing that **p** and having an "interrogative attitude" towards the question of whether **p**. Given that Friedman includes a much broader range of attitudes under this heading, her claim is stronger.

[25] Bratman (1999).

However, it is true that were we not to exercise enough of these permissions, constant deliberation and revision would undermine our capacity to pursue any long-term ends.[26] So even if [SETTLE] fails to establish a requirement, [STABILITY] might succeed. There must be a more general requirement that prevents us from becoming "reconsideration monsters". Reconsideration is an activity that interferes with many of our goals; we need to ensure that we don't reconsider so much as to prevent our engagement in other important activities. As we saw above, these activities, together with the principle of instrumental reasoning, already impose a demand not to reconsider too much. Moreover, on no one's view should plans never be cancelled, and not even the most rational being can always be relied on to proceed as expected, so a reasonable view forbids only too much reconsideration rather than positing a general prohibition against reconsideration. It is also worth noting that we do not need a rational requirement to ensure the ends of coordination and stable pursuit of long-term ends. What we need is that agents can be *expected* to proceed as they intended (often enough), not that they be *required* to proceed as they intended (in the right circumstances). But if at t_0 I intend to ϕ at t_1 and nothing interferes between t_0 and t_1, then I will still be intending to be ϕ-ing at t_1, which means that, in the absence of interferences, I will be ϕ-ing at t_1. Of course, reconsidering the intention is a possible source of interference, but the fact that I am not required to refrain from reconsidering does not entail that I expect that I will reconsider (let alone that I will reconsider and change my mind). Thus the mere absence of a requirement not to reconsider (or something similar) does not prevent rational agents from coordinating and forming stable plans. Snowball effects, our other ends, the other demands on our time and mental resources, and even the very fact that in intending to ϕ I (typically) acquire a belief that I will ϕ, already conspire to make our intentions relatively stable.

It is worth pausing for a moment and considering how we should understand the function of FDIs. Many authors emphasize the importance of our capacity to deliberate and form decisions that significantly predate the time of the resulting actions. Given our limited resources, it would be disastrous to always make up our minds at the last moment, so our lives clearly go better if we can form and act on FDIs. Note, however, that this is part of a more general lesson about *pursuing an end*. We tell our students not to write their

---

[26] Including, of course, second-order ends to realize larger ends (the end of having a career, to engage in meaningful activities, etc.).

papers at the last minute, not because we think there is something intrinsically better about a pattern of distribution of effort over time, but because we know that limited powers of concentration, susceptibility to fatigue, and competing ends, could interfere with the successful pursuit of the student's end. Of course, this temporal management of our ends makes sense only if our ends tend to persist through time; if it was unlikely that our students still had the end of doing well in the course at the end of the term, this advice would be useless. In sum, *expecting* that my ends will persist is necessary and sufficient for the rationality of engaging in the pursuit of certain means to our ends earlier than strictly necessary by the nature of the end. In fact, forming FDIs can be seen as a limiting case of this general temporal management of our pursuits. As I see the need to paint the fence, I could get an early start by painting the first yard, the first foot, the first inch, or just by *forming the intention* to paint it in the near future. Forming the intention is just the limit case of early engagement in the pursuit of certain means to an end, not any different than engaging in a gappy action, except that the relevant gap is prior to the fully active parts of the action.[27]

5.3 Reconsideration and Vague Ends

Reconsideration does have a problematic structure, a structure very much like the structure we have seen in the case of the puzzle of the self-torturer. Quite often reconsidering is not too costly, and for (almost) any particular plan, abandoning just this plan will not undermine more general ends. But reconsidering in too many cases can have a devastating cumulative effect: were I to reconsider my intentions at every permitted opportunity, I would forgo pursuing many of the ends I care about. And were reconsideration to lead me to revise plans often enough, my life would be a pathetic alternation of momentary or soon-to-be-abandoned pursuits. On the one hand, no *particular* intention must "resist reconsideration"; the requirement not to reconsider too much applies only to the total set of one's intentions. On the other hand, we can only satisfy this requirement if we avoid reconsidering particular intentions, none of which we are required not to reconsider.

---

[27] Moran and Stone (2011) and Ferrero (2017) argue for thinking of intentions as not being essentially different from actions on similar grounds. I am particularly sympathetic to the latter account of the relation between intentions and actions. See also Russell (2018) for an attempt to draw a principled distinction between intentions and later stages of the action while still accepting the claim that future-directed intentions are forms of acting.

General requirements on (non-)reconsideration, and a two-tier model in particular, might be thus defended as determining what counts as rational agency for agents who face this kind of problematic structure. Given that on any particular occasion there is no reason to refrain from reconsidering, an agent will risk reconsidering too much, and thus jeopardize her plan and her ends, if her habits and dispositions were not such that her intentions were reconsideration-resistant sufficiently often, or, more generally, if there were no reasons or requirements pushing against reconsideration. As we pointed out in the previous chapter, this problematic structure is widespread: we can give endless examples of activities such that it would be at least apparently rational at various particular instances to engage in these activities, but also such that it would be disastrous to engage in such activities in every such instance.

However, all, or nearly all, such cases are instances of the derailment of long-term plans, projects, and so forth by conflicting momentary (or short-term) ends and preferences; the problem seems to be precisely a problem about how general intentions should guide our momentary actions. In the "good case", a rational agent implements her general policies despite this problematic structure of her particular choices. Yet, she can only succeed in implementing her policies by refraining from reconsidering her policies on too many particular occasions. Thus it might seem that rational agency in the face of this kind of problematic structure must involve acting on principles, and conforming to requirements governing intention (non-)reconsideration.

We have already considered planning solutions to the puzzle of the self-torturer in the previous chapter; here, we'll consider more systematically whether there are any advantages to accepting basic principles of rationality governing FDIs that are not available to ETR. As I said above, although we will be considering these advantages just in terms of the rational structure added for intention (non-)reconsideration, the arguments generalize to any requirement for intention stability that is supposedly generated by this problematic structure.

5.4 Extended Action and Policies

As we saw earlier, most of our actions are gappy. Not only are most actions gappy, but there is also no principled reason to limit the width of the gaps between the fully active parts of these actions. There are very few, short gaps in cooking an omelette, larger gaps when taking a walk, and even larger gaps in writing a book. But once we note a continuum of indefinite length of gaps between fully active parts, various things that we do not ordinarily classify as actions naturally belong in this continuum. The peripatetic philosopher is engaged in an action much like taking a walk; it is in fact the action of contemplating while taking a walk with much wider gaps and stretched through a much longer period of time.

The structure of activity of the peripatetic philosopher is not significantly different from the structure of the activity of someone who has adopted a policy. In both cases, there is (we suppose) a good to pursue, or a reason to engage in certain activities (walking and philosophizing, for the peripatetic philosopher; running, swimming, etc., for the person who has a policy of exercising). Success in being a peripatetic philosopher involves engaging in these activities often enough, and similarly success in implementing one's policy of exercising involves engaging in its characteristic activities often enough. My suggestion is that any kind of policy, project, long-term action, and so forth[28] can be understood in these terms; that is, as a continuous (though "gappy") action. However, I am not concerned here about the metaphysics of actions or policies; I only claim that from the point of view of the theory of rationality, there are no differences between actions and policies. Perhaps actions require certain bodily movements, while policies don't. Perhaps actions are events or processes while policies are states. In fact, it is a consequence of ETR that policies and projects must be treated as ordinary actions. If our given attitude is "pursuing ends (intentionally)", then it is hard to deny that having a policy or a long-term project is a way in which I am pursuing an end intentionally; that is, one of the things I am currently pursuing if I have a policy of exercising regularly is exercising regularly.

As we saw, a long-term action will consist in part of the undertaking of many momentary, or at least short-term, actions. The rationality of the set of momentary actions will be in part (and perhaps fully) a function of how the momentary actions contribute to the execution of the long-term action and its ends. Preheating the oven is an expression of my rational agency (partly) because it contributes to my baking the cake. Similarly, the "gaps" in the production of the cake count as an exercise of the same power partly due to their relation to the larger action; whatever I do while I am baking a

---

[28] For simplicity, I will mostly mention only "policies" hereafter.

cake should not interfere with the production of an acceptable cake. For ideally rational agents engaged in a long-term action ϕ, some momentary actions in its interval are constitutive or instrumental means (where "means" is conceived broadly) to ϕ, while the gaps between these momentary actions will include only actions that are not incompatible with (or don't seriously endanger) the completion or continuation of ϕ. If we then treat a policy as an ordinary action, acts in accordance with one's policy will be fully active parts of this action, and actions in the gap between two instances of execution of a policy must be such as not to be incompatible with (or not seriously endanger) the maintenance of the policy. In the case of ordinary actions, the rationality of momentary actions and gaps is evaluated in relation to the *completion* or *maintenance* of the larger action. This pair of notions applies to actions that are, respectively, (roughly) the referents of Vendler's "activity terms" and "accomplishment terms".[29] Some actions (activities) are completed at any point at which they are interrupted (if I was running, I have (gone for a) run); some actions (accomplishments) are only completed at the end of the process (I can't infer that I have built a house from the fact that I was building a house; I have only built a house if the process of building a house was completed).[30] Policies have the same structure as activities: the rationality of a policy must be understood in terms of its maintenance or perseverance. Of course, we should not conclude, at least not by definitional fiat or by the examination of the grammar of certain sentences, that instrumental rationality requires that once we engage in an activity we not abandon it. What the principle of instrumental reasoning requires is that we pursue the means to our ends. In the case of activities and policies, the constitutive and instrumental means for the end of the activity are for its continuation or perseverance, not for its completion. The principle of instrumental reasoning only applies as long as you still have the end, while you are still engaged in the activity.

One might worry that, unless we postulate a diachronic requirement that I continue an activity after I start it, instrumental requirements cannot apply to activities or policies; after all, if I do not pursue necessary means for my ϕ-ing, then I am not ϕ-ing, and thus I am not failing to pursue the means to what I am doing. It is true that there could not be any non-diachronic instrumental requirements for activities if we assumed that non-diachronic requirements must be momentary. In formal epistemology,

---

[29] Vendler (1957) and also Mourelatos (1978). See Chapter 2.
[30] See, for instance, Thompson (2008) and Steward (2012).

a view that defends the existence of diachronic norms of rationality (let us call it "the diachronic view") is contrasted with the "time-slice" view, a view according to which norms of rationality apply fundamentally to instantaneous time-slices of the agent.[31] But at least on one understanding of "diachronic norms", this contrast need not be exhaustive. A diachronic norm N of X-ing[32] can be defined as a norm such that whether an agent complies with N at t depends on facts that obtain at some time t^* such that $t^* \neq t$.[33] But the time-slice view follows from the denial of the possibility of diachronic norms only if "t" refers to moments; if the formulation is neutral between moments and intervals, a "synchronic" norm is not necessarily a time-slice norm. Given that ETR takes as our basic attitudes actions and pursuits that extend through time, a norm that is synchronic to X's occurrence could depend on facts that are not circumscribed within any particular moment in time without depending on facts that do not coincide with the time of X's occurrence. Of course, if one assumes that the rationality of an agent at an interval must supervene on the rationality of the agent at each moment within the interval, then rejecting the diachronic view implies accepting the time-slice view. But this amounts to taking for granted the falsity of the NON-SUPERVENIENCE THESIS.

At any rate, one can be *pursuing* the end of φ-ing even while *at the same time* failing to take the necessary means to φ-ing, as long as pursuing an end extends through time. Let us look at two distinct cases of such a failure. The first case is an adaptation of Anscombe's understanding of the "contradiction" of the expression of an intention in action. If I am replenishing the water supply and at the same time I am making holes in the pipe with an axe then I am being instrumentally irrational in pursuing the end of replenishing the water supply.[34] Although it seems a rather bizarre agent who would act irrationally in this way, we can think of less far-fetched examples. Suppose I am trying to run a six-minute mile. A six-minute mile is an accomplishment and I can be instrumentally irrational in ordinary ways in bringing this about; I can give in to temptation and slow down at various points, and thereby end up taking longer to finish the mile. But a similar

---

[31] See, for instance, Moss (2015) and Hedden (2015).

[32] "X-ing" here could refer here to a state (such as "believing" or "deciding") or to a "doing".

[33] Typically, t is later.

[34] Anscombe (2000), p. 55. The original example is not an illustration of instrumental irrationality but of contradictory expressions of intentions by two different persons.

syndrome could be present if I am running at a six-minute-mile pace.[35] Here too at various points I could give in to tiredness or distraction and slow down my pace. And this could all be happening while I am simultaneously acting in ways that are intelligible only if taken as means to my (failing) pursuit of running a six-minute mile; I could be at the same time putting a great deal of effort into breathing in the way necessary to keep a six-minute-mile pace (but superfluous if I am trying to run at slower paces). At those intervals I would be instrumentally irrational exactly because I am pursuing the end of running a six-minute-mile pace yet not taking the necessary means to it.

But the possibility of instrumental irrationality for activities is even more apparent in some gappy activities. For instance, suppose I am holding a rope tied to a pole and I need to ensure that it is always within a certain height (we need it to be, say, always roughly within 10cm of one meter above the ground for our jumping competition). The rope slowly slides down the pole so I need to keep pushing it up. But because it can be a bit further up or down, I can push it up and then do something else quickly before I need to push it up again. So I could glance away from the rope for a few moments in order to check out the beautiful cat across the street since I know I have a bit of time before I need to give the rope another tug. But here I could linger too much, and irrationally fail to take the necessary means to my pursuing the end of keeping the rope at around 1 metre. Yet there is no question that I am still engaged in the activity;[36] there is no other (explanatory) reason why I am holding on to the rope other than the fact that I am trying to keep the rope tied to the pole in this way. The gappier the activity, the easier it'll be to make room for its irrational pursuit. In keeping a diary, I can keep postponing writing my next entry, until it is no longer true that I am keeping a diary. Just as one can be instrumentally irrational in relation to the action of writing a book, one could be instrumentally irrational in relation to the end of keeping a diary. I skip a day or two, but that's fine; my end of keeping a diary does not require that I have an entry for every single day. But if I keep skipping days at some point I am not succeeding in the pursuit of my end of keeping a diary. And as I write the occasional entries

---

[35] Keeping a six-minute-mile pace (at least for ordinary runners) is not a matter of keeping a precise constant velocity of 10 mph. As long as I average roughly six minutes per mile, and my pace is reasonably steady, I have kept a six-minute-mile pace.

[36] At least if the activity is characterized as "trying to keep the rope in this position". More on trying in Chapter 9.

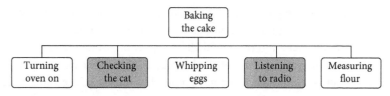

Figure 5.1 Baking the cake

after long intervals, I am still pursuing the end of keeping a diary while not taking adequate means to it.

With these clarifications in mind, ETR's treatment of policies and projects that exhibit the problematic structure discussed in the previous section is quite straightforward. Let us look again at how the principle of instrumental reasoning applies to a "mundane" long-term gappy action such as baking a cake. We then see how to extend it to a policy such as "exercising regularly" on the assumption that policies should be understood as just instances of long-term gappy actions. Let us go back to our extended, gappy action diagram (Figure 5.1).

As we mentioned before, there is a difference between the rational relation of the larger action to the fully active parts, and the relation of the larger action to its gaps: I measure the flour for the sake of baking the cake, but I do not check the cat for the sake of baking the cake. The smaller actions are, however, constrained by my interest in performing the larger action. I should only listen to the radio as long as it does not interfere with my baking the cake.

So here we can put forward the following contention:

(SUFFICIENCY) For my actions to be instrumentally rational in relation to the end of φ-ing (baking the cake), it is sufficient that I φ-ed (baked the cake) through my actions in the knowledge that so doing would result in my having φ-ed (the cake baked).[37]

(SUFFICIENCY) states a consequence of the fact that the principle of instrumental reasoning is our only principle of derivation, and that intentional action is our basic given attitude. If (SUFFICIENCY) is true of my pursuit of φ-ing, then I did take the necessary and sufficient means to

---

[37] I am ignoring further constraints that my end might have; it might be important for me to have the cake baked by a certain time etc. "In expected ways" is supposed to rule out deviant causal chains.

φ-ing. The "in the knowledge…" clause ensures that the relation between the pursuit of the end and the pursuit of the means is non-accidental; I baked the cake through the exercise of my rational powers. (SUFFICIENCY) is relativized to particular end, so it does not guarantee that all my actions in the range of φ-ing are rational. Had I successfully baked a cake but by means that involved (expectedly) that I set the house on fire I would have ensured that I did not take sufficient means to other ends I was pursuing. (SUFFICIENCY) does not express a necessary condition for rational agency even relative to an end given that stepmotherly nature might have intervened with my best attempts to bake a cake.

If having a policy is like being engaged in an ordinary action, then the same forms of rational control hold between the policy and its instances as between the larger actions and its parts. Let us take, for instance, a policy of exercising regularly. We find here a similar structure of rational relations that can be depicted in a similar diagram (Figure 5.2).

If policies exhibit the same rational structure as actions, then a suitably modified version of (SUFFICIENCY) is true of policies. In particular, ETR is committed to the following claim:

> (SUFFICIENCY$_p$) For my actions to be instrumentally rational in relation to the end of executing my policy P (e.g. exercising), it is sufficient that I execute the policy (e.g. exercise enough) through my actions in the knowledge that so doing would result in my executing the policy.

On ETR, (SUFFICIENCY$_p$) is just an instantiation of (SUFFICIENCY); there is no special role for FDIs to play in this context.

Let us look at cases in which a certain policy can potentially apply. For instance, the policy "drinking occasionally", or a general policy against drinking that allows for occasional exceptions, puts no constraints on my action if I am, say, walking on a campus in which no alcohol can be found.

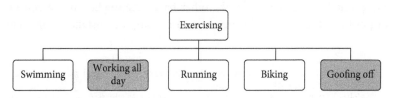

Figure 5.2 Exercising

It will apply if I am at a party at which alcohol is available in large quantities. I will focus on two-tier models (TTM) of the rationality of (non-)reconsideration, but as I explained above, this results in no loss of generality. In fact, as will be clear in a moment, I will extend the reach of the focus on (non-)reconsideration by assuming that policies such as "drink occasionally" work as follows:

(a) The "default" way in which one acts is not to drink.
(b) Deciding to drink is an instance of reconsideration (the other possible form of reconsideration would be to open the question of whether one should drink and deciding against it; for simplicity's sake, I'll mostly ignore this possible outcome of reconsideration).

On this view, once a policy applies, the two-tier model assesses the rationality of (non-)reconsideration at two levels.[38] Instances of (non-)reconsideration are deemed rational if they are the outcome of reasonable principles, habits, or dispositions of (non-)reconsideration.[39] Dispositions are deemed reasonable if they reliably promote our ends. Let us now distinguish two versions of the two-tier model (TTM) depending on how they read the first tier:

(*TTM Strong*): Instances of (non-)reconsideration are deemed rational if, and only if, they are the outcome of reasonable dispositions of (non-)reconsideration.

(*TTM Weak*): Instances of (non-)reconsideration are deemed rational if they are the outcome of reasonable dispositions of (non-)reconsideration.[40]

TTM Strong only evaluates an agent as rational if she is manifesting a reasonable disposition. An agent might fail, according to *TTM Strong*, in two ways. On the one hand, some of her dispositions of (non-)reconsideration might fail to be reasonable, in which case *all* manifestations of such disposition would be irrational. On the other hand, she might have reasonable dispositions that she fails to manifest in certain circumstances. On some

---

[38] Recall that we are examining only rational requirements governing (non-)reconsideration.

[39] Henceforth, I'll just use "dispositions".

[40] Holton (1999), p. 248 implicitly makes a similar distinction and endorses the stronger view.

occasions, something might interfere with her reasonable dispositions or she might act "out of character" and (fail to) reconsider when, were her actions to manifest her reasonable dispositions, she would not (would) have reconsidered. *TTM Weak*, on the other hand, deems all manifestations of a reasonable disposition rational, but is silent on those cases in which the agent's disposition is not reasonable, or those in which her reasonable disposition is somehow inert.

5.5 ETR vs *TTM Strong*

In order to evaluate how *TTM Strong* fares against ETR, let us first distinguish between two kinds of policies: loose and strict. Strict policies are those that call for the performance of the relevant action on every occasion in which the policy applies; a loose policy allows for occasional exceptions. So, for instance, for many people a policy of loyalty to their partner is a strict policy. On the other hand, one can have a more Leonard Cohen-like fidelity policy, which only requires you to be "faithful, Ah give or take a night or two".[41] Using Bratman's distinction between rejecting a policy and blocking a policy, one can say that strict policies can be rejected, but not blocked.[42] Larry may decide that he is no longer interested in being loyal to his spouse and no longer adopt a policy of loyalty, but insofar as he maintains a strict policy, he cannot rationally continue having the policy while deciding that it does not apply on special occasions, like his birthday. The Leonard Cohen version of a fidelity policy also illustrates that loose policies can be of two kinds. The phrase "give or take a night or two" suggests that this version of the policy does not specify precise exceptions. Another loose policy might be more precise in specifying when certain exceptions are allowed. So, for instance, one can have a policy of not drinking more than two pints of beer per evening, or a policy of drinking moderately, or just a general policy not to drink that allows for occasional exceptions. The first is a loose, but precise, policy, the second and third ones are loose and vague.

---

[41] "Everybody Knows", © Universal Music Publishing Group, Sony/ATV Music Publishing LLC. Jim Conant has pointed out to me that I completely butchered the lyrics here. I suppose I am grateful to him.

[42] Of course, they can also be violated. The distinction between "blocking" and "rejecting" a policy was introduced by Bratman (1999).

Now *TTM Strong* and ETR cannot give different verdicts on strict policies, for each must classify every action that fails to conform to such a general policy as instrumentally irrational. The same holds for loose but precise policies, as any violation not covered by a precise exception will be deemed instrumentally irrational by both views given that such violations are straightforward violations of the principle of instrumental reasoning. If I have a strict policy never to talk to strangers, any time I talk to a stranger will count as a violation of the policy. However, we need to appeal only to the policy and the principle of instrumental rationality to account for any irrationality here. If "never talking to strangers" is one of my ends and I talk to a stranger on my walk, I have failed to pursue the necessary (constitutive) means to my end. This instance of irrationality will be explained along the same lines by ETR and by any view that takes intentions to be the basic given attitudes. The former explains the irrationality as failure to *pursue* the necessary means to the end *I am pursuing*, while the latter explains it as a failure to *intend* the necessary means to the end *I intend*.

It is in the case of vague policies that the potential for disagreements and differences comes up. Suppose I have a policy of having fruit for dessert instead of chocolate. Suppose my reason for adopting this policy is health-related: I like chocolate better, but I am concerned about my health. The best policy in this case would then be a vague one; this is a policy whose application a rational being would block in certain circumstances. There are various ways of representing this policy, but for our purposes, it will be the best to think in the following terms: the policy in question is just a general policy, "Eat fruits for dessert". Since this is not a strict policy, I allow myself some exceptions; sometimes I can block the policy without thereby rejecting it. In other words, I can decide not to follow the policy today without in any way giving up on, or even weakening, my commitment to not eating chocolate for dessert. I'll assume that the policy is executed if nothing interferes with its execution. In our example, in the absence of interference, when it comes time for dessert, I'll eat fruits. Much can interfere with the successful execution of a policy in a particular case. There might be no fruit available; I might be force-fed chocolate; I might be fooled by chocolate cleverly disguised as a piece of fruit. But the only relevant case of interference for us is reconsideration. In reconsidering I might end up blocking the policy and thus not eat dessert on this particular occasion. Of course, I might also not change my mind after reconsidering, but, once again, to make matters simpler, I'll assume that whenever I reconsider I do change my mind and thus prevent the execution of the policy on that occasion. But given that the policy is vague, the fact that reconsideration interferes with the execution of policy does not make it, on its own, irrational to reconsider. In fact, given that occasionally enjoying sweets is also one of my ends, I *should* reconsider from time to time.

According to *TTM Strong, some* instances of reconsidering would manifest irrationality: a rational agent has dispositions that guide her in implementing a policy on particular occasions, and she is rational only insofar as her reconsidering on a particular occasion manifests such dispositions. Suppose I ate chocolate after dinner yesterday; that is, yesterday I reconsidered and decided to block the policy. We can now ask whether this is an instance of rational reconsideration. According to *TTM Strong*, reconsidering the policy counts as irrational if (and only if) this instance of reconsideration fails to manifest a rational disposition (that is, if it fails to manifest a disposition that the first tier classifies as a rational disposition). As we will see in a moment, ETR and *TTM Strong* do give divergent verdicts of rationality with respect to some such cases of blocking a policy,[43] and, for this reason, they are good test cases for comparing the two understandings of rational agency in the face of this problematic choice structure.

Let us return to my policy of eating fruits for dessert. According to ETR, as long as my actions exhibit the overall pattern in which I don't eat too much chocolate, there is no further question of the rationality of my conduct. (SUFFICIENCY$_p$) implies that the existence of a pattern of eating in accordance with the policy guarantees that I was instrumentally rational in relation to the policy.[44] On *TTM Strong*, on the other hand, at least in some cases in which I had sweets for dessert, I might have failed to act in accordance with rational habits and dispositions of reconsideration. Suppose, for instance, I have a reasonable habit of only reconsidering my intention not to eat chocolate for dessert in certain unusual circumstances;[45] when the chocolate is especially good, or goes particularly well with this liqueur, and so forth. Suppose now that this is not one of these evenings, but I reconsider anyway, and in light of my current preference for eating chocolate, I simply do it. My reconsideration here is not a manifestation of a rational disposition, and thus, on this version of TTM, this is a case of irrationality. Doubtless, if this kind of reconsideration keeps happening, the general *pattern* of activity could turn out to be irrational. But if ETR is correct, this

---

[43] I consider the other possible divergences in the next section.

[44] At least as long as the pattern was brought about by my actions in a non-deviant manner.

[45] The relevant habits and dispositions will probably be more general than this, but it simplifies matters to consider a rather specific habit.

particular action cannot, on its own, ground any assessment of instrumental irrationality in relation to this policy.

But if the agent's "dessert behaviour" still conforms to his vague policy, why should such an action count as irrational? Doesn't (SUFFICIENCY$_p$) correctly evaluate such patterns of activity as rational relative to the policy? David Gauthier gives an argument for something like *TTM Strong*. In considering a (vague) policy to have fruit for dessert, Gauthier argues that I could not choose chocolate in a particular occasion simply because at the time of the decision, I want (prefer) to have chocolate on this occasion:

> In considering my choices between chocolate and a fruit, I am supposing that if it were rational for me to deliberate on some basis for any such choice, it would be rational for me to deliberate on that basis for every such choice. For there is nothing to distinguish one choice from another... [Thus] choosing on the basis of one's proximate preferences is not rational.[46]

In a nutshell, according to Gauthier, if I am ready to make an exception in a case without relying on any special features of the situation, then, by parity of reasoning, I would be willing to make an exception to my policy every night. In such a case, I don't really have a policy of eating only fruit for dessert, or if I do, I am failing to comply with it. We can present Gauthier's argument as follows:

[VIOLATION] If I eat sweet desserts on too many occasions, I act irrationally.

[CULPRITS] If eating sweet desserts on too many occasions is irrational, then if I do eat desserts on too many occasions, then on at least some *specific* occasions it must be irrational to eat dessert.

[GENERALITY] If eating sweet desserts is irrational on some occasions, it must be irrational on every other relevantly similar occasion.

[VIOLATION] is a straightforward consequence of the principle of instrumental reasoning and our stipulations; since we stipulated that my end is to follow the policy, violating it must be instrumentally irrational. I do not want to quibble with [GENERALITY]; some fans of extreme versions of

---

[46] Gauthier (1997), p. 21.

particularism might take issue with such an assumption, but I find [GENERALITY] overwhelmingly plausible. What about [CULPRITS]? [CULPRITS] essentially claims that if a certain extended pattern of activity was irrational, then some of the momentary actions that constitute the pattern were irrational. If we accept the idea that policies have the same rational structure as extended actions, [CULPRITS] would say that there could be no policy that is irrational without some of its momentary parts being irrational. In other words, [CULPRITS] is the denial of the possibility of top-down independence and thus of the *NON-SUPERVENIENCE THESIS*. But if top-down independence is possible, then there can be a *pattern* of activity that is irrational relative to the policy without any of the momentary actions that constitute the pattern being irrational. Suppose, for instance, I have a policy of not drinking too much at parties. We might ask what would count as a successful execution of this policy. It seems plausible that there is no precise set of momentary choices that constitute *the exact maximum* amount of drinking allowed in a party. Given the vague nature of what counts as success in the policy, there'll be clearly acceptable choices, clearly unacceptable choices, and a certain penumbral area. Because of the penumbral area, there'll be no point at which it would be right to say that if I were to drink one more drop of alcohol I will have at this point violated my policy, or at least that I would have done so knowingly. In this case, at each momentary choice node, there might be no decisive reason for me not to block the policy; but if I always choose to block the policy I will fail to execute it. Having a policy with such a vague end is not essentially different from having a vague policy as defined earlier; in fact, there is no important difference between this policy and a policy not to drink at parties that allows for some unspecified exceptions.

We have already argued in the previous chapters that we should accept the *NON-SUPERVENIENCE THESIS*. But we can give now further reasons to accept the thesis in this context. First, the plausibility of (SUFFICIENCY$_p$) on its own suggests that manifesting such habits and dispositions is only *one* way in which an agent can be rational relative to a vague policy. If the agent implements the policy in an acceptable manner, and if she does so not by chance but through her knowledge of how to realize her end, then she is complying with any plausible instrumental requirement, whether or not she also manifests commendable habits or dispositions. Even if she fails to manifest such habits or dispositions, she is exercising her instrumentally rational powers flawlessly; she is, after all, non-accidentally taking sufficient means to her end of implementing the policy.

The structural parallel between (SUFFICIENCY) and (SUFFICIENCY$_p$) suggests stronger grounds to accept the possibility of top-down independent policies. After all, baking a cake is also a vague end; it is unlikely that there is a precise set of "distractions" such that even one more second of listening to the news would prevent me from baking a cake. The predicate "x is a cake" is probably vague, but this is not the main reason why my end here is vague or indeterminate. Awful-tasting cakes, or cakes that weren't ready until after the party was over, will not count as realizing my end of baking a cake, but there is no precise last-second or minimum "tastiness" that my end specifies. [SUFFICIENCY] here seems extremely plausible. It seems hard to defend the proposal that we could not judge an agent who success-fully bakes a cake in ordinary circumstances to be rational unless we can determine first that all her distractions were the manifestation of the right kind of dispositions.[47] As long as I ended up with an acceptable cake in a non-deviant and not too lucky manner, my baking of the cake is a proper exercise of my rational powers. Why would instrumental rationality require more from us than the non-accidental successful completion of my action of baking the cake? In other words, the only disposition a rational agent needs in this context is the disposition to comply with the principle of instrumental reasoning.

In fact, once we accept [SUFFICIENCY], we are already committed to the possibility of top-down independence as a feature of almost any extended action or pursuit. Let us look at a case in which I bake an acceptable cake through a series of interruptions that were not all manifestations of more specific rational dispositions. By [SUFFICIENCY] all my actions (while I was baking the cake) are instrumentally rational in relation to the end of baking the cake, including the actions that constituted the gaps (my check-ing the cat to see if it had moved, my calling grandma on the landline, etc.). But now compare this case with a case where I failed to bake a cake. Let us stipulate that in such a case there are *more* interruptions, but that there are no relevant differences between the added interruptions and the original ones. Thus, by [GENERALITY], we must conclude that the new interrup-tions are also rational actions. But, assuming that I kept the end of baking the cake throughout this time, we must conclude that the general pattern of

---

[47] Unless we trivialize the notion of "manifesting the right kind of disposition" in this con-text, such that it counts as manifesting the right kind of disposition whenever I comply with [SUFFICIENCY].

activity is irrational relative to the end of baking the cake. After all, I did fail to bake my cake even though the necessary means were fully under my control, and there were no unexpected circumstances; all the interruptions were due to my own agency. So if [SUFFICIENCY] is correct, we can easily build a case in which we must reject [CULPRITS]; [SUFFICIENCY] thus already implies the possibility of top-down independence.

There is one way to try to block this argument: namely, one might deny the coherence of our stipulations that there are no relevant differences among all interruptions in the case in which I failed to bake a cake. Of course, it is easy to imagine that each extra time the cat is in the same position, I am just as bored, the cake is at a relevantly similar stage, and so forth. But, one might argue, at least some interruptions will be importantly different; some of them must be such that, given that so many interruptions had occurred, they would prevent the cake from being baked in an acceptable manner. In other words, there must have been some momentary action *MA* such that before I performed *MA*, it was still possible for me to bake an acceptable cake, but after I performed *MA*, it was no longer possible for me to bake an acceptable cake. In that case, *MA* is our culprit; *MA* is the irrational momentary action (or at least one of the irrational momentary actions). This, however, would amount to the denial of the possibility of properly indeterminate ends. We argued in the last chapter that similar attempts to try to show that indeterminate ends are incoherent or impossible, or showing that they collapse into fully determinate or precise preference orderings, would rule out rationally innocent ends that most of us seem to have. However, it is worth noting that the argument of this chapter is independent from accepting this claim from the previous chapter. As we argued above, the existence of such patterns was the best chance to establish the intentional autonomy thesis; if there were no vague policies, the arguments of the first sections would suffice to repudiate the intentional autonomy thesis.

5.6 ETR vs *TTM Weak*

TTM Weak claims that conformity to reasonable dispositions is permissible but not mandatory; in other words, *TTM Weak* delivers verdicts of "rational action" but not of "irrational action". Thus *TTM Weak* could only conflict with ETR if it is more permissive than ETR; if it allows that certain cases of failing to execute a policy would count as rational, but these would be irrational by ETR's lights. But since [SUFFICIENCY] and [SUFFICIENCY$_p$] specify only sufficient conditions for rational agency, we have so far formulated no precise principle of evaluation in this context that could determine that some actions are irrational. So let us put forward the following principle:

> [NECESSITY] In cases in which there is no risk, no relevant change of information, and in which φ-ing (executing a policy P) is (known to be) fully under my control, for my actions to be instrumentally rational in relation to the end of φ-ing (executing policy P), it is necessary that I φ (execute the policy) through my actions in the knowledge that so doing would result in my having φ-ed (executed the policy).

[NECESSITY] merely replaces "sufficient" with "necessary" in replacing "sufficient" in [SUFFICIENCY] and [SUFFICIENCY$_p$]. In other words, it is a "completeness" clause for the principles of instrumental rationality of action under knowledge; it simply says that there are no principles other than the principle of instrumental reasoning that could also make an agent instrumentally rational in relation to an end or policy under these conditions.

TTM Weak will be incompatible with [NECESSITY] if the following is true according to this version of TTM:

> [RATIONAL NON-EXECUTION] There are cases in which an agent manifests rational dispositions of reconsideration (and thus dispositions that generally result in successful execution of the policy) in every occasion she reconsiders, and in which the agent had all the relevant information at the time she reconsiders, but in which she fails to execute the policy. In such cases, the agent does not act irrationally.

A habit of reconsideration that reliably prevents the agent from making too many exceptions to her policy might, in some adverse circumstances, lead a rational agent astray. In such a case, according to [RATIONAL NON-EXECUTION], the agent would not be irrational, but just unlucky. This seems rather plausible at first. But could someone rationally fail to live up to the policy of, say, drinking moderately[48] in this way? Perhaps we can imagine a situation like the following: Mary has reasonable habits of

---

[48] That is, she failed in her pursuit of the end of, say, drinking moderately in general, rather than that she engaged in the occasional excess that is compatible with a general policy of drinking moderately.

reconsideration; for instance, she only reconsiders her policy not to drink if there is some special occasion in which drinking would be especially appropriate. For Mary, weddings are such occasions; these are unique circumstances in which we can express our sympathetic joy by toasting to brides and grooms. Unfortunately, weddings keep coming up, and Mary's actions end up amounting to a clear failure to realize her end. Should we conclude that Mary's failure to keep up her policy was not a failure of rationality, that it was simply bad luck (one of these unfortunate occasions in which stepmotherly nature frustrates the efforts of flawless rational agency)?

It doesn't seem so. If Mary is going to a wedding every day, she must realize that her dispositions of reconsideration are leading her astray; the fact that these dispositions are rational in other contexts cannot excuse her if she is in a position to know that they are inadequate in the present context. *TTM Weak*, understood this way, is clearly too permissive. It sounds like a joke to say in this situation that Mary was unlucky: "she had such reasonable dispositions, and she is overall such a rational agent but, alas, there were just too many weddings".

It might seem that we are ignoring something obvious; we seem to have targeted a particularly implausible version of *TTM Weak*. If in the current context the disposition is leading Mary astray, isn't this enough to show that the disposition is not a rational one? Wouldn't all rational dispositions be sensitive to the presence of too many weddings? Indeed, if we say that the correct dispositions are those which *ensure* that the agent complies with her policies, then *TTM Weak* will deliver the same verdicts as [NECESSITY]. However, [NECESSITY] allows us to get these results without positing irreducible norms governing FDIs. We can get the exact same verdicts by simply relying on the principle of instrumental reasoning; *TTM Weak* is thus either too weak or entirely superfluous.

One might complain that ETR cuts down on rational principles only by inflating what goes into the traditional conception of the principle of instrumental reasoning; after all, [SUFFICIENCY$_p$] is not part of the traditional conception of instrumental rationality. However, strictly speaking, [SUFFICIENCY$_p$] is just an instance of [SUFFICIENCY] applied to policies. [SUFFICIENCY$_p$] does not *add* to the content of [SUFFICIENCY]; [SUFFICIENCY$_p$] is simply an *implication* of [SUFFICIENCY] within ETR's framework. The more general principle is already needed to understand what counts as rationally pursuing the end of baking a cake, and it cannot be replaced by a principle governing FDIs. The focus on mental attitudes rather than extended actions might have obscured this for us, but applying the principle of instrumental reasoning to vague or indeterminate pursuits (which are nearly all our pursuits) already commits us to top-down independence.

5.7 Conclusion

It has been a general assumption of theories of instrumental rationality that their principles must apply primarily to mental states, and only derivatively to actions; in other words, on this view, intentional actions cannot be the basic given attitudes. I think Bratman, among others, correctly noticed that principles governing the agent's beliefs, desires, or preferences could not exhaust the theory of instrumental rationality; he went astray, however, in thinking that the fix was to add one more mental state to the pile: FDIs. A theory of instrumental rationality is a theory of rationality in action, and thus we need to turn our attention to the actions themselves.

However, the thesis of intentional autonomy is not fully refuted here. I focused mostly on pragmatic defences of the intentional autonomy thesis; that is, I tried to show that rational requirements governing intentions cannot be explained as part of the coherent pursuit of the agent's ends, as agents who violate such requirements do not undermine the pursuit of their ends (or in the cases of permissions, agents who do exercise the relevant permission would undermine the pursuit of their ends). However, there might be requirements that are internal to the nature of having an FDI itself or that are implied by a constitutive relation between FDIs and the nature of (some aspect of) our agency. Perhaps it is simply incoherent to form an FDI and fail to act in accordance with it (or give it up prior to the action) in certain contexts, or perhaps some constitutive ends of (a form of) agency, such as self-governance, are bound up with certain intention-specific requirements. Of course, the two types of arguments ("pragmatic" and "internal") are not so easily disentangled, and the division is a bit artificial. Still, the arguments that I will be considering in Chapter 6 are different enough to deserve separate treatment.

6

Persisting Intentions

6.0 Introduction

In the previous chapter we focused mostly on pragmatic arguments for principles or requirements of intention stability, and, in particular, requirements and principles that could potentially govern a rational agent's disposition to reconsider the future-directed intentions (FDIs) they had previously formed. The principles or requirements were supposedly grounded on the functions of FDIs, such as intra- and interpersonal coordination in the pursuit of long-term goals, efficient use of deliberative resources, resisting temptation, and the successful pursuit of vague policies and ends through momentary actions. The question was whether the importance of planning, coordination, and so forth in the unfolding of our extended agency could ground legitimate principles or requirements governing how we maintain and revise FDIs. I argued that a better understanding of how the principle of instrumental reasoning applies to extended action, and of how a rational agent pursues indeterminate ends through arbitrarily long intervals of time, allowed us to see that the purported principles or requirements were superfluous (or outright invalid).

However, there might be more fundamental principles or requirements of diachronic coherence for FDIs. Just like we accept that there are principles of synchronic coherence governing intentional action (or intention in action),[1] there might also be principles of diachronic coherence through time governing FDIs (or the relation between FDIs and intentional action). Just as it is incoherent to act with the intention of both replenishing the water supply and the intention of destroying the pump (thus knowingly making it impossible that the water supply be replenished), it might be also incoherent, at least in certain circumstances, to intend at t_0 to replenish the

---

[1] This is ETR COHERENCE in our view. Of course, philosophers who are sympathetic to the view that intentions are among the basic given attitudes also think that there are synchronic requirements governing FDIs.

water supply at t_2 and to then at t_1 to abandon this intention and intend instead to destroy the pump so that the water supply will not be replenished at t_2. As I said before, the division is a bit artificial, given that pragmatic considerations might be relevant in determining what counts as coherence over time. Still, the grounds for principles and requirements governing FDIs we discuss in this chapter deserve separate consideration.

In Section 6.1, I formulate the main putative requirements that will be the topic of the first four sections of the chapter: what I call "persistence requirements". Section 6.2 looks at the main arguments in support of these persistence requirements. Section 6.3 argues that the intuitions that support such requirements depend on an illicit move from the irrationality of certain patterns to the irrationality of instances of the pattern. Section 6.4 argues that to the extent that there are rational requirements in the neighbourhood, they are better accounted for by ETR. Section 6.5 discusses a somewhat different way to introduce similar requirements; namely, arguments for the view that certain diachronic requirements for FDIs are constitutive of self-governance (and that self-governance is a central aspect or end of human agency).

Finally, since the chapter relies on the role that evaluative or normative judgments have in guiding rational agents, it seems to rely on the correctness of certain enkratic requirements; that is, rational requirements to do what we judge to be all-things-considered good to do, or what we ought to do all-things-considered. However, one might object that accepting the correctness of such requirements conflicts with the claim that ETR COHERENCE and ETR DERIVATION are the only principles of coherence and derivation. So this chapter ends with an appendix explaining how enkratic requirements can be part of the theory of instrumental rationality presented here.

This chapter completes our argument against the view that FDIs are among the basic given attitudes. Since Chapters 2 to 4 argue for the superiority of ETR over views that take desires or preferences as the basic given attitudes, this chapter ends the presentation of the main part of the book's argument in favour of ETR. Chapters 7 and 8 extend ETR to include not only principles but also virtues and vices of instrumental rationality, and Chapter 9 explains how ETR can be extended to cases of risk and ignorance.

6.1 Persistence Requirements

Choice situations in which our substantive reasons do not determine a specific course of action are ubiquitous; often, if not always, we have to choose among incompatible possible future actions such that none is better supported by our reasons than the others. I might have sufficient reason to go for lunch to any of the many restaurants near my office; I might be justified in spending the evening reading, watching TV, or playing cards; my next vacation could be justifiably spent either hiking in the mountains or doing volunteer work helping refugees. In all these cases my reasons do not settle on a uniquely rational, or justified, course of action.[2]

In such situations, forming an FDI might play a particularly important role. Namely, an intention commits us to a course of an action *even when our reasons run out*. Thus, one might argue that rationality requires that, *ceteris paribus*, we do not revise our intentions. In Chapter 5, we looked at whether we should reconsider our intentions in cases in which reconsidering my reasons could lead me to conclude that I have better reasons to form a different intention. But the proposal here is that I might have reasons not to revise an intention when *I know that* I have no decisive reason to choose one course of action over another. In such cases, it might seem that it is of the very nature of an intention that it settles the matter and thus gives rise to a requirement not to revise it; someone who forms such an intention and later abandons it for no particular reason might arguably be manifesting a form of incoherence over time.

Let us suppose I decide to go on vacation in December. There are various destinations that interest me, so I start deliberating about where I should go. I conclude that several of these destinations would be equally good, but, of course, I must settle on one of them. I finally form the intention to go to Paris, even though I know that I would be equally justified in deciding to go to Madrid. Does this intention generate any special reasons or requirements? Let us consider the temporal progression illustrated in Figure 6.1.

Since no intention is formed prior to t_2, there can be no intention-specific requirement prior to this point. But it is unlikely that we need to appeal to an intention-specific requirement to explain my normative situation at any point

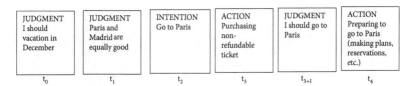

JUDGMENT I should vacation in December	JUDGMENT Paris and Madrid are equally good	INTENTION Go to Paris	ACTION Purchasing non- refundable ticket	JUDGMENT I should go to Paris	ACTION Preparing to go to Paris (making plans, reservations, etc.)
t_0	t_1	t_2	t_3	t_{3+1}	t_4

Figure 6.1 Judgment, intention, and action

<hr />

[2] Acceptance of the ubiquity of this kind of situation is what Joseph Raz calls "The Basic Belief" in Raz (1999).

after t_3. After all, after this point I seem to have reasons to prefer Paris over Madrid that are independent of my having intended to go to Paris at t_2; namely, given I have bought tickets it is now cheaper to go to Paris than to equally good Madrid. Insofar as there are any important intention-specific requirements, they must be most salient to my normative situation between t_2 and t_3. What would such requirements look like? Here are a few possibilities:

[NONREV] An agent should be disposed not to revise her intention, unless certain special circumstances obtain.

[PERSIST] An agent should not abandon her intention without reconsidering unless certain special circumstances obtain.[3]

[NOGRAT] Reconsideration alone should not suffice to abandon one's intention unless certain special circumstances obtain (no gratuitous change of mind).

The clause "unless certain special circumstances obtain" is left here for the benefit of proponents of such principles; I will not try to spell it out further.

[NONREV] is probably best supported by the kind of pragmatic considerations we considered in the last chapter; that is, considerations that appeal to the limits and obstacles encountered by the particular circumstances in which human beings exercise their rational capacities.

On the other hand, both [PERSIST] and [NOGRAT] can be given non-pragmatic justifications; one might argue that it is a form of incoherence to revise one's intentions without a change in the assessment of our reasons to act.[4] On such views, intentions would count among our basic attitudes, and acting from principles such as [PERSIST] and [NOGRAT] would count as manifestations of the agent's rational powers. Given that they are amenable to very similar kinds of justification, I'll refer to [PERSIST] and [NOGRAT] together as "intention-persistence requirements". These intention-persistence requirements will be the focus of the next few sections. In the final section,

---

[3] Broome (2013) defends a more precise version of this principle. See also Bratman (2012) for a similar principle. Paul (2014a), Holton (2009), and arguably Bratman (1987) (see Chapter 5) defend requirements similar to (NONREV). I'm not aware of anyone who explicitly defends (NOGRAT) but it should be congenial to anyone sympathetic to intention-persistence requirements (though Broome explicitly rejects similar requirements in Broome (2001)). Ferrero (2010) makes a persuasive case that it's not clear how any persistence requirement can be accepted once we reject principles like (NOGRAT).

[4] Just as it is arguably incoherent to update our beliefs or credences without any change in the evidence.

I consider Bratman's recent attempts to establish similar requirements on the basis of an end of self-governance.

6.2 Persistence of Intention

Let us look at two cases in which our reasons run out:

(a) *Ties*   Often when we pick from a restaurant buffet, get something from our pantry, choose dates to travel, pick a time to go to the bookstore, and so forth, we need to pick among indifferent alternatives.[5] Forming an intention in such a case settles which of the indifferent ends one will pursue.

(b) *Incommensurability*   From deciding between going to a movie or a restaurant to the decisions about which career to pursue, we face choices between alternatives that do not seem to be comparable.[6] Forming an intention in such cases settles which of the incommensurable ends one will pursue.

Given that in these cases, the FDI settles among alternatives left open by the balance of reasons, they seem particularly well suited to justify a requirement not to change our mind, to persist in the intentions we form in these scenarios, at least absent any new information or any other improvement in our epistemic situation. We can provide a rough formulation of this idea as follows:

Persistence   Forming an FDI, by its very nature, settles among alternatives previously left open. It is thus incoherent to settle and then "unsettle" later without new reasons or relevant deliberation.

In cases in which our reasons leave us no option but to form a specific intention, there is no need to appeal to persistence requirements to explain the rational agent's continuous commitment to the intention; the grounds upon

---

[5] Ullmann-Margalit and Morgenbesser (1977) famously argued for the ubiquity of cases of "picking" (selection under indifference). Some of the cases of what they call "second-order picking" are cases of incommensurability and will be discussed separately.

[6] How to understand these cases more precisely is a matter of much debate. For some suggestions, see Chang (2002), Griffin (1997), and Gert (2004). Even describing such cases as cases of 'incommensurability' is controversial; see Chang (2017). I intend the term to be merely picking out these cases, rather than committing to a particular theoretical account or explanation of these phenomena.

which the agent formed the intention in question would also explain its persistence.[7] However, given that we often have independent reasons to form intentions prior to the time of action in the case of ties or incommensurability, there might be good reasons to insist on persistence requirements exactly in those cases. Perhaps a rational agent who needs to (or may) form an intention in such cases will, *ceteris paribus*, hold on to such intentions up to the time at which she acts.

6.2.1 Ties

Let us start with the following vignette:[8]

> There will soon be a fork in the road. Both branches take me to my destination in the same amount of time, without any significant difference in the landscape, gas costs, and so forth. I form the intention now that I will take the left branch.

A few minutes pass and I now reach the fork. Of course, if I carry out my intention, I act rationally (*ceteris paribus*). But suppose that my driving comes to an unexpected conclusion. Let us take a look at those two alternative endings:

(a) The intention slips my mind, and I turn right.
(b) I still remember having formed the intention to turn left, but I abandon it for no particular reason, and turn right.

Are these alternative endings instances of irrationality? Given that I successfully and non-accidentally did something towards which I was (rightly) indifferent compared to the option of taking the left branch, it seems hard to explain why this would be irrational. It certainly seems that I did not violate any instrumental requirements, since the path I took was just as good from my practical standpoint as the one I forsook. However, one could argue that I did violate a requirement; after all, what would have been the point of forming an FDI in the first place, if it turned out that it made no

---

[7] Of course, this justification would not apply to the persistence of ill-formed intentions, but a rational requirement for the persistence of ill-formed intentions is particularly implausible.

[8] Taken from Bratman (1987).

difference to what it was rational for me to do? We can put the argument in favour of the view that I must have violated a rational requirement in the form of a dilemma. Either (i) there was a reason to form my intention and thus there would be reason to carry it out;[9] or (ii) there is no reason to form my intention and thus it was irrational to form it. The fact that we can come up with such a dilemma arguably suggests that the combination of forming the intention and not carrying it out is a case of incoherence.

However, this argument suffers from an ambiguity. The first horn of the dilemma is true only if there is decisive reason to form the intention. That is, even granting that a reason to intend to φ must also be a reason to φ, it would follow that I now must φ only if the reason in the case was decisive; in other words, only if there was not just as good a reason to do something else. But, *ex hypothesis*, there is just as good reason to turn right. On the other hand, the second horn of the dilemma is only true if there was no sufficient reason to φ and thus no sufficient reason to intend to φ. Even if there was no decisive reason to form the intention (that is, even if there was also sufficient reason to form another, incompatible, intention), it would not be irrational to form the intention as long as there was sufficient reason to form it. Yet, the dilemma does seem to have an intuitive appeal. How could intentions settle what we do if it were not for the fact that they are going to persist? And if a state does not settle what we do, how can it count as an intention?

Doubtless, in paradigmatic cases, agents who have an FDI to φ are likely to φ at the relevant time. It is exactly because intentions tend to persist that they can serve the function that they do. In our earlier case of choosing among travel destinations, it was important to start planning for a trip, since I had decisive reason to go somewhere; even if I need not do anything right now, it might be worth deliberating now as it might be costly later.[10] Whatever justification I had in intending to φ, the justification would typically be preserved together with the judgment. But if my justification for my preserved intention *permitted* the intention, but did not *require* it, then I am no more required to φ now than I was required to form the intention to φ then.

---

[9] Perhaps in some cases there are reasons to form an intention to φ when there is no reason to φ, as in the Toxin puzzle (Kavka (1983)). There are complicated issues here, but all parties to the debate would accept that our vignette is not a special case in which the reasons to form the intention are completely independent from the reasons to perform the action.

[10] Ferrero describes this role of intention as a part of a division of deliberative labour. See Ferrero (2010).

We can agree that the function of an FDI is to settle an issue without conceding that there are intention-specific requirements. Barring interferences (including forgetfulness), intentions persist till they are acted upon. This is indeed part of the constitutive nature of FDIs: FDIs are exactly mental states such that an agent who has an intention *will* act with that intention in the absence of interference. This non-normative fact is enough to explain how they can serve their "settling function". In our original vignette, the point of forming the intention was, no doubt, that it would save me from having to deliberate while impatient drivers wait for my decision. Given that I was justified earlier in forming the intention to turn left, I am still justified in acting on this intention when I reach the fork. FDIs serve their settling function because in the normal course of events at the time of action they become intentions in action.[11] But this fact does not imply that my interfering with this normal course of events is (even *pro tanto*) irrational.

It is rather implausible that FDIs can generate persistence requirements in cases of "ties". Such ties are by definition matters of indifference, so it is hard to see how an agent who took one of two indifferent courses of action could have done anything wrong; if the original intention was the manifestation of rational power in virtue of picking among two indifferent alternatives, it seems that the later intention to choose the second alternative would be the manifestation of a rational power on the same grounds. On the other hand, cases of incommensurability might be a more promising stage to find a special role for FDIs to play in the theory of rationality. Unlike tie cases, in cases of incommensurability one can invest a great deal into the pursuit of one alternative without altering the comparative relation between two choices. If my buying a non-refundable ticket to Paris sufficed to make going to Paris a superior alternative to going to Madrid, given the now higher cost of the Madrid alternative, the same cannot be said for the choice between, say, giving a large sum of money to my favourite charity or spending the money on a very expensive family reunion. These alternatives might still be on a par even after my travel agent offers a discount on the family reunion package.[12] In such cases, we might think that there is a more important role to be

---

[11] McDowell (2010), following Sellars, says that FDIs "mature" into intentions in actions "provided that the subject realizes the time for acting has arrived, and does not change her mind, and is not prevented from acting" (p. 61).

[12] I am using Chang's notion of "being on a par" (Chang (2002)), but this point, of course, does not depend on accepting a particular view on this issue. See below for my preferred treatment.

played by the stability of an FDI and this might be, consequently, a better context for the justification of persistence requirements.

6.2.2 Incommensurability and Reflective Preferences

Raz's famous proposal defines two alternatives, A and B, as incommensurable when it is neither the case that A is better than B nor that B is better than A, nor that A and B are of equal value.[13] But it is also possible to talk about values being incommensurable, if, for instance, trade-offs between different kinds of value are not always comparable.[14] So a choice between watching *Tokyo Story* and going to dinner at Chez Panisse might be incommensurable, but, more generally, the values of cinematic appreciation and gastronomic enjoyment might be incomparable; incommensurable alternatives often arise from choices among incomparable values.

ETR allows for a straightforward understanding of these relations of incommensurability, at least from the point of view of the theory of instrumental rationality. As we saw in the first two chapters, neither the agent's Pareto Preferences nor her reflective preferences necessarily provide a complete preference ordering across options involving the better and worse actualizations of two ends. An agent might pursue the end of cinematic appreciation and the end of enjoying gastronomic pleasures. Each of these ends have better or worse actualizations, but there might be no combined gastro-cinematic end that the agent pursues that would settle every single potential conflict between these two.

The agent might also have reflective preferences[15] between various actualizations of each end. Reflective preferences are grounded on second-order ends to give priority to one pursuit over another. One might, for instance, have the end[16] of giving priority to cinematic enjoyment of rare, exceptional movies over gastronomic enjoyment of any kind, and perhaps also have the end of giving priority to rare opportunities to enjoy excellent meals over watching run-of-the-mill commercial movies. Such an agent would also have Pareto Preferences, preferences for actions that actualize both gastronomic

---

[13] Raz (1986), p. 342. Of course, one could define the notion similarly in terms of preferences.
[14] For an example of the latter use, see Wiggins (1978). Chang (1997) distinguishes between incomparability and incommensurability along similar lines and provides a very useful guide to the various ways of understanding "incommensurability" and similar notions.
[15] See Chapter 2.
[16] Given our conclusions of the last chapter, these second-order ends can be understood as policies.

enjoyment and cinematic appreciation better than their alternative. If my choice is between watching *Tokyo Story* and having dinner at Chez Panisse, on the one hand, and watching *Battlefield Earth* and eating at Subway on the other, I will choose the former.

Let us call the ranking of possible actions generated by the better or worse actualizations of an end, a "ranking within a teleological dimension".[17] So there'll be the ranking generated by my pursuit of cinematic appreciation, and a different ranking generated my pursuit of gastronomic enjoyment.[18] Let us take our two teleological dimensions, "cinematic appreciation" and "gastronomic enjoyment", and represent the respective rankings from each dimension as an ordered pair such that each item is assigned a value for each dimension such that the higher the value, the higher the ranking along the corresponding dimension. In our options above we could either [go watch *Tokyo Story*, eat at Chez Panisse] or [go watch *Battlefield Earth*, eat at Subway]. Each option gets assigned a pair of values, respectively, [1,1] and [0,0]. The first option gets higher values on both dimensions as *Tokyo Story* is a better movie and Chez Panisse a better eatery. As we said before, as long as no indeterminate ends are generically implicated, a rational agent chooses according to her Pareto Preferences. For ease of exposition, I'll assume from here on that no indeterminate ends are generically implicated in any of our cases. We can thus formulate the following Pareto Principle:[19]

[PP] if $x_a > y_a$ and $x_b > y_b$, then choosing $[y_a, y_b]$ in a choice between ($[x_a, x_b]$; $[y_a, y_b]$) is not rationally permitted.

ETR generates thus at least this additional requirement for cases of incommensurability. But our opponent wants to argue that in such cases, we also

---

[17] This proposal bears some similarities to the representation of value relations in Rabinowicz (2008).

[18] Note that understanding this type of incomparability in terms of the pursuit of different ends, instead of in terms of competing values that we can realize, has some important advantages. Not all cases in which trade-offs are not comparable can be plausibly described as cases in which we realize different kinds of values. If I am lucky enough to have two friends, various choice situations involving the two of them will have a similar structure to the choice situations in which I could realize two kinds of values. But it would be implausible to describe, say, helping Jane train for the marathon and helping Jay train for the marathon as the realization of two different kinds of values, though obviously my friendship with Jane and my friendship with Jay are two independent ends that I pursue. For a similar point (on the topic of rational regret), see Hurka (1996).

[19] For simplicity's sake, I will look only at the two-dimension case, but it should be clear how to generalize it to more complex cases.

need intention-specific requirements. Let us start examining this claim by looking at the simple case below:

(SIMPLE)
I can watch either *Better Movie* or *Movie* at *Town Theatre*. My other option is to go to *Fancy Restaurant*. I don't prefer *Fancy Restaurant* over either *Better Movie* or *Movie* or vice versa. However, I form the intention to go see *Better Movie*. I start driving through *Road to Everything* but just before I need to turn to *Better Movie Road*, I abandon my intention to go to the movie, and take *Restaurant Road* instead.

Cases like (SIMPLE) seem not to justify any persistence requirement. If we were persuaded by the argument that I violated no requirement when I turned right in our above vignette, we should be equally convinced that I have violated no requirements in (SIMPLE). However, if the only constraint on permissible choices we have in these cases is [PP], it seems that we need to allow much more radical changes of mind if we do not introduce intention-specific requirements. And, arguably, a rational agent would not change her mind in this way. Let us look at the following case:

($200 WASTED)
Larry is deciding between being a professional footballer or a stay-at-home dad. In order to become a professional footballer, he must buy a $200 ball and net set. If he wants to be a stay-at-home dad, he needs to buy the *How to Be a Stay-at-Home Dad* DVD for $200. Larry forms the intention to become a professional footballer, goes to the store, and buys the ball and net set. Ten minutes later he abandons his intention, calls the Barcelona manager, and says that he no longer wishes to be on the team as he is now a stay-at-home dad.

This seems to be a case in which it is plausible to say that this decision is one in which Larry finds the two options (stay-at-home dad; professional footballer) incommensurable, and that a difference of $200 dollars in the cost of either alternative would not suddenly make one of the options better than the other. In our preferred way of understanding such cases, Larry has no reflective preferences that would lead him to choose either alternative if we add $200 to one of them. Taken in isolation, neither choice is rationally mandated. That is, choosing to be a professional footballer at the first juncture is obviously permissible. But it would also have been permissible to choose to become a stay-at-home dad if the cost of this option was $200 higher. Yet it seems that something went awry here. Larry seems to have done something foolish; after all, he just wasted $200. However, ETR seems unable to locate this irrationality; certainly Larry has not violated (PP). There are two teleological dimensions relevant for Larry's choice; we can call them the "professional" dimension and the "family" dimension. Now if A = [stay-at-home dad], B = [stay-at-home dad and loss of $200] and C = [professional footballer] and D = [professional footballer and loss of $200], then A, B, C, and D are assigned the following set of values: A = [0, 2], B = [0, 1], C = [2,0], D = [1,0]. But we can now see that neither Larry's earlier choice of C nor Larry's later choice to move to B violates [PP]. After all, when Larry chose B the strictly preferred option A was no longer available, so the choice was between B and C, neither of which is Pareto superior to the other.

However, we have good reason to doubt the intuition that Larry is irrational.[20] Let us start by looking at a variation of ($200 WASTED):

(SQUAD/RIYADH 1)
Larry faces the same situation and forms the same intention and buys the same ball and net set. Larry then thinks he gets a call from his team manager (Ernesto) and thinks he hears Ernesto say, "You're dropped from the squad." He then abandons his intention to be a professional footballer (as he now thinks that this career is no longer available to him). Before he even has time to consider what he'll do instead, the phone rings again. It's his cousin Honesto. Honesto tells him he was the one who called him and that what he said was, "I got ear drops in Riyadh." Without considering the matter further, Larry immediately forms the intention to become a stay-at-home dad.

It seems hard to distinguish (SQUAD/RIYADH 1) from ($200 WASTED) in terms either of the intuitions they elicit regarding Larry's rationality or the well-groundedness of these intuitions. Yet (SQUAD/RIYADH 1) could not possibly be a case of failing a requirement not to abandon an intention. Assuming that Larry was justified in forming the belief that he had been

---

[20] Considering a similar example, Broome (2001) argues that an agent in Larry's situation is rational as long as he repudiates his previous intention. But it is not clear even why such repudiation is necessary, and as Ferrero (2010) argues, it is not clear why, if repudiation can be done on any grounds or even on no grounds at all, it should make a difference whether or not I repudiate my intention.

dropped from the squad, then his abandoning his intention was perfectly rational; in fact, keeping the intention would be irrational in light of this belief. He also could not be under a requirement to re-form the intention to be a professional footballer; given our stipulations, it would be no less rational to form the intention to become a stay-at-home dad.

But now we can see a further problem with postulating persistence requirements if we think about a small variation to this case:

(SQUAD/RIYADH 2)
Same as (SQUAD/RIYADH 1) except that Larry does form the intention to become a stay-at-home dad between the first and the second phone call.

Would Larry now be under a requirement to continue to intend to be a stay-at-home dad after he learns about his mistake? It would be implausible to say "yes". Given that he was planning to be a professional footballer before the confusion, wouldn't it be equally rational for Larry to go back to his original intention? And wouldn't the rationality of this course of action be independent of the content of further deliberation or reconsideration or even of whether any further deliberation or reconsideration occurs? But it is hard to see how an advocate of persistence requirements can accept this conclusion. It is true that Larry does get new information, so his updated belief state might be seen as "covered" by the *ceteris paribus* clause of the correct persistence requirement. However, the new information does not make a difference to any of the relevant values or evaluations in Larry's situation. It is still true that neither choice of profession is better than the other, and it is still true that they are not of equal value. This suggests that something might have gone wrong with our apparently intuitive judgment that Larry's actions were irrational at any point.

6.3 Pattern and Instance

Let us take a different perspective on Larry's choice in ($200 WASTED). Suppose that Larry did change his mind and became a stay-at-home dad, and everything went as he expected. He was happy with such a life, his assessment of the value of such a life was overall correct, and there were no surprises, twists, and so forth that would be relevant for our later assessment of Larry's life. Larry is also (correctly) aware that had he chosen the path of

a professional footballer, he would also have realized an end of his; he neither regrets[21] his decision from this vantage point nor thinks that his life
would have been worse (or better) had he chosen to be a professional footballer. Does it still seem that Larry originally acted irrationally? Should we
say that, fortunately, everything turned out well, but that his decision to
become a stay-at-home dad was irrational? It seems that given that his life,
predictably, did not turn out to be worse than had he held on to his intention to become a professional footballer, his choices were all permissible. Of
course, often irrationality is harmless and sometimes it might even pay off.
But, in general, these are cases in which circumstances luckily conspire to
make it the case that irrationality does not lead us astray. But in our case,
Larry's judgments are, *ex hypothesi*, all correct: nothing unexpected happens, he is not ignorant of any relevant information, and so forth.

This vantage point on Larry's choice suggests that an inclination to judge
Larry irrational lies somewhere else. Notice that were Larry to continue
changing his mind in this way, the results could be disastrous. Suppose that
every time Larry switches from one intention to another, he gives away the
book or the ball and net set to avoid clutter. Thus every time he changes his
mind it costs him $200. If he keeps doing this, he will be much impover-
ished and yet his life options would be the same. Doubtless, if Larry keeps
changing his mind in this manner, he has behaved in an irrational fashion.
It is hard not to project onto Larry this kind of fickle disposition; such dispositions are vices of rationality.[22] However, the irrationality of proceeding
this way need not appeal to any intention-persistence requirement; it is simply a consequence of his general end of happiness for which he needs general means such as money. Given this fact, his repeated changes of mind
would lead him to an unacceptable actualization of his pursuit of enough
financial resources.

One could try to defend an intention-persistence requirement exactly on
the grounds that multiple instances of such changes of mind are irrational.
If multiple instances are irrational, and all these instances are alike, then there
should also be a requirement against any instance of failure of persistence.
But this is just a version of Gauthier's (adapted) argument from the

---

[21] There is an interesting question about justified regret from the point of view of later
attachments and values that were not present when one made a potentially mistaken decision,
and what this regret tells us about this decision. See Harman (2009), Wallace (2013), and
Coates (2017). But my case is essentially different, as it does not presuppose here any significant shift in Larry's practical standpoint.

[22] More on virtues and vices of rationality in Chapter 7. See also Ferrero (2012).

previous chapter.[23] It fails for the same reason that Gauthier's argument failed: it assumes the falsity of the *NON-SUPERVENIENCE THESIS*.

6.4 Further Constraints

There is a way to fill in ($200 WASTED) in which Larry might be violating a rational constraint, but not an intention-persistence requirement. Let us look at a modified version of (SIMPLE):

(MANY ROADS)
I jotted down a series of notes on the movies showing tonight and instructions on how to get to the *Town Theatre* and how to get to *Fancy Restaurant*. I can barely understand them now given my poor handwriting. I can't tell from my notes whether the movie showing at the *Town Theatre* is *Movie* or *Better Movie*. I understand just enough of my notes to conclude the following: Road A will take me to the restaurant if and only if *Better Movie* is showing. Road B will take me to the restaurant if and only if *Movie* is showing. Road C takes me to the restaurant. Road D takes me to the movie, no matter what it is. I take Road A.

There seems to be something incoherent in my attitudes in (MANY ROADS). I could have chosen just to go the movie no matter which one was showing, and I could have also chosen to simply go to the restaurant. I could have made it the case that I would go the movies, if *Better Movie* were showing and otherwise to the restaurant. Instead, I chose to go the movies if *Movie* was showing, but to the restaurant if *Better Movie* was showing. The only overall ranking of the alternatives that could be read off from my choosing in this manner is, from higher to lower, {*Movie, Fancy Restaurant, Better Movie*}. But I rank *Better Movie* higher than *Movie* along the cinematic teleological dimension; the introduction of another option (*Fancy Restaurant*), even if incomparable with my movie options, should not lead to a choice disposition that inverts this ranking. In other words, my reflective preferences are incompatible with the internal preferences generated by my end of watching movies. Although choice situations similar to MANY ROADS are rare, the incoherent attitudes are arguably present as choice dispositions

---

[23] See Section 5.5.

even in the absence of such options. That is, my attitudes seem to be incoherent if I would choose to go to *Movie* over *Fancy Restaurant*, but if I were to learn that *Better Movie* were showing then I would choose to go to the restaurant instead.

This problematic combination of attitudes does not violate [PP]; we need a Further Ordering Constraint [FOC]:

[FOC] If [xa, xb] ≥ [ya, yb] and za ≥ xa and zb ≥ xb, then [za, zb] ≥ [ya, yb]

Does Larry violate [FOC] in our original case? Since we did not specify what his general attitudes were in describing ($200 WASTED), we left it open whether his attitudes were, at the initial point, that he would choose to be a professional footballer over being a stay-at-home dad, but he would choose the latter if it would cost him an extra $200 to be a stay-at-home dad. So Larry's preferences are at least *possibly* in violation of [FOC]. However, [FOC] is a synchronic requirement on pursuing ends (or on choices or choice dispositions), not a diachronic requirement on intention persistence through time. So there is a way of reading ($200 WASTED) that makes Larry incoherent, but even in such a reading Larry's incoherence is not due to the violation of a intention-persistence requirement.

Can ETR explain (FOC)? Notice that there is nothing wrong with Larry simply changing his mind in favour of the restaurant as soon as he learned that he could watch a better movie. Even a stable but "brute" disposition to change his mind this way would not be problematic. If he is somehow wired to change his mind in this way whenever *Better Movie* becomes an option, he might indeed be a bit eccentric. But as long as he has no comparative views between *Better Movie* and restaurant, there is nothing malfunctioning in his rational agency. The problem is really when he has reflective preferences that violate FOC. But if we are right that such reflective preferences are grounded in second-order ends, in having such a reflective preference he is pursuing incompatible ends. The typical end of cinematic appreciation requires that, at least if he reflects on this issue, he forms the end of giving priority to better movies over worse movies. But the other second-order ends that violate FOC are incompatible with this end, and thus this combination of ends does violate ETR's principle of coherence; Larry cannot pursue all these higher-order ends at the same time.

To sum up, there are a number of difficulties in trying to hold on to the view that a persistence requirement is violated in ($200 WASTED). Moreover there are a number of irrational attitudes in the neighbourhood that might account for whatever inclination one has to judge that Larry is being irrational in this scenario. I hope that these considerations are enough to lay to rest the claim that cases such as ($200 WASTED) suffice to establish the cogency of intention-persistence requirements.

6.5 Self-Governance and Intention Persistence

I am self-governing or act autonomously, very roughly,[24] when my actions are guided or caused by attitudes that I can identify with, or that express where "I really stand" with respect to the matter at hand. The contrast would be with being manipulated, being "dragged" by "alien" desires or motives, and so forth. Self-governance over time or diachronic autonomy should thus be understood as an extension of this general idea to the case of agency extended over time.

Arguably, if certain ways of acting potentially undermine the agent's self-governance, then the nature of self-governing agency will make normative demands on our agency. Of course, if self-governance is just an end like any other end, such putative demands are irrelevant to the theory of instrumental rationality. However, if self-governance is constitutive of human agency, or if only the attitudes that I "identify with" are among the basic given attitudes, then the normative demands of self-governance might have a significant role to play in the theory of instrumental rationality. And if the demands of self-governance force us to accept principles of instrumental rationality governing FDIs, then they do pose a significant threat to ETR's claim that intentional actions are the only basic given attitudes.

The idea that our (interest in) diachronic autonomy or self-governance makes demands on us finds many adherents, but I'll focus here on the papers collected in Bratman (2018).[25] Bratman has the most developed defence of the claim that principles of diachronic coherence for intentions are grounded in self-governance in the literature, and his views are, thus, the most directly relevant to our concerns.[26] Bratman's understanding of self-governance relies on Frankfurt's notion of an "agent's standpoint", the

---

[24] Of course, what exactly self-governance or autonomous action consists in is a subject of much debate. Bratman mostly relies on the understanding of the agent's standpoint developed in Frankfurt (1987) (among other places), and I'll assume, for the purposes of this section, that some such understanding is roughly correct.

[25] For some other examples, see Velleman (1997), Ferrero (2010), and Paul (2014a).

[26] We discuss the other views mentioned above in Nefsky and Tenenbaum (forthcoming).

idea of certain attitudes that "speak for the agent"[27] (Bratman (2018), pp. 48, 96) and thus represent where the agent stands regarding, for instance, a certain end E. Certain principles are, on this view, constitutive of synchronic self-governance. If I have incompatible ends (such as being healthy and smoking), at most one of these attitudes represents where I stand with respect to the choice between smoking and leading a healthy life. Since, according to Bratman, we have "intrinsic reason to govern our own lives" (98), we presumably have also reason not to pursue incompatible ends at the same time.

I'll not challenge here anything Bratman says about synchronic self-governance; I'll just grant that our *synchronic* self-governance is, somehow, a source of reasons for action or that it can ground synchronic principles of coherence.[28] But how do we move from this notion of synchronic governance to a notion of self-governance *over* time and, from there, to the claim that diachronic self-governance makes normative demands on our agency?

Let us start with the principles that Bratman thinks are grounded on the fact that we are agents capable of diachronic self-governance:

Diachronic Plan Rationality (DPR)
If S is...capable of diachronic self-governance then the following is...*pro tanto* irrational of S:

(a) S is engaged in a planned temporally extended activity....
(b) Given her present standpoint, a choice to continue with her planned activity would cohere with that standpoint and...in part for that reason, with her diachronic self-governance. And yet
(c) S makes a choice that blocks her continued diachronic self-governance. (Bratman (2018), p. 217)

Rational End of Diachronic Self-Governance (REDSG)
If S is...capable of diachronic self-governance then it is *pro tanto* irrational of S to fail to have an end of diachronic self-governance. (Bratman (2018), p. 220)

As stated, these principles just say that I have reason to adopt the end of diachronic self-governance and ensure that I do not undermine my diachronic

---

[27] See Frankfurt (1987).
[28] Notice that a notion of synchronic self-governance is unproblematic for ETR, since it would at most give us reasons to conform with, or further grounds for, (ETR DERIVATION) and (ETR COHERENCE).

self-governance. But, if the end of diachronic self-governance requires only that I do not have incompatible ends at a time, or only that I pursue the means to my ends, then the principles are superfluous; they do not demand from the agent anything beyond what the principle of instrumental reasoning already demands. However, according to Bratman these principles do generate further demands, given the nature of diachronic self-governance. In particular, (DPR) requires that an agent acts on her prior intention in cases of ties and incommensurability (rather than "shuffling" from one decision to another supported by her reasons). The end of self-governance required by (REDSG) tips the balance in favour of sticking with one's prior intention at least in some cases of temptation in which, in the absence of my commitment to the end of self-governance, my evaluation of the situation at the time of the action would shift in favour of succumbing to temptation. Thus falling into temptation in these cases, or "shuffling" from one choice to another as in the case of Larry, would block one's continued self-governance. I'll call this interpretation of the (DPR) and (REDSG) in which they make these normative demands in cases of potential shuffling or temptation, the "substantive version of the diachronic principles of self-governance", or just "the diachronic principles" for short.

But what conception of diachronic self-governance could underwrite the diachronic principles? Some relatively straightforward ways to extend the notion of synchronic self-governance will certainly not do the job. For instance, we could propose an "additive conception of diachronic self-governance". This conception simply defines self-governance over t_0–t_n as self-governance at each moment that lies between t_0 and t_n. Obviously, the additive conception of diachronic self-governance cannot generate any principles of rationality above and beyond those generated by the demands of synchronic self-governance.[29]

Is there a different notion of diachronic self-governance over time that would ground the diachronic principles? Such a notion of diachronic self-governance would need to validate the following theses:

(1) *Ubiquity Thesis*. The reasons we have to be self-governing over time apply *to each particular action* for which diachronic coherence is an issue.

---

[29] Bratman explicit rejects the idea that the additive conception exhausts the notion of self-governance over time (see Bratman (2018), p. 226).

(2) *Strawsonian Thesis.* Self-governance over time is a fundamental aspect of our practical lives such that it is deeply entrenched in our agency (and it is hardly a live option for us to give up being self-governing agents).

(2) is put forward by Bratman at various places (see, for instance, Bratman (2018), pp. 46–7) as a way of endowing the reasons that are grounded in self-governing agency with something like "normative inescapability" without accepting full-blown constitutivism. The claim is, roughly, that even though self-governance over time is not constitutive of agency as such, it is so thoroughly interwoven with central aspects of *our* planning agency that it is not a realistic option for us to give up being diachronic self-governing agents. As we said above, if the end of self-governance is an optional end for us, it will not generate norms or principles that belong to a theory of instrumental rationality. We need the Ubiquity thesis if the diachronic principles are not merely to recommend that we do not shuffle too much, or that we do not fall into temptation too often. As we saw in the previous chapters, we do not need any intention-specific requirements to deliver this result. The diachronic principles supposedly apply to *each particular occasion* in which we face temptation or the possibility of shuffling, and they are supposed to (*ceteris paribus*) give us a reason (though possibly not a decisive reason) not to shuffle or succumb to temptation on *each occasion.*

Compliance with the diachronic principles would certainly prevent someone from having a life of irresolution and constant shuffling. Moreover, it seems correct that something is amiss in a life in which constant irresolution and shuffling prevents an agent from pursuing long-term ends and projects. We can even grant that what is amiss in such a life is that the agent lacks self-governance *over time* (even in cases in which she is self-governing at each particular time). So perhaps self-governance over time requires that we pursue a reasonable number of long-term ends, and arguably even that we have the pursuit of long-term ends itself as a second-order end. We can thus define a more robust notion of self-governance over time, which I will call "the extended conception", as follows:

An agent A is self-governing over an interval t_0–t_n if and only if:
(a) A is self-governing at every moment t_m within the t_0–t_n interval.
(b) At the t_0–t_n interval, A is rationally pursuing a sufficient number of long-term ends.
(c) A has the end of pursuing a sufficient number of long-term ends.

The extended conception of self-governance over time satisfies the Strawsonian thesis, but it does not satisfy the Ubiquity thesis. This conception only gives us a reason not to shuffle *too much* or to be resolute in the face of shifting judgments or preferences *some* or even *most* of the time. Given the vicissitudes of life and the failures of our will, in some contexts, the only way we can avoid shuffling too much is ensuring that we treat our prior intentions like divine commands not to be quibbled with. Of course, insofar as this is true of us, in such contexts we had better act in compliance with the diachronic principles. The extended conception of self-governance tells us to comply with the diachronic principles in such circumstances. But these are extreme circumstances; the fact that we can face this kind of predicament here and there does not show that the diachronic principles are general principles of rationality.

Let us imagine beings who are self-governing over time according to the extended conception, but do not comply with the diachronic principles. Such beings sometimes form intentions in "temptation" cases, trust that they will (often enough) not reconsider them, and similarly, form intentions in cases of incommensurability and ties, and expect that they will (often enough) not reconsider. We can even imagine that if such beings find themselves shuffling too much or being irresolute, they adopt the second-order intention to stick to their prior intention in such situations *as a means* to their more general end to satisfy the extended conception of diachronic self-governance. These seem to be, at least as far as we described them, instrumentally rational agents. Yet these beings are under no instrumental requirements not explained by ETR. More importantly, these beings are not essentially different from the average human agent. An agent that satisfies the extended conception of diachronic self-governance, but does not comply more generally with the diachronic principles, is not missing any fundamental features of human agency. Thus the diachronic principles cannot be essential to any conception of self-governance that satisfies the Strawsonian thesis.

There is indeed something wrong with an agent who is inconstant, irresolute, or lacking in self-control. But the problem is not that they fail to follow a certain principle of rationality; resolution, constancy, and self-control are instrumental virtues of a rational agent that cannot be reduced to compliance with principles of rationality. These are character traits or dispositions that enlarge one's general capacity to pursue ends, but such traits cannot be understood in terms of principles that evaluate local failures or success of this capacity. Or so I'll argue in the next chapter.[30]

---

[30] For a more detailed discussion of the issues in this section (6.5), see Tenenbaum (2019).

6.6 Conclusion

I have been arguing that, in formulating the principles of instrumental rationality, we should take intentional actions as the only basic given attitudes. In the course of arguing for this point, we learned that the rationality of extended action through time does not supervene on the rationality of momentary choices of the agent. In the next two chapters, I'll argue that the rationality of the agent also fails to supervene on compliance with principles of rationality more generally. One of the lessons we learn by shifting our attention to extended action is that an instrumentally rational agent exhibits some virtues of character that are not reducible (except trivially) to compliance with principles of practical rationality. The instrumental rational power of an extended agent is manifested in her temporally extended character and actions. In other words, not all ways of acting or being a rational agent through time are ways of acting or being a rational agent at each point in time.

6.7 Appendix

We have said nothing systematic about how the evaluative and normative judgments an agent makes are relevant to our evaluation of their rational agency. Do an agent's views about what they ought to do or about what is good (or good for them) introduce new coherence requirements for a theory of practical rationality? And if so, do such requirements challenge the view that the principle of instrumental reasoning is the only principle of derivation or, more likely, the view that the prohibition on the pursuit of incompatible ends is the only principle of coherence?

In order to answer these questions, we need to distinguish two different understandings of normative and evaluative judgments. The first is that at least some such judgments are genuine practical judgments. On this view, the normative and evaluative judgments in question are inseparable from certain practical attitudes: our intentions or intentional actions express our normative or evaluative judgments.[31] I'll come back momentarily to these views. On another view,[32] all such judgments are theoretical attitudes; in other words, all such judgments are instances of theoretical judgments or beliefs that happen to have evaluative or normative contents.[33] On

---

[31] This is the view that I myself accept. See Tenenbaum (2008, 2007a). It is worth noting that such a view allows that there are also "detached" or "third-person" normative or evaluative judgments that are not in any way tied to a practical attitude. However, on such a view, these detached judgments are irrelevant to the evaluation of the agent's practical rationality.

[32] Broome (2013); Scanlon (2014).

[33] From here on, I'll talk about evaluative judgments or normative judgments depending on the context, but none of the arguments of the chapter depends on choosing one or the other in a particular context.

such a view, of course, an agent's evaluative judgments are subject at least to the same rational and coherence requirements that govern any belief, but such requirements are the province of the theory of theoretical rationality. However, some philosophers also accept the existence of enkratic requirements,[34] rational requirements that, roughly, state that an agent ought to act in accordance with her own judgment about what she ought to do. Such requirements seem to go beyond pure theoretical rationality as they pertain to the rational relations that hold between beliefs and actions, rather than among different beliefs we hold. However, the enkratic requirement is not an additional requirement of instrumental rationality in the relevant sense, or so I'll argue momentarily. Let us put forward a rough formulation of the enkratic requirement, which will be serviceable enough for our current purposes:

(*ENKRATIC*)   It ought to be the case that [if α believes that she ought to ϕ, then she ϕ-s].

Now (*ENKRATIC*) does not clearly qualify as a putative principle of instrumental rationality according to our classification, given that it connects a *theoretical* attitude (a belief) with a practical attitude.[35] But one could take this as evidence that there is a problem with our classification, or that the category of "instrumental rationality" is not particularly interesting; at the very least, we want to know how principles like the enkratic principle fit within our overall theory. There are at least three ways in which the relation between normative judgments and one's action can potentially explain why the rational agent acts in conformity to her normative judgments.

(1) STIPULATIVE/CONCEPTUAL/METAPHYSICAL: The rational agent α is, by definition (or by her nature), an agent who has an effective desire, or motivation, to act in accordance with her normative judgments (or who normally acts in accordance with her normative judgments).[36]

(2) REASON RESPONSIVENESS: The rational agent is the one who responds to the correct reasons. The same reasons that an ideally rational agent would respond to in forming the relevant normative judgments would also be the reasons she would respond to in acting.[37]

---

[34] See, for instance, Kolodny (2005), Broome (2013), and Coates (2013). For doubts about whether they are in fact rational requirements, see Reisner (2013).

[35] For a similar reason, Kiesewetter (2017), pp. 17–18 calls akratic irrationality a form of "second-order" structural irrationality.

[36] Scanlon (1998) and Broome (2013) arguably fall under this interpretation.

[37] See Lord (2017) for a view that would support this interpretation.

(3) ACTION IMPLIES BELIEF: Every case of α intentionally φ-ing is also a case in which α believes that she ought to φ.[38]

In none of these cases does the enkratic principle end up being an independent instrumental principle. If one accepts (2), the enkratic principle is not a separate principle at all, and a violation of this principle is not a *further* violation of rationality; it is at best a symptom that one has failed to properly respond to some reason. If one accepts (3), the irrationality of the *akratic* agent is theoretical, rather than practical; the agent holds inconsistent beliefs.[39] (1) is a bit more complicated, given that we can think of two ways in which an agent α might fail to comply with the enkratic principle in this case:

(1A) α does not have the end (overall desire) to act in accordance with her normative judgment.

(1B) α has the end (overall desire) to act in accordance with her normative judgment, but the desire, or motivation, is not effective.[40]

If (1A) is true, then we should distinguish two cases. In one case, the agent fails to have a general desire to act in accordance with her normative judgments. It is doubtful that this is a real possibility for a rational agent, as it would be a systematic violation of a general condition of practical rationality; after all, according to (1), having this kind of motivation is constitutive (metaphysically, conceptually, or definitionally) of being a rational agent. On the other hand, if the agent has the general end of acting in accordance with her normative judgments and yet does not have the end to do so in this specific occasion, she violates the principle of instrumental reasoning, as she would be failing to pursue constitutive means to her ends. Similarly, if (1B) is true, the agent has violated the principle of instrumental reasoning; the agent has an end (or overall desire), but does not take the sufficient means to this end (or does not act from this overall desire).

On the view that intentional actions express evaluative or normative judgments, things are slightly different. Of course, one version of the enkratic requirement is

---

[38] This would be a stronger version of what I call the "content version" of the guise of the good (or guise of reasons) view. For the label, see Wald and Tenenbaum (2018) and Tenenbaum (2018b). For examples of the view, see Oddie (2005), Raz (2010), Gregory (2013), and Milona and Schroeder (forthcoming).

[39] This is in the spirit of cognitivist views such as those of Wallace (2001).

[40] Scanlon, for instance, does not think that rational agents have a separable extra desire to act on a normative judgment; rather, he thinks that the agent's "judgment leads to action via the processes that are normal for a rational agent, and the agent is moved to act by the consideration he judges to be conclusive." But Scanlon grants that in cases of irrationality, "the agent is not *motivated* by these considerations [*sc.* the normative reasons]" (Scanlon (2014), pp. 55–6; emphasis mine). Since this does not make a difference to our argument below, I'll ignore it. Scanlon's view collapses into either (1A) or (1B).

trivially satisfied whenever an agent acts on this view;[41] it is impossible that one does not act in accordance with one's evaluative judgment, since the evaluative judgment is determined by the action itself. Specific instances of violations of the enkratic requirement will be, again, violations of the principle of instrumental reasoning. My judgment, say, that I ought to run the marathon is, on this view, nothing other than my pursuing the end of running the marathon. And my failure to act on it is nothing other than my failure to pursue sufficient means.

However, on any plausible version of such a view, it is still possible that an agent has independent beliefs with evaluative content. Thus, any plausible version of such a view needs to explain the relation between such evaluative beliefs and the evaluative judgments expressed in action,[42] but it need not conflict with anything that ETR says about the nature of instrumental rationality and it would likely be unrelated to issues about instrumental rationality.

Of course, these are not exhaustive of the ways that one can try to explain the enkratic requirement and I cannot fully discuss the merits of each view here; in fact, one might even see it as a basic coherence requirement that is not explained by anything else. But I hope this appendix at least makes a plausible case that such requirements are compatible with ETR.

---

[41] Such views are compatible with characterizing *akrasia* in different ways. See Tenenbaum (2007a, 2018b).

[42] I try to provide such an explanation in Tenenbaum (2007a); see also Wald (2018).

7

Instrumental Virtues

7.0 Introduction

When philosophers think about rationality, they mostly think in terms of the principles of rationality, and the rational agent as one who complies with the principles of rationality.[1] The aim of this chapter is to argue that an account of instrumental rationality in terms of compliance with principles cannot be a full account of instrumentally rational agency. The chapter argues that an ideally instrumentally rational agent not only complies with the principles of rationality, but also possesses what I call "instrumental virtues".[2] This chapter examines the virtue of courage as our central example of an instrumental virtue, while Chapter 8 will examine a particular instrumental virtue (practical judgment) that ETR helps explain and make apparent.

Section 7.1 starts by looking at an apparent disagreement between Kant and Aristotle on the question of whether courage can be exhibited in the pursuit of bad ends, and briefly discusses the different conceptions of the virtue of courage that they imply. In particular I distinguish a Kantian conception of courage as a general capacity to pursue ends (whether good or bad) and an (arguably) Aristotelian conception according to which, roughly, courage manifests a proper assessment of the relative values of different goods in a certain context. Section 7.2 examines these two conceptions and argues that, at least for certain theoretical aims, the Kantian conception is preferable. Section 7.3 then argues for the indispensability of instrumental virtues for ideal rational agency by drawing on the Kantian conception of

---

[1] This is not quite true about "reason fundamentalists" as they might think that rationality is simply a matter of responding to reasons, and that principles of rationality as such play no special role in explaining rational agency. For a recent example, see Lord (2017). But I hope it'll be clear that the argument of the chapter would apply in the same way to reason fundamentalist positions.

[2] Some philosophers argue that rationality itself is best understood as virtue (see, for instance, Wedgwood (2017) and Schafer (2019)). As it will be clear in this chapter, I am sympathetic to their view, but the more specific view I defend is not strictly implied by the claim that rationality is a virtue. One could accept the claim and yet think that the virtue consists in a capacity or disposition to comply with certain principles.

courage (and instrumental virtues more generally). Section 7.4 provides a more general theoretical framework in which to locate the claim that the instrumental virtues are rational powers. Section 7.5 discusses some potential problems for the Kantian conception defended in the chapter. Finally, Section 7.6 looks at some of the consequences of the discussion for other instrumental virtues, such as resolution.

7.1 Kant and Aristotle on Courage

According to Kant,

> Courage, resolution, and perseverance in one's plans, as qualities of temperament, are undoubtedly good and desirable for many purposes, but they can also be extremely evil and harmful…Moderation in affects and passions, self-control, and calm reflection are not only good for all sorts of purposes but seem to constitute a part of the inner worth of a person…but [these qualities] can become extremely evil.   (*Groundwork*: 4:393–4)[3]

On the other hand, Aristotle seems not to allow for the possibility that courage can manifest itself in evil action. For instance, he says that "if someone is confident when he is going to be whipped for his crimes, that does not make him courageous" (*Nicomachean Ethics* III, 6.24).[4] These quotes seem to express an important disagreement between Kant and Aristotle about the nature of courage, and more generally, certain virtues that have been often classified as "executive virtues".[5] Kant seems committed to the view that at least some forms of "confidence" exhibited by villains count as courage, whereas Aristotle's colourful example expresses his view that courage-like behaviour in the pursuit of evil, or in the forbearance of the deserved punishment that evildoing brings about, should not be classified as instances of courage. It is hard to settle who has the edge with regards to ordinary usage. On the one hand, it is hard to resist calling "courageous" the daring thief who sets up a heist that requires fearlessness in the face of great danger; on

---

[3] All translations of Kant's work are from Kant (1996); here pp. 49–50.

[4] Aristotle (1999), p. 71. Irwin translates *andreia* as "bravery". I am rendering it "courage" so as to make it consistent with Kant's *Mut* and my own use of "courage".

[5] Pears (1978); Williams (1986). This is made a bit more complicated by the fact that Aristotle does not think that self-control is a virtue.

the other hand, many of us hesitated in calling the 9/11 terrorists "courageous".[6] It is worth noting that it is not only in contexts that are traditionally classified as "moral" that the pursuit of a wrong end calls into doubt whether the action is courageous. If I swim across the shark-infested water to recover a five-dollar bill I see floating in the ocean, we might hesitate in calling my action "courageous". It is tempting at this point to classify the disagreement as merely verbal; sometimes, when pursuing bad (or imprudent) ends, agents behave in ways that are similar to the patterns of behaviour exemplified by agents who are courageous in the pursuit of something actually good. We can remark on the similarity and now decide whether we extend the word "courage" to such cases or not. If we care to ensure that the word covers only actions that are good, then we will refuse to mess with the boundaries of the concept in this way. If we want the word to mark the similarity in the pattern of behaviour describable independently of the goodness of one's ends, then we will use "courage" more broadly.

However, the dispute is not merely verbal, or at least it need not be. It is a substantive question whether all these instances of behaviour express a common power (or a common quality of the mind, or a common something else). Aristotle insists that those who show confidence that is unrelated to good ends are not necessarily courageous on the battlefield. Those who do not fear the pains of shame and public humiliation that their evil deeds might confer on them might flee at the first sight of an enemy spear. Kant takes qualities of temperament such as courage as "gifts of nature", while acting well is a self-grounded activity for Kant. Thus, for Kant, the manifestations of such passive dispositions cannot be classified together with the manifestation of the same active powers that determine whether our actions were good or evil. Moreover, on some views, we define courage in such a way that we cannot pick out instances of courage independently of our assessment of the moral quality of the action. If courage is understood as, for instance, giving proper weight to certain goods,[7] then there is no way to subtract the part of the conception that requires that the end pursued be a good end and thereby define a broader conception of courage. On such an understanding, the expression "an act that is just like a courageous act except that is not in the pursuit of a good end" denotes the empty set.

---

[6] See Weber (2005) for an interesting discussion.   [7] Hurka (2000), ch. 4.

But even here it is not clear that we have identified a substantive disagreement. Aristotle is doubtless correct that those who can pursue their ends undeterred by the danger of social ostracism might easily tremble upon meeting an enemy army. But it's not clear that bravery on the battlefield is a uniform phenomenon; some of those who do not fear the spear might panic when confronted with guns. On the other hand, if there are people who fight both good and evil battles, it is likely that their resolve will be the same whether they are on the side of the angels or on the side of the opposing team. And Kant would be the first to acknowledge that the virtuous agent has traits that are at least superficially similar to qualities of temperament such as courage, but that are the effect of virtuous willing rather than gifts of nature. It seems that Kant and Aristotle are carving up different powers or capacities for largely different theoretical purposes, and just happened to have used the same term (or different terms with similar English translations) for these different capacities.

I will definitely not try to settle who has a better claim to have captured the ordinary notion of courage. But I do want to argue for a Kantian position that there are what we might call "instrumental virtues". My claim is that in listing these virtues as not having unconditional value, Kant has correctly identified a set of powers and capacities that are part of instrumentally rational agency. A finite agent is more rational (or closer to the ideal of rational agency) to the extent that she manifests such powers or capacities. Correlatively, these powers are essential to our understanding of instrumental rationality. More specifically, I'll try to show that a proper conception of instrumental rationality must make room for the existence of certain capacities that are not reducible to the principles of instrumental rationality. An ideally rational agent is not just an agent who abides by certain principles; she also manifests certain instrumental virtues. This general conclusion is compatible with other conceptions of practical rationality, but in giving a central place to the management of means to overlapping extended actions over time, ETR is particularly well placed to explain the role of these instrumental virtues. In Chapter 8, I argue that there is a particular instrumental virtue that cannot be accommodated by standard conceptions of instrumental rationality.[8] I call this virtue "practical judgment". The existence of such a virtue explains the irrationality of common failings, such as procrastination.

---

[8] More specifically, it depends on accepting top-down independence.

7.2 Purely Evaluative Understanding of Courage and the Unified Power/Disposition View

It is common ground among all that a lack of courage will undermine the possibility of achieving a number of good ends. No matter how committed I am to fighting injustice, if I fear the loss of my job, or, in certain extreme cases, if I flee in the face of physical danger, I will not be able to carry out my noble plans or contribute significantly to my lofty ideals. It is thus tempting to provide an account of courage in which courageous acts are acts in which we do not overvalue danger (Pears (2004)) or that I do not desire my safety in a way that is disproportionate to its value (Hurka (2000), ch. 4). Such accounts of courage and other instrumental virtues are "Aristotelian"; that is, they take it that courage is a form of correct evaluation. On these views, the courageous person is necessarily substantively rational, or necessarily responding to the right reasons, at least to the extent that they are courageous.

However, if virtuous traits are powers or capacities,[9] it seems that the person who can pursue her ends in the face of serious danger exercises the same capacity whether she is pursuing good or bad ends. Let us consider a sailor who does not fear the high waters. The sailor might on Mondays and Wednesdays cross the seas to feed the hungry on a distant island, on Tuesdays and Thursdays she sails the same seas for money, and on Fridays to conduct an illicit affair with her lover. She regularly faces frightening situations which she manages exquisitely and without any sign of fear. It seems that in an important sense, on all these days, she manifests the same capacity[10]—the same "talent of the mind" is manifested in the pursuit of all those ends. In fact, if we witnessed her actions on the sea we would not need to consult our calendar to know that she was acting courageously.

---

[9] Hurka (2000) and Adams (2008) start from virtuous actions, others understand virtuous actions in terms of virtuous agents, such as Hursthouse (1999). I am not taking a position on this debate; I certainly do not deny that someone can act courageously without a stable courageous disposition. My only point is that a courageous person is someone who has the character trait, and thus the general capacity or power to perform courageous acts. Whether the trait or the act is primary is irrelevant to my argument.

[10] Of course, if someone individuates capacities (or abilities) in a very fine-grained way, these will not be the same capacity (see Hyman (2015) for an example of a fine-grained individuation of ability). However, I agree with Small (2017) that we independently need a more coarse-grained notion of ability or capacity if capacities are to play any explanatory role in intentional action. Although I am sympathetic to Small's account of practical abilities, any suitably coarse-grained account would work for my purposes. In a different paper (Small (forthcoming)), Small argues that virtues are not abilities, but his argument would not apply to instrumental virtues.

There is, of course, *something* different about her actions on Mondays and Wednesdays. There is something particularly admirable about her commitment to the island dwellers that she is willing to brave dangerous seas to meet their needs. But this speaks for the quality of her benevolence, not the quality of her courage. The fact that she courageously discharges her duty to help others shows the depth of her commitment to the ideals of benevolence. But the fact that she expresses her courage in benevolent ways says nothing about the quality of her courage. Although there is no such thing as commitment to courage (exactly because courage is an instrumental virtue), we can talk about degrees of courage, and the measure of one's courage is not given by the nature of the ends that one pursues courageously, but by the nature of the dangers one faces, or is capable of facing, without abandoning one's end.[11]

Similarly lack of courage, resolution, self-control, and so forth can also appear in the pursuit of bad ends. As we are driving to the bank we intend to rob, we see that Larry is shaking and whining in fear, and we decide he is only good for the lookout job. And yet, as soon as he sees someone whom he believes could be a cop, he runs away from his post. He calls us later to ask if he's still entitled to at least half his cut, as he was doing his job for half the time, and as we threaten him, he whimpers, begs for forgiveness, immediately agrees that he deserves no money, and obsequiously thanks us for sparing his life. Larry seems to be a coward, but it seems difficult to describe his shortcoming as the overvaluing of his safety or the undervaluing of his potential ill-begotten gains.

Finally, sometimes we exhibit courage in engaging in supererogatory acts. Some people undergo serious risks in order to be live liver donors for complete strangers;[12] the very thought of undergoing such surgery fills the heart of many with dread. However, someone's refusal to be a live liver donor does not show that she's overvaluing her safety; it is perfectly reasonable to refuse to make such a sacrifice for a stranger. Yet, doubtless undergoing such surgery is a paradigmatic case of courageous behaviour; lack of willingness to undergo such a procedure does not make someone a coward but it is some evidence of a lesser degree of courage.

---

[11] It is true that if one's ends are truly foolish, we no longer regard the action as courageous (if I run through artillery fire to recover a lost paper clip, I don't seem to be displaying courage). More on this issue below.

[12] For one such story, see www.bbc.com/news/health-21143602.

Interestingly enough, courage seems to fail Aristotle's test for whether something should count as a virtue rather than a craft.[13] As Aristotle points out, the bad shoe produced by a shoemaker is no evidence that she is not a good shoemaker if we know that, out of spite, vindictiveness, or simply as a joke, the shoemaker intended to make a defective shoe. On the other hand, the fact that someone acts unkindly on purpose is exactly what makes her unkind. But courage seems to line up with shoemaking rather than with kindness; the fact that Jane fails to risk her life to help Larry does not speak against her courageous character if we learn that Jane held a lifelong grudge against Larry and thus had no desire to save his life.[14] This means that having the virtue of courage does not necessarily make an agent virtuous, and does not even necessarily contribute to the virtue of the agent. In other words, if we accept this broader conception of the virtue of courage as being the same power whether in the life of the kind or the cruel person, it will not be true that a person who has the virtue of courage is to that extent more virtuous than the person who lacks it.

Insofar as we've been accepting Kant's view on courage, we need also to accept the conclusion that a courageous criminal is no better than a cowardly one for being courageous. It might seem that a consequence of this view is that courage is not in fact a virtue; after all, if something doesn't even make a positive contribution to someone's overall virtuous character, why should we call it a virtue?[15] Now, for our purposes, we need not answer this question. My concern is with our rational powers, and insofar as we accept that courage, so described, is a genuine rational power, we need not be concerned with the question whether courage is also a moral virtue. Nonetheless, courage, on this picture, does make a positive contribution to one's virtue; a kind person who is courageous is for that very reason more virtuous; it is simply that it does not *always* make a positive contribution to the agent's virtue. Here we can fully side with Kant: the instrumental virtues do contribute to the "worth of a person", but their contribution is conditioned by their good will, or, in other words, by the extent of the person's noninstrumental virtues. Instrumental virtues are conditionally good and, like

---

[13] *Nicomachean Ethics* book 6, chap. 5, 1140b22–5.

[14] Since courage does not have an internal end, like shoemaking, one might argue that the analogy is not perfect. But, still, the point stands: acts contrary to the way a courageous person would act in a certain circumstance do not speak against the person's courage, if acting in this manner was intentional.

[15] This is arguably Kant's conclusion in the *Groundwork*.

all instrumental goods, they are only good *simpliciter* when at the service of something that is good.

But since I have no intention to argue with those who are jealous of the word "virtue", I should list the main claims I defend in this chapter. Insofar as one thinks that these claims do not suffice to show that the instrumental virtues are real virtues, they can simply see this chapter as a defence of the claims:

(a) The instrumental virtues denote the same powers or dispositions whether they are manifested in the pursuit of good ends or bad ends.

(b) The instrumental virtues are powers and dispositions that are constitutive of the agent's instrumental rationality, and thus they are (instrumental) rational powers or dispositions.

(c) It is possible for an agent to always comply with the principles of instrumental rationality and yet fail to be instrumentally rational because she lacks some of the instrumental virtues.

I think (a)–(c) suffice to make instrumental virtues genuine instances of virtue because I also accept:

(d) Virtues are rational powers or dispositions.

But since (d) is not relevant to the aims of the book, I will not try to defend it here.[16]

I will not say much more about (a) than what I have already said in this section. The remainder of the chapter is mostly focused on (b) and (c).

7.3 Instrumental Rationality and Instrumental Virtues

Most contemporary theories of instrumental rationality have assumed that being instrumentally rational is a matter of conforming to certain principles. Philosophers, of course, disagree about which principles are essential to our understanding of instrumental rationality. I have been arguing for the prominence of the principle of instrumental reasoning, while others focus on the axioms of decision theory; some think that there are diachronic

---

[16] But see Section 7.4 below.

requirements, some take all requirements of instrumental rationality to be synchronic. But it is generally taken for granted that being instrumentally rational is a matter of complying with certain principles. I'll argue now that this view is at best incomplete. More specifically, I will argue in this section for the following two claims:

I.   Certain failures to have (in full) or manifest (in full) instrumental virtues cannot be explicated in terms of failures to comply with the principles of rationality.
II. Agents who exemplify the above failures thereby fall short of ideal instrumental rationality.

It is worth defining the opposing view here, as committed to the following Eliminability Hypothesis (EH):

(EH) An agent who fails to manifest the instrumental virtues will fail to comply with the principle of instrumental reasoning.

Since I'm mostly concerned with defending this view in the context of ETR, I will be taking for granted ETR's claim that the only fundamental principle of instrumental rationality is the principle of instrumental reasoning. But the central arguments of this chapter are largely independent from the rest of the book.[17] In particular, I hope it will be clear that the problems with EH will generalize to any version in which we replace EH with any non-trivial[18] principle or set of principles.

Could one be cowardly (or irresolute, lacking in self-control or decisiveness) without ever violating the principle of instrumental reason? At first, it might seem that this is not possible. Suppose I have as my end to find the Holy Grail. But the path to the Holy Grail, as we all know, is filled with dangers and temptations. If heavily armed creatures are guarding the Holy Grail, I'll fail in the pursuit of my end if I'm not courageous enough; the same will happen, of course, if I lack self-control or give in to

---

[17]   In fact, much what I say here about adjusting our ends due to our instrumental vices could be similarly said about forming adaptive preferences in light of restrictions to the set of feasible options due to these instrumental vices. However, if we focus on momentary decisions, rather than on extended agency, it'll be difficult to explain why these instances of "adaptive preferences" count as failures of rationality. For scepticism about the irrationality of adaptive preferences, see Bruckner (2009). For attempts to understand when adaptive preferences are irrational, see Elster (1985); Bovens (1992).

[18]   "Non-trivial" here rules out principles such as "Be courageous" or even "Be rational".

temptation—if, for instance, I abandon my quest as soon as the guards offer me exquisite Turkish delight in exchange for giving up on the Holy Grail. Thus it seems that any agent who complies with PIR will thereby manifest all the instrumental virtues.

However, this moves too quickly. The way the story is told, our agent retains the end of pursuing the Holy Grail while akratically giving in to temptation or running away in fear. But this need not be how it happens. Our agent might simply change her ends as she faces these situations.[19] As she meets the terrifying bunny in her pursuit of the Holy Grail, she might give up her end, or at least revise it ("My end is to pursue the Holy Grail conditional on its no longer being protected by the terrifying bunny" or "I shall pursue the Holy Grail once the terrifying bunny is dead"). On a wide-scope reading of the principle of instrumental reasoning, this is just as good as taking the means to the end. But even in a narrow-scope reading, of course, giving up the end also leaves one under no requirement to pursue the means.[20] Let us give names to our two cowardly (potential) pursuers of the Holy Grail: let us call the one who holds on to his end while cowardly failing to pursue it "Sticker". And let us call the one who cowardly abandons her end in the face of danger "Shifter". Philosophers have raised doubts about the possibility of Sticker, or at the very least about the possibility that Sticker's attitudes make sense on a purely instrumental theory of rationality.[21] After all, if Sticker fails to continue on his quest once he faces the terrifying bunny, in what sense does Sticker still have the end of retrieving the Holy Grail? In a way, this qualm makes no difference to our purposes.[22] If Sticker is not a conceptual possibility, then Shifter is the only possible case, and since my challenge to EH depends solely on the possibility of Shifter, it is of no consequence to the argument if Sticker turns out not to exist; he is here just as a contrast case.

In some versions of Shifter, Shifter is self-deceived. Shifter could be just a version of Sticker with a false belief: she is convinced that she no longer has this end. This, of course, would collapse the two cases. Or Shifter might have discarded her ends through some kind of mechanism of self-deception.

---

[19] This is how much of the psychological literature describes the akratic agent (except that they use the language of preference instead). For a classical example, see Ainslie (2001).

[20] Of course, "widescopists" are often criticized exactly because they treat all resolutions of incoherence on a par. See Kolodny (2005).

[21] Korsgaard (1997).

[22] However, in Chapter 8, I argue that the apparent difficulty of understanding the possibility of Sticker is itself a consequence of focusing on momentary mental attitudes.

Perhaps she started looking for evidence that there is no Holy Grail or that the Holy Grail is not all that it's cracked up to be. Such cases of self-deception would introduce distracting complications, so I'll ignore them. Instead I'll look at the case in which Shifter abandons her end exactly because she understands that she is a coward; she understands that she'd likely fail to stick to her end of retrieving the Holy Grail. Our question will be "Does Shifter exhibit any kind of (instrumental) rational failure?" But even after making this stipulation we need to tread carefully. There is certainly a version of Shifter that is perfectly rational. Suppose Shifter thinks the Holy Grail would be a nice addition to her trophy collection. She thinks it is more interesting than the Super Bowl ring she could acquire on eBay, but not significantly better. Once she realizes that she needs to get past the terrifying bunny to get the Holy Grail, she reasons that it is better to invest in the Super Bowl ring (which already had the advantage of being more affordable anyway). Here Shifter just revises her ends as she receives new information in a way that is obviously appropriate. Here is how I will stipulate that Shifter revises her ends:

(SHIFTER)
For any end that Shifter has, Shifter is likely to abandon it or fail to pursue it in the face of a certain level of danger, irrespective of how much she cares about or values these ends. Shifter knows this and revises all of her ends in the face of risk exactly for this reason.

Here we take Shifter's cowardice as a general pattern of agency; that is, a general pattern of revising ends. In other words, cowardice is a character trait that manifests itself in the way that Shifter is disposed to change her ends throughout her life (or throughout a significant stretch of time). Given this characterization of Shifter, Shifter will never fail to conform to the principle of instrumental reasoning; as soon as danger threatens, Shifter will simply give up the end. But Shifter does fall short of perfect instrumental rationality, or at least there is an important sense in which we must regard Shifter's overall attitudes as manifesting a diminished rational capacity. Shifter's cowardice restricts the range of ends that she can pursue; not only is the Holy Grail beyond her reach, but any end whose pursuit will involve a certain level of danger, irrespective of the nature of the end or the importance that the end initially has for her. Of course, there are many other restrictions on the ends an agent might pursue. Any end that will require unaided flight, divination, or bilocation is not possible for human beings. But these, of course, are factors extrinsic to the will; while cowardice is a "quality of the will". Leaving aside some difficult questions about freedom, Shifter could go towards the terrifying bunny by willing (or, more straightforwardly, engaging in) the relevant action; Shifter changes her ends because she foresees that she'll not will in this manner when the time for action comes.

It is worth pausing a moment for a few clarifications. I am not claiming that Shifter is *acting* irrationally. Let us take Shifter's disposition to manifest itself in explicit deliberation about whether to stick to, or shift away from, her ends that would require her to face dangerous situations. In such a case, Shifter is deliberating, as some philosophers would put it, from a third-person perspective about her action; rather than focusing on the content of her reasons, desires, and so forth, she is looking at her future self's decisions as possible risky outcomes, and reasoning on her credences (or knowledge of likelihoods) about how she'd proceed if she were facing the terrifying bunny. It is worth comparing Shifter with Jackson and Pargeter's Professor Procrastinate,[23] who knows that he is unlikely to ever complete a book review even if he originally forms the intention of doing it. Many think that Professor Procrastinate should not say "yes" to the request, especially if we imagine a case with a high cost of dereliction (if, for instance, the book's author's job hangs on getting her book reviewed). Similarly, if Shifter knows that many of her loyal followers will have to make great sacrifices in the pursuit of the Holy Grail, while she judges that very likely she'll just run away as soon as she sees the terrifying bunny, it might be rational for her not to get started in the quest. But this in a sense is grist for my mill. Shifter is correctly following the principles of instrumental rationality in such cases. But the fact that Shifter finds herself in such a position manifests an imperfection in her will, an imperfection not in what Shifter cares about or pursues, but an imperfection in her powers to pursue whatever she might care to pursue; that is, an imperfection in her instrumental rational powers.

In the first chapter, we distinguished between substantive and instrumental rational powers. Substantive rational powers are our powers to pursue what is in fact good, or what we have good reason to pursue, (somehow) guided by our understanding that this is the case. Instrumental rational powers are those powers to pursue whatever ends we have by employing the necessary means at our agency's disposal. Violations of the principle of instrumental reasoning are a defective manifestation of our rational powers;

---

[23] Jackson and Pargetter (1986).

our capacity to pursue means to our ends somehow fails to manifest itself in our actions. In other words, violations of the principle of instrumental reasoning are failures of our powers to carry out our ends in specific instances. So they are problems with particular instantiations of the power. But an ideally rational agent also has no "self-imposed" restrictions on the *extent* of the power, no restrictions that are neither the effect of external obstacles nor the consequences of her understanding of the good (or what she ought to do). An ideally rational agent not only takes means that are available to her will in pursuing her ends, but her power to pursue ends is also not restricted by the internal shortcomings of her own will.

In other words, cowardice undermines the agent's powers to bring about ends not necessarily by leading the agent into incoherence in the pursuit of certain ends, but by simply restricting the ends that are available to the agent. The same goes for other instrumental vices. Irresolution does not allow the agent to pursue ends whose execution would require overcoming temptation. A similar thing can be said even about lack of moderation, or at least insofar as lack of moderation implies lack of reasonable self-control. Someone who has the virtue of moderation can set his sights on a life peppered with occasional desserts and even voracious eating from time to time. Those who lack such a virtue must choose between gluttony and self-denial.[24] In the next section, I will try to develop this view in a bit more detail by trying to distinguish between two rational powers in the practical realm.

7.4 Rational Powers

In this section, I will put forward a Kantian account of how these virtues are constitutive elements of our rational capacities. This particular understanding of rational powers will depend on a number of controversial assumptions that I'll not be able to defend. But I do hope that the general framework of understanding the instrumental virtues as rational powers or capacities, and the theory of instrumental rationality as containing indispensably an account of such powers or capacities, might be available even to those who reject the controversial assumptions.

---

[24] See Rachlin (2000) on this issue; in Chapter 8 I discuss the related virtue of practical judgment.

On Kant's view, practical reason is the capacity to act from the self-conscious representation of a law,[25] and more generally the capacity to act from the representation of an object that is determined to be good by a practical law. Avoiding some complications and controversial aspects of Kant's practical philosophy, we could say more generally that practical reason is a power to act from the representation of an object as good. This, of course, commits us to a version of the guise-of-the-good thesis, but a rather mild one.[26] This version of the guise-of-the-good thesis says only that rational action, as opposed to all action, is action under the guise of the good.[27] Of course, the power in question is not a mere contemplative power, but a practical power. So the representation of the good in question must be an effective representation; that is, in representing an action as good, I do it.

We can now distinguish two causal powers that would correspond to the powers that Kant represents, respectively, by the categorical and hypothetical imperatives.[28] We can think about the general power to act from the representation of something that is actually good as characteristic of the rational powers that constitute the categorical virtues. Of course, there are many theories of the virtues, but insofar as one accepts that the virtues are a capacity to respond to good reasons of a certain kind in action, one should not object to the claim that they consist, at least in part, of certain rational

---

[25] G 412.

[26] I defend a much stronger version of the guise-of-the-good thesis in Tenenbaum (2007a).

[27] Notice that this restriction can even accommodate a position according to which our final ends are never desired as good; in such a view, practical reason is purely instrumental, selecting the means to a final end F by representing these means as good for F. Such a view would, however, under the assumptions I am making, allow only for the possibility of instrumental virtues, and it would rule out the possibility of virtues such as kindness. On some views, virtuous action does not represent its object as good; rather, a virtuous action is motivated directly by nothing other than the good-making features of the action (Arpaly and Schroeder (2013); Markovits (2010)). But not much would need to be changed in the general view presented here to accommodate these positions; the rational powers would be the power to act by representations of properties that are in fact good, rather than the power to act by the presentation of an object as good. For some reasons to prefer the guise-of-the-good view of virtuous actions, see Wald (2017).

[28] Some people prefer to think of the categorical and hypothetical imperatives as representing normative principles, rather than powers of the agent; imperatives are governed by "oughts", and thus they are not causal principles of any kind. However, it is common ground that Kant thinks that the same principles would not be imperatives for the perfect will, but would simply determine them to act. So they would certainly be causal principles for the infinite intellect. It seems then that the most natural way to understand these principles is not that they get demoted from causal to normative principles when determining the infinite or finite intellect, but the "ought" represents the possibility of interference in their determination of the finite intellect. Unfortunately, settling complex issues of Kant interpretation is beyond the scope of this chapter.

powers or their manifestation.[29] We can now think of a virtue as a general power or capacity of the will to pursue good ends; that is, a general power to bring about the content of certain attitudes by representing their content as good. And we can now think of our distinction between substantive and instrumental rational powers as a distinction between the power to pursue something we represent as good immediately, and the power to pursue something we represent as good conditionally or inferentially. If we understand instrumentally rational powers this way, as inextricably connected in the successful and paradigmatic case with the power to pursue good ends, then it is clear why instrumental virtues are constitutive of such rational powers. Restrictions internal to the will are restrictions to the general power to pursue the good; in this case a restriction on the ends the agent can pursue whenever only certain means are available to her.

Of course, not everyone will accept the Kantian picture of our practically rational powers outlined here. Nonetheless, it suffices for our purposes that the varieties of failures and successes presented in the previous sections cannot be accounted for as failures and successes of merely acting in compliance with the principle of instrumental reasoning (they must be understood instead as failures and successes in manifesting certain virtues). The indispensability of the appeal to instrumental virtues in explaining these failures and successes is enough to show the plausibility of the view that the instrumental virtues are constitutive of instrumental rationality. In this section, I simply tried to propose theoretical foundations for this conclusion.

7.5 The Evil, the Foolhardy, and the Unity of Virtues

What about the shamelessly evil and the foolishly foolhardy? Aren't they counterexamples to the idea that courage is a purely instrumental virtue? Let us go back to Aristotle's claim that those who do not fear disgrace are not courageous (book 3, ch. 6). I take it that what Aristotle means here is that those who do not fear that what they do is actually shameful or disgraceful are not made courageous by this lack of a fear of acting badly. This (obviously correct) observation poses no problem to the Kantian view proposed here. Since what is actually disgraceful and shameful is the pursuit of evil ends, the capacity not to "fear" shame and disgrace is simply the capacity to

---

[29] Some views of the virtues also emphasize the role of emotions and other attitudes. So, for instance, Adams (2008) and Hurka (2000) talk about "loving the good".

pursue evil ends;[30] as such, it is not a manifestation of a power to pursue ends irrespective of their content. On the contrary, it is an (in)capacity to pursue a particular type of end—the evil ones. This kind of capacity is not an instrumental virtue, and, of course, it is not a virtue of any kind, as it is certainly not any part of a power to pursue good ends.

Some complexity is added if you think of the fear of shame and disgrace as the fear of being perceived by others in dishonourable ways. Not to fear the "court of public opinion" seems a more general capacity to pursue ends, whatever they happen to be. Certain forms of failure to listen to the court of public opinion manifest a lack of epistemic humility and capacity for self-criticism; these intellectual vices are arguably themselves instrumental vices.[31] As we'll see in a moment, the manifestation of certain vices may undermine, at least to some extent, the possibility that certain actions manifest an instrumental virtue. But lack of fear of adverse public opinion is indeed a manifestation of courage, and if we can ever separate instances of fearlessness of dangers to one's reputation from instances of arrogance and similar vices, it'll be plausible to classify such cases as cases of courage; in fact, we often do admire people for their courage when they express unpopular opinions even when those opinions do not coincide with ours.

Thus no form of the Aristotelian concern regarding lack of fear of the shameful threatens the Kantian view. But the possibility of certain forms of foolhardiness seem to present a more serious threat. For it seems that in our example above, the person who braves the sharks to retrieve five dollars manifests the general instrumental capacity to pursue ends in the face of danger. Yet we hesitate to classify this action as a courageous one, and it seems that we hesitate exactly because of the trivial nature of the end; contrary to Kant's position, whether one is courageous or not does appear to depend on the particular end we pursue.

It definitely seems wrong to say that the foolish swimmer is courageous. But the Kantian view is actually in a good position to explain why this is so, mostly because this Kantian view can support a moderate (and novel) form of the unity of the virtues thesis. A very strong version of the unity of the virtues thesis says that an agent can never manifest any particular virtue unless she possesses all the virtues. I'm not sure anyone defends such a view;

---

[30] In Kant's own view this would be described as an incapacity, a misfiring of our power to pursue the good, much the same way as it would be strange to describe one's liability to make certain mistakes in addition as a "capacity to resist carrying when adding two numbers".

[31] Kant discusses a similar vice under the heading "logical egoism". See Kant (2006), 7:128–9.

it certainly puts a very high bar on what counts as manifesting a virtue. A slightly weaker version of the thesis says that one cannot have any of the virtues in full perfection unless one has all of them in full perfection. On this view, perfect kindness requires perfect justice and vice versa; only those who are infallibly brave can be infallibly self-controlled.[32] A similar view, that is neither stronger nor weaker than this view, strikes me as particularly plausible; namely, that there are some relations of dependency between the virtues. On this view, for instance, some failures of justice (beyond a certain degree? Lack of justice in a particular sphere of action?) might be incompatible with certain forms of kindness (above a certain degree? In a certain sphere of action?), and there is only so much self-control that a coward could exhibit. These seem overall plausible: the fact that I pay no attention to what is owed to a person must put limits on how kind I can be to them, and there are probably some forms of self-control that I cannot have if any danger scares me senseless.

There are many ways that one could define this version of the unity of virtues, but the first thing we need to note is that if we accept the Kantian view that there are two types of powers that constitute the virtues, then there are four different versions of the unity of the virtues theses that one might examine. The substantive virtues might depend on the instrumental virtues (SI), the instrumental virtues might depend on the substantive virtues (IS), the substantive virtues might depend on each other (SS), and the instrumental virtues might depend on each other (II). I have no horse in the (SS) race, though as I said above, some version of it seems plausible. (SI) seems undeniable; someone who is too afraid to do what is just cannot be a just person; being a coward certainly puts serious limits on one's justice or kindness. Now, it is a consequence of the Kantian view that (IS) is false;[33] if it is indeed the same power we exhibit when we are courageous in pursuing good and bad ends, then can we have any degree of this power irrespective of the goodness of our ends? In fact, our sailor from before could be perfectly courageous in braving the rough seas, and her courage would be in no way diminished if she meets her lover more often and helps the children less often. This does not seem implausible; I don't think our pre-theoretic judgments speak much in

---

[32] See McDowell (1979).

[33] One could argue that the Kantian view expounded here is still compatible with there being *some* dependence; one could accept the Kantian view and still think that perfect courage, for instance, is only possible for the virtuous agent. I cannot rule out in advance that someone could make this argument, and its soundness would ultimately not affect the conclusions of this chapter. But since I do not see how this argument could be made, I will let the stronger claim (that is, that (IS) is simply false) stand.

favour of one position or the other on this issue, and the Kantian position provides a principled "regimentation" of these judgments.

But what about (II)? Does lack of self-control put limits on how courageous one can be? Let us look at the possibility of, for instance, an act of something that seems like akratic courage. I think the most obvious instances of such putative akratic courage are dares. Suppose I dare you to go the wrong way full speed down a one-way tunnel in the middle of the night.[34] Although cars rarely drive through it at late hours, there is a real chance that someone will be using the tunnel at that time. In such a case you and the unsuspecting driver would be involved in a serious crash. You hesitate, but I double-dare you, and you go. You know it is a dumb idea; nothing to be gained, and much to be lost. But the thought of my uttering clucking sounds while making wing motions is too much for you, and you akratically step on the gas. Although you were not deterred by the thought of danger in the pursuit of your end, it's not clear that you exhibited courage; your action seems just plain stupid.

Yet we can explain why this is not a courageous act within the confines of the Kantian view. The power of instrumental rationality is the general power of an agent's will to pursue ends, whatever they happen to be. Within this general capacity or power, we can identify various possible types of failures and successes as specific ways in which one could (fail to) manifest this capacity. So courageous acts are manifestations of this general capacity in the face of danger, and the trait of courage is a disposition to manifest the general capacity in circumstances involving danger. But lack of courage is not the only way in which failures of the will can narrow the range of ends available to an agent. Lack of self-control, akrasia, hesitation, irresolution, and procrastination are also capable of undermining our agential powers. If in circumstances where you do not fear danger you also exhibit at the same time a significant failure of the will, you do not manifest the general capacity at all. When you accept my dare, you are failing to pursue your ends appropriately. Although, of course, you successfully pursued the end of carrying out the dare, you failed to pursue your end of protecting your life in an acceptable way. So (II) holds because having an instrumental vice can prevent fearlessness, for instance, from being a manifestation of the general power to pursue given ends—rather, this case is mostly a manifestation of my incapacity to resist temptation. Similarly, our five-dollar swimmer does

---

[34] This was supposed to be a common dare in Rio de Janeiro in the 1980s. More likely, it's an urban legend.

not manifest courage, at least as long as his pursuit of the five dollars exhibits severe forms of akrasia, thoughtlessness, irresolution, avarice, or any other instrumental vice.[35]

7.6 A Vain Search for Principles

If the above considerations are correct, my claim that the principle of instrumental reasoning is the only fundamental principle of an agent's instrumental rational power should not be equated with the view that instrumental rationality is purely a matter of being properly guided by PIR; an ideally rational agent must also have certain instrumental virtues. In the previous chapters, I argued against various attempts to defend principles of diachronic rationality that prohibit or restrict reconsideration of (or require the persistence of) intention. I propose now to offer a tentative general diagnosis of what goes wrong with such attempts. There is no doubt that the agent who lacks any kind of self-control or who never exhibits resolution is instrumentally irrational. The mistake is to think that such irrationality must be captured by identifying a principle with which such agents fail to comply. The problem with these agents is not that they fail to comply with a principle on specific occasions; rather, such agents lack a general disposition of the will. Between trying to locate the irrationality of the agent at a momentary failure and trying to understand all such failures as violations of principles, traditional conceptions of instrumental rationality left themselves with no room to understand irresolution and weakness.

Although this understanding of instrumental virtues is relatively independent of the general theory of instrumental rationality that I have defended in this book, it is clearly congenial to a conception of rationality that takes as its given attitudes extended action; after all, capacities are not something that easily show up in a snapshot of the agent's mind. In Chapter 8 I argue that ETR is committed to a particular instrumental virtue, a virtue that I call "practical judgment" that would have no role to play in a theory in which the basic given attitudes are momentary mental states. As I said above, I take it that the plausibility that there is such a virtue (and its corresponding vices) to be further support for ETR.

---

[35] Of course, someone who had a fetish for five-dollar bills or had no reflective preferences between seriously risking their lives and marginally adding to their wealth might be exhibiting courage on my account. But insofar as this seems odd to us, it is a symptom of how unlikely such a possibility is for a human rational agent.

8

Practical Judgment and Its Corresponding Vices

8.0 Introduction

In this chapter, I describe an important but overlooked virtue, the instrumental virtue of practical judgment. This is a virtue that finitely rational agents need exactly because of the extended temporal structure of their agency. Practical judgment is a complex virtue with two aspects (roughly, an executive part and a corrective part). According to the *NON-SUPERVENIENCE* thesis, an agent can act rationality at each moment in time *from* t_1 to t_n without having been rational *through* t_1 to t_n. This possibility implies that a perfect rational agent has the following executive capacity: she must be capable of undertaking all the necessary means to a long-term action even when she can act rationally at each moment in a way that would undermine her long-term ends. Thus there are instrumental virtues that are the "excellence" of these long-term executive capacities. Just as in the case of courage, this excellence cannot be reduced to conformity to a principle. I could compensate for the lack of this capacity by adopting ends that can be executed in momentary or nearly momentary actions; yet, this would be no less of a failure of my general power to pursue any given end. In the rest of the chapter, I present the virtue of practical judgment and its corresponding vices in more detail; this will also help us get a fuller picture of the nature of extended instrumentally rational agency.

Section 8.1 presents two dimensions of the virtue of practical judgment (the "horizontal" and "vertical" dimensions of the virtue) and defines its corresponding vices: procrastination and extended akrasia are the correspond-ing vices of the horizontal dimension, and inflexibility is the corresponding vice of the vertical dimension. Section 8.2 looks at the ways in which a limited rational agent adopts and revises intermediate policies or actions in an attempt to understand better how these two dimensions of the virtue inter-act. Section 8.3 argues that, despite the characterization of the vice of pro-crastination as made possible by the indeterminate structure of our ends, and the intermediate vague policies we adopt to pursue them, we cannot escape succumbing to the vice by trying to adopt only very strict and precise policies or making our ends more determinate. Rational human agency inescapably depends on manifesting the virtue of practical judgment (in both dimensions). Finally, Section 8.4 argues that this understanding of the vice of procrastination shows a serious flaw in a popular argument against instrumentalism (that is, the view that the principle of practical reason is the principle of instrumental reasoning); although I am not committed to instrumentalism, this result shows the independence of the principle of instrumental reasoning from substantive principles of rationality.

8.1 Practical Judgment and Corresponding Vices

Let us suppose an aspiring author is writing a novel. The diagram below shows the gaps and the fully active parts of her pursuit (see Figure 8.1). According to [SUFFICIENCY], if the agent completes the novel in an acceptable manner, she is instrumentally rational relative to the end of writing the novel. However, in pursuing the end of writing a novel, the agent might also have engaged in intermediate activities, activities that stand between the "top" action of writing a novel and the "bottom" actions of typing on a computer, revising the manuscript, and so on. For instance, she might have settled on a policy[1] of writing at least a page a day. Of course, she might also have had no need of any such intermediate policies in order to successfully write a novel. In fact, the ideally rational agent would *not* need any such intermediate ends or policies. After all, if she only cares about writing a page a day for the sake of writing the novel, but it is not strictly necessary that one writes a page a day to finish it in a timely manner (one could easily compensate for non-writing days by writing two pages on a day, or even delaying finishing the book by a couple more days), then imposing on herself such a rule arbitrarily restricts the pursuit of her ends. On the other hand, given human limitations, we often need to make largely inflexible plans about how to ensure that we engage in enough fully active parts of writing a book as we pursue other ends.[2] But this is indeed a consequence of our *limitations*; ideal rational agents would not have such shortcomings. Of course, even ideal agents must implement their intentions in particular ways, but

---

[1] As we saw in Chapter 5, on ETR these policies are instances of extended action.
[2] See Gollwitzer (1999) for a classic study on the need of implementation intentions.

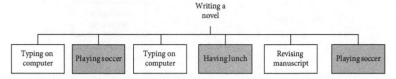

Figure 8.1 Gaps and fully active parts

they need not *restrict* the means available to them solely for the purpose of ensuring that an extended action is carried out.

An ideal agent needs to carry out the writing of her book at particular times, but she would be able to do this without having to rely on an inflexible schedule; instead, she would manage her time with maximum flexibility for the pursuit of her diverse ends without thereby compromising the pursuit of any of her ends. I will call an *intermediate policy* one that an agent adopts with the sole purpose of ensuring that she engages in enough fully active parts of the pursuit of some of her ends. So the policy of writing one page a day would be an example of an intermediate policy. An ideal agent is capable of pursuing all her ends without relying on intermediate policies. To the extent that we approximate this ideal, we exhibit the virtue of practical judgment. The virtue has a "vertical" dimension and a "horizontal" dimension. The vertical dimension corresponds to the agent's general capacity to pursue a long-term end without the need of (too many) intermediate actions or policies. The horizontal dimension corresponds to the agent's capacity to successfully pursue her ends by means of the intermediate actions she has chosen. For instance, we might be both writing a book and training for a marathon, and we both have the intermediate policy of training three days a week and writing three days a week. But I might need to specify the actual days in which I do each in order to successfully carry out these policies, while you can remain flexible about which days of the week will be dedicated to each activity. So my "action tree" will be vertically longer than yours (see Figures 8.2 and 8.3).[3]

On the other hand, we might have intermediate policies at the same level of depth, but my poor execution of these policies might force me to revise my original end (instead of writing an excellent book, I now need to content myself with writing a decent one) or give up or revise other ends (because I procrastinated on my training I need to give up on doing the Sunday *New York Times* crossword puzzle this weekend). This would

---

[3] Figures 8.2 and 8.3 contain only the fully active parts of the action in order to keep their size manageable.

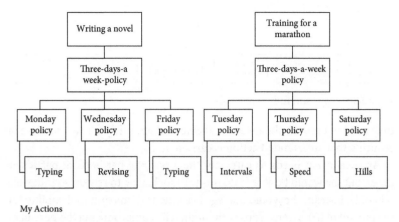

My Actions

Figure 8.2 My Actions

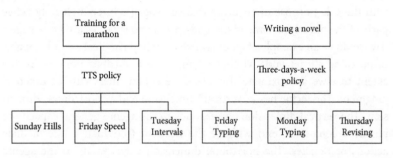

Your Actions

Figurre 8.3 Your Actions

manifest a difference between us with respect to the horizontal dimension of the virtue.

Back to the vertical dimension, insofar as I need a further (or a more restrictive) intermediate policy of training Tuesdays, Thursdays, and Sundays, I exhibit to a greater extent what I will call *the vice of inflexibility* (though in this case, it would probably be more charitable to describe me as exhibiting, to a lesser extent, on the vertical dimension, the virtue of practical judgment). Again, even an ideal rational agent would need to exercise at particular times, so she might actually run Tuesdays, Thursdays, and Saturdays, and she might even decide that these are particularly convenient days of the week to exercise. But she does not adopt a more specific policy merely to ensure that she will realize her end of exercising regularly. In other words, she does not adopt the policy of exercising Tuesdays,

Thursdays, and Saturdays so as to avoid manifesting what I will call the *vice of procrastination* or as to avoid manifesting what I will call the *vice of extended akrasia*. These two vices pertain to the horizontal dimension of the virtue of practical judgment. My policy of exercising regularly is compatible with my not exercising at any particular moment considered in isolation. But if I keep failing to pursue the fully active parts of exercising, if I keep postponing engaging in specific instances of exercise, I exhibit the vice of procrastination. If my policy is one of refraining from a certain action (say if I am dieting and thus avoiding fattening treats), I can exhibit a similar failure in engaging *too often* or *too much* in instances of the action that I am avoiding. In such a case, I exhibit the vice of *extended akrasia*. We can understand the virtue of practical judgment better by contrasting it with its corresponding vices. But since, for our purposes, the difference between procrastination and extended *akrasia* is unimportant, I will focus on the vices of procrastination and inflexibility.

Let us start with procrastination. In the absence of unexpected circumstances, an agent violates [NECESSITY] if she continuously engages in a long-term activity through an interval but does not take the necessary means to complete the long-term activity in an acceptable manner. In such cases, the agent chooses the end but fails to take the necessary means to bring it about. Of course, our author might fail due to specific temptations at particular discrete moments in time; these would not be cases of procrastination. For instance, it would not be a case of procrastination if our aspiring author failed to complete her project because she gambled away all her writing utensils. However, she might also fail to write her book due to a more general inability to manage her momentary actions so that she failed to engage in enough fully active parts of her actions in the relevant interval; in such a case, she would manifest the vice of procrastination. Our writer might have written a few sentences, or a general outline of the novel, but then seldom took any further steps to complete the novel. There is no question that she was engaged in pursuing the end, but procrastination prevented her from realizing the end of her action of writing a book.

Two things should be noted here: first, in order to attribute this form of procrastination to an agent, we only need to understand the long-term end that the agent was pursuing, and the pattern of management of her momentary actions. In many cases, manifestations of the vice of procrastination are themselves straightforward violations of the principle of instrumental rationality. If I never get around to write my book, but at each moment I always choose to do something else, at some point it will no longer be possible for me to complete my book (let us assume there is a looming deadline), in which case, I will have been pursuing the end of writing the book without taking sufficient means to it. But often the vice of procrastination is manifested not in failing to bring about the end with respect to which I procrastinate, but some other end, or at least in forcing me to revise my end. So I might plan to do all my grading tonight so as to be able to go to a play tomorrow that I would love to go to, but don't do my grading, and have to miss the play the next day. Even if I do complete my grading the next day, procrastination prevented me from also realizing my end of attending the play. Understood as a general failure of the capacity to pursue one's long-term ends through the intermediate policies one has adopted, procrastination can come in varying degrees, depending on the extent of the ends that procrastination will generally force me to abandon or revise. But as such, it need not imply any direct violation of the principle of instrumental reasoning; I might abandon and revise ends as I procrastinate in such a way that I am never pursuing an end and failing to pursue sufficient means at the same time.

Similarly, practical judgment and practical inflexibility are the extremes on the gradient of a certain instrumental power (much like cowardice and courage). But in order to understand better how these two dimensions of the virtue interact, we need to look at how agents adopt and revise intermediate policies and actions.

8.2 Intermediate Policies, Revisions, and Failures of Practical Judgment

Let us look back at our example of the ordinary action of baking a cake. We can imagine that as I am baking the cake, some things turn out badly. As I beat the eggs, I notice that they are not getting the texture I expected. I might then check the egg beater, see if there's anything stuck in it, or change my plans for how to move my hands. Part of being a rational agent is, of course, that we check the progress of our actions and revise the actions undertaken as means (as well as the ends themselves) in light of what we learn in the course of acting. However, the complications and difficulties introduced by the vagueness of what counts as an acceptable outcome will give rise to further complications about how a rational agent revises the actions undertaken as means to more general ends.

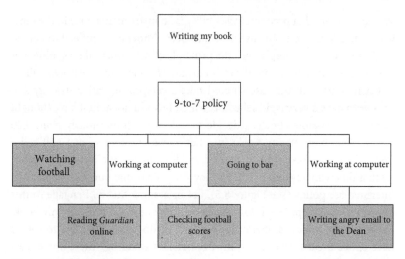

Figure 8.4 Writing my book

Suppose that I decide to write a book, and after a while I look back at my actions and see that I have exemplified the pattern outlined in Figure 8.4. I might have two distinct attitudes in relation to these actions. I might think that this is an overall slow start, but it is to be expected given that the World Cup was on, it was hard to leave the Dean's outrageous actions unanswered, and so forth. Since these initial choices are fully compatible with writing my book in an acceptable way, I might think that I am engaging in the appropriate actions in pursuit of my end of writing a book. But it is unlikely that this kind of judgment is warranted. More likely, I should realize that I cannot write my book without further planning; I will not write a book unless I adopt intermediate policies such as "write at least two pages a day", "do not go online before writing at least one page", and so forth. Cases in which we recognize the need for further planning seem to allow us to locate failures of rationality more precisely than just in the general pattern of activity: if I can't expect to write a book without an intermediate policy, the failure to adopt the intermediate policy is itself a failure of rationality.

Suppose that I recognize the need to have an intermediate policy. This conclusion must lead me to revise the sets of choices that are feasible, as well as some of my other ends. Perhaps my intermediate policy to write at least two pages a day is incompatible with my end of having one day a week in which I do no work at all. Given that our menu of options has shrunk, we might find acceptable now what we previously thought should be ruled out, just as someone who has weight-control problems might end up reluctantly adding a life without chocolate desserts to the list of acceptable outcomes.

We can see here that practical inflexibility is an instrumental vice in the same way that cowardice is an instrumental vice; although an inflexible person might never fail to comply with the principle of instrumental reasoning, her power to pursue ends is significantly curtailed by a failure of her own will.

Let us start with the case where I take a very conservative strategy and choose to have a very rigid schedule, which I would not at first have thought to be an acceptable choice. I decide to, say, work continuously from 9:00 a.m. to 7:00 p.m. on my book; in other words, I adopt what I will call a "9-to-7" policy. To simplify matters, I will look first at the unlikely possibility that this is an absolutely strict policy. This is our diagram for my planned intermediate policy (see Figure 8.5). Let us assume that as I engage in this new intermediate policy, I do make good strides toward finishing my book. However, the policy is obviously too strict; it does not allow me to eat, to have coffee breaks, or to go to my best friend's wedding. There are at least two ways I can react to this. I can just allow certain exceptions from time to time and transform my 9-to-7 policy into a loose and vague policy. In the case of a loose and vague policy, I expect to be writing my book most of the time between 9:00 and 7:00, but I allow that, from time to time, I take a break to do other things. Or I can form a policy that is essentially like my 9-to-7 policy, but I also now incorporate into the policy precisely specified conditions under which breaks are acceptable.

Note that the vague intermediate policy leaves us with a problem much like the one we faced in the original project of writing a book. I might be quite good at managing a few exceptions here and there, but it is also perfectly possible that my actions controlled by my vague intermediate policy are identical to the ones that were directly controlled by the project of writing a book (see Figure 8.6).

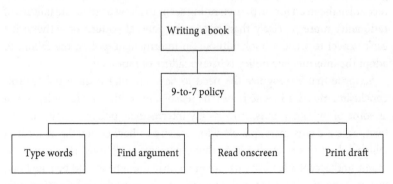

Figure 8.5 Writing a book I

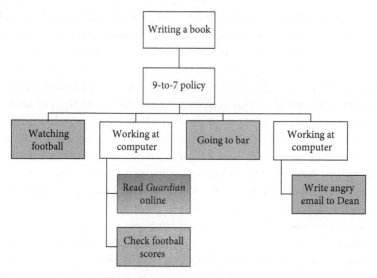

Figure 8.6 Writing a book II

But notice that, again, none of these momentary actions on their own are instrumentally irrational; after all, each exception on its own is compatible with my 9-to-7 policy. Just as in the case in which the agent does not adopt an intermediate policy, the irrationality of the agent consists solely in the fact that these choices do not constitute an execution of the end of the intermediate policy. In sum, adding intermediate policies, as long as they are vague, still requires that the agent has some amount of practical judgment to implement them; she must be capable of managing her momentary action in such a way as to bring about the 9-to-7 policy.

Instead of following a vague policy, I could choose a less demanding but still strict policy, or have a loose but precise policy.[4] I could cut down on the hours I expect myself to be writing a book or incorporate precisely laid-out exceptions to my plan. And here one might think that I move from a vague policy that allows unspecified exceptions to a precise but less strict policy for the same reason that an intermediate policy was adopted in the first place; that is, the agent suspects that the vague policy is not a feasible one. But even

---

[4] One might ask what is the difference between acting on a policy or simply being disposed to act in a certain way. Of course, I need not be committed to a particular answer to this question as long as it is agreed that there is a distinction here. However, my preferred view is that policies must be possible answers to Anscombe's question "Why?"; that is, they'd be among the reasons for which the agent acts.

a less demanding but still strict policy will probably not be ideal. Not all exceptions can be thought out in advance, and it would be a great cost not to allow wiggle room in unexpected circumstances. A policy whose system of exceptions is part of the policy itself, or is limited only by pre-existing rules and regularities, is almost always a second-best option; the flexibility of leaving open when and how many exceptions are permitted is likely to be advantageous to the pursuit of the agent's other ends, as long as this is a feasible option for the agent. As we pointed out in Chapter 5, most of our strict policies are either policies that we think are intrinsically choiceworthy or desperate reactions to powerful temptations. Avoiding extramarital affairs and not betraying friends fall under the first category, while quitting smoking completely and becoming a teetotaller fall under the latter.[5]

At any rate, as I find out that the direct implementation of a vague policy proves difficult for me, I might tweak it either by revising how to carry out my policy one level up or by implementing it with a further policy one level down, which could be more or less precise. Of course, excessive tweaking or fine-tuning might be itself a failure of the will. Again [SUFFICIENCY] determines, plausibly, that whether particular tweaks and fine-tunings add up to a manifestation of irrationality depends on whether my end has been accomplished; that is, as long as I write the book, I was instrumentally rational relative to this end. Suppose I open a file, write the title of the book, and write the first paragraph of the preface before the pattern of potential procrastination gets started. I then revise my understanding of the necessary means to pursue my end of writing a book, and decide to adopt some intermediate policies. Even though my initial engagement might not have contributed much to the final product, it is part of the overall pattern of activity, much as my missteps in baking a cake are part of the process of baking a cake. If my adopting intermediate policies delivers a decent book after a certain time, I ended up hitting on an acceptable set of choices, one that happens to include these seemingly procrastinating actions in my first days at the job of writing a book. In fact, if anything, the set that includes those early misdeeds can only be better than one that replaces some of these early misdeeds with more instances of book writing, at least if further instances would not have significantly improved the quality of the book. After all, I also realized my ends of watching football and reading newspapers. Since the outcome was good, and it was non-accidentally brought about by

---

[5] See George Ainslie's famous discussion of the need for bright lines in trying to overcome addictions in Ainslie (2001), ch. 6.

my acting with the goal of writing a book, there is no reason to think that my actions exhibited any kind of failure to comply with the principle of instrumental reasoning.

I suggested in the previous chapter that resolution is also a fundamental virtue that is not reducible to compliance with certain principles of practical rationality.[6] Resolution can be roughly described as the executive virtue that ensures that temptations or shifting judgments will not render us too fickle to pursue a wide range of ends. In particular, the virtue of resolution allows us to pursue higher-order ends of having stable projects and long-term significant commitments. An irresolute person changes her mind too often and too easily, preventing her, at least in extreme cases, of realizing any significant long-term project. But practical judgment is a different kind of instrumental virtue insofar as someone can entirely fail to exhibit practical judgment while being perfectly resolute; that is, without at any moment changing her mind about the importance of her end. Procrastination is indeed not a form of irresolution exactly for that reason; procrastination does not involve a change of mind or rejection of a previously accepted plan or project;[7] it is simply a failure to properly pursue enough fully active parts of a gappy, indeterminate, long-term pursuit. In order to realize long-term ends, we need both virtues; we need resolution and practical judgment.

Practical judgment involves both the capacity to carry out vague policies (and long-term actions in general) in the absence of an intermediate policy and the capacity to adopt and revise intermediate policies that are effective but not overly inflexible. Fully virtuous agents would exhibit only the first aspect of the virtue; not needing any intermediate policies or plans, they would simply engage in the long-term activity by choosing an acceptable set. But a less than perfect degree of virtue will require both that one can effectively execute fairly vague policies and also that one can choose well among intermediate policies when direct execution of long-term activity is not feasible. As I argued above, we can fail in this virtue in two ways. I exhibit practical inflexibility if I need to adopt a very detailed intermediate policy in order to pursue my end. In fact, someone who is practically inflexible in this manner often needs the help of external incentives and constraints. I might need to disconnect the internet, go to a retreat, or join a

---

[6] Except, again, trivial principles such as "Be Resolute".

[7] The procrastinating agent might abandon an end as she realizes that due to her procrastination the end is beyond her reach. But this is not a change in her practical perspective, since she doesn't alter her assessment of the value of the end.

self-help group in order to effectively engage in my pursuit of writing a book. But as long as my intermediate policy is not so detailed as to leave out any vagueness and indeterminacy, I'll still need the virtue of practical judgment in order to implement my "lowest level" policy—that is, the policy that is not being implemented by means of further intermediate policies. Practical inflexibility is not the contrary of procrastination; one can combine both vices. I can drive dozens of miles to the nearest 24/7 store that would have floss late at night due to my need for an overly strict policy of flossing every night, and yet still procrastinate when I arrive home, and fall asleep on the couch before I have a chance to floss. We procrastinate when our attempt to realize an indeterminate end fails because we engage in the characteristic activity on too few occasions, or we engage in other activities on the wrong occasions. This account also explains an intuitive feature of procrastination: it seems to be a vice of inaction. I succumb to temptation when I do something that I have conclusive reason not to do, but I procrastinate when I fail to do something I have conclusive reason to do. As an instrumental vice, it is a failure to realize my action's end by failing to execute enough fully active parts of the action.[8]

This understanding of procrastination does not depend on any kind of discounting or preference reversal for greater rewards in the present.[9] This might be considered a disadvantage of the view, but I think not. Suppose that I actually enjoy writing more than performing household chores. However, every time before I begin to write, I decide to engage in the household chores so I will not forget to do them, or I just think that it is better to do the things I do not enjoy before I engage in something I do enjoy. If I keep thinking, "I will just get this one more thing out of the way, and then I will start writing", I do exhibit procrastination. After all, I put off engaging in the fully active parts of my actions, and as a result of putting them off in this way, I fail to achieve the end of my action. Of course, this is not to deny that often what causes procrastination, what prevents me from displaying the virtue of practical judgment, is exactly the kind of hyperbolic discounting described by Ainslie (and others).[10] However, procrastination on its own does not require preference shifts, let alone hyperbolic discounting;

---

[8] In some accounts of value and reason, this distinction is spurious; values are comparative, and decisive reasons are all-things-considered reasons. So, by failing to do something that I had decisive reason to do (or by failing to choose the option of greater value), I thereby did something that I had no decisive reason to do (or I thereby chose the option of lesser value).

[9] Andreou (2007) makes a similar point.   [10] Ainslie (2001).

one can procrastinate even if one is a perfect Sidgwickean agent who counts every good the same way irrespective of its temporal location.

But this is not the only way in which the capacity of practical judgment can fail along this dimension. We already mentioned extended *akrasia*, but there is also a vice that is the contrary of procrastination, a vice we might call *the vice of rigidity*. Such a vice consists in either an incapacity to treat a vague policy as one that allows for exceptions, or a tendency to be too hesitant to make exceptions in the execution of the policy. In other words, the vice of rigidity is a vice of performing the characteristic actions of our policy too often or at the wrong times. I manifest the vice of rigidity if, for instance, I hear that my friend has been suddenly hospitalized, but I do not visit him because my schedule requires that I write two pages today, or if I keep to my diet plans and do not eat cake at my child's wedding.

8.3 Procrastinating Further

I have been assuming that procrastination requires a vague policy; adopting a strict policy to avoid having an opportunity to procrastinate could itself be a failure of the virtue of practical judgment (a manifestation of inflexibility), but at least, on the account presented so far, it would be a successful way of making procrastination impossible. However, it is hard to see how we could have a policy that is strict enough so as to render procrastination impossible. After all, even a strict policy needs to be implemented through various steps. Let us go back to my 9-to-7 policy. If I am going to act on this policy, I need, for instance, to start writing at 9 a.m.; we could write down my first step as "Begin writing at 9:00 a.m." But this first step has the same structure as a vague policy; it does not determine a precise moment in which my finger needs to hit the keyboard, but it can be executed by a number of different choices (idle finger drumming from 9:00:01 to 9:00:05, finger hits keyboard at 9:00:07, etc.). And here, too, we will need the virtue of practical judgment to avoid frittering away time until, without my noticing, my choices clearly are not within an acceptable set (i.e., it is already 9:01, and my fingers are still drumming). Thus even relatively short-term actions are prone to procrastination. This should come as no surprise; all actions are extended and no representation of my choice is fully particular. The only difference is a difference of degree: some actions extend for longer periods of time, and some pursuits leave more or less room for latitude (what Kant calls "Spielraum"; Kant (1996), 6:390, when discussing how we comply with imperfect duties) in determining the precise way to bring about their ends. For instance, suppose that I want to bake a cake for my wife, and I want it to be a nice cake, not put together at the last moment. However, as the day goes by, I check the internet, I go out to buy coffee and bagels, and so forth. By the end of the day, I only have time to bake a cake from a boxed mix, an outcome that surely was not one that I had first considered acceptable.

As I said above, one can be very strong-willed (capable of resisting temptation) and yet be a serious procrastinator. Of course, at some point, one will expect that if one is strong-willed enough to move to a precise enough policy, one will not have trouble in executing the policy without the help of further policies or habits or dispositions. But there is at least the theoretical possibility that this is not the case; it might be possible that without a more specific policy that makes my starting time more precise, I cannot execute an intention to start working at 9:00 a.m. As the milliseconds pass by, I can see no reason to start working *right now* rather than at the very next moment; I can continue on this path of inaction until I realize that it is already 9:01 without at any time having succumbed to any specific temptation.

If ETR is right, it should not surprise us that failures of practical judgment can extend to arbitrarily short-term actions. All action is extended and shares the same rational structure independently of how far it extends into the future and how gappy it is. Of course, the longer and gappier the action is, the more difficult it is for a limited, finitely rational agent to manage its pursuit. But, in principle, the potential failures and successes are the same for all of our intentional pursuits: short or long, continuous or gappy, all our intentional actions are manifestations of the same rational powers.

8.4 Practical Judgment and Instrumentalism

There is a further important implication of this understanding of practical judgment. Christine Korsgaard argues for the incoherence of a view according to which the only principle of practical reason is the principle of instrumental reasoning.[11] I do not count myself among such instrumentalists,[12]

---

[11] Korsgaard (1997), pp. 229–30.
[12] I have been arguing that the principle of instrumental reasoning is the only principle of instrumental rationality. But, of course, this does not imply that there are no other non-instrumental principles of practical rationality.

so it saddens me to say that I bring good tidings for those who do. Korsgaard's argument against the instrumentalist is complex, and I do not claim to address it here in its entirety. However, one aspect of her argument loses its force in view of our account of practical judgment and, more generally, in moving the focal point of our analysis of instrumental rationality from momentary mental states to extended actions.

Korsgaard argues that an instrumentalist will ultimately be unable to account for the possibility of violating the principle of instrumental reasoning. Let us take a seemingly typical case of violating the principle; an agent refuses to undergo a lifesaving operation out of fear. However, as we explain why the agent violated the principle of instrumental rationality we at the same time identify an end of the agent that *is* furthered by such an action; namely, the end of avoiding pain (or avoiding certain procedures). But if this is the case, why shouldn't one say that the agent did *not* violate the instrumental principle? Why can't we say that she abandoned an end and efficiently pursued a different end? It seems that the instrumentalist faces a dilemma. Either the instrumentalist will have to identify certain things as the "real ends" of the agent (and claim that violations of the instrumental principle are failures to pursue the agent's real ends), or she will have to treat any apparent violation of the instrumental principle as adoption of a different end that is, in fact, furthered by the agent's actions. In either case, instrumentalism turns out to be false; in neither case is it true that the principle of instrumental reasoning is the sole principle of practical rationality. The first strategy amounts to implicitly accepting a second principle of rationality; namely, that one ought to pursue one's "real" ends. The second deprives the instrumental principle of any content: if no action, or combination of actions, could count as a violation of the principle of instrumental reasoning, then the principle does not prescribe anything.

When we look at momentary actions, this argument seems persuasive.[13] Suppose that I spend the bonus I earned on Monday on a nice watch, instead of saving it to procure nourishment on Tuesday as I had planned to do before I cashed my bonus cheque. When the instrumentalist looks at my action on Monday, it seems that she has only two options. She could say that given that I chose the watch, my end (or my most preferred option) on Monday was to buy the watch rather than to have a proper meal on Tuesday; in other words, I must have changed my mind after I cashed the cheque. But if the instrumentalist always reads off my ends from my actions in this

---

[13] I do, however, have some doubts that it is ultimately persuasive even in this case; see Tenenbaum (2003).

manner, no violation of the principle of instrumental reasoning seems possible. On the other hand, the instrumentalist might not want to say that all cases in which I choose to buy the watch are cases in which my end (or my most preferred option) is to buy the watch. The instrumentalist might insist that at least in some such cases, for the purposes of assessing my rationality, my real end on Monday is to eat properly on Tuesday. But then we're back at the second horn of the dilemma. The instrumentalist seems to have smuggled in an (additional) principle of rationality: the principle that prescribes the pursuit of those ends that the instrumentalist identifies as my real ends.

However, this problem for the instrumentalist disappears when we look at some cases of procrastination. It is worth focusing again on the case of my writing a book. Suppose that I procrastinate and never finish writing the book. Here we seem to have a simple case of adopting an end without taking the necessary means that were available (and known to be available) to me. In order to understand this failure of instrumental rationality, we need not ascribe to the agent a real end hidden behind the ends he actually pursues. My end of writing a book is revealed precisely by my pursuit; despite the fact that I fail to achieve my end of writing a book, I do engage in its pursuit.

Notice that, unlike the case of my buying a watch, in many of the ways of filling out my failure to write a book, the fact that I changed my mind at a certain point in time will not make the charge of irrationality go away. This point is easier to see if we assume that I have a deadline to write the book by. I might need to have it sent to the publishers by a certain date (say, a year from today). Suppose I write a few words every couple of days, but I do not make enough progress to finish the book by the deadline. Given the indeterminacy of my end, it is likely that I will still be trying to write the book when it is no longer feasible to finish it in time. But now let us look at two points in time at which one could say that I changed my mind: before I engaged in the last fully active part of my writing a book (or while I was engaged in that action) or after that point. If one chooses to locate the change of mind before I stopped taking means to writing the book, if I no longer had the end of writing a book even before I stopped, then I was instrumentally irrational by virtue of engaging in the characteristic activities of writing a book without having any end that was furthered by this activity. If, more plausibly, one locates the change of mind after I stopped taking such means, then at the moment before I changed my mind, I would have been instrumentally irrational. It was true then that I had the end of writing a book but had taken insufficient means to bring it about.

Of course, one could claim that we must attribute to me in this case a certain gerrymandered end rather than the end of writing a book. Perhaps one can argue that I did not (ever?) have the end of writing a book but only had ends such as typing the words "It was a dark and stormy night" on the paper or engaging a number of times in the characteristic activities of writing a book. But since these ends would not be capable of explaining my actions as well as the simpler end of writing a book, there is no reason to think that the instrumentalist must stop short of attributing to me the end of writing a book. And obviously, what I say about the case of my writing a book extends to many cases of extended pursuits, and more generally to other cases in which top-down independence holds. We started the previous chapter by proposing that a theory that focuses on extended action makes room for a conception of instrumental rationality that extends beyond compliance with principles of rationality, by also requiring possession of certain virtues. However, a closer look at these virtues reveals another surprising advantage of the focus on extended actions: we end up with a clearer picture of the independence of the principles of instrumental reasoning from the other principles of practical rationality.

8.5 Conclusion

I have so far argued that taking extended actions as the basic given attitudes of practical reason provides a simpler and more compelling understanding of instrumental rationality than starting from preferences or intentions. I have so far mostly assumed that the agent had all the relevant background knowledge, and thus we have not seen how the theory incorporates risk. However, preferences have been at the basis of a powerful mathematical theory that seems to be particularly successful in accounting for cases that fall short of knowledge, such as cases of decision under risk and uncertainty. If ETR cannot account for the exercise of instrumental rational agency in such contexts, it seems to have a major flaw exactly where decision theory is most powerful. In Chapter 9 we look at the prospects of extending the view to cases of risk and uncertainty. The main contention is that nothing fundamental changes about the nature of the theory when we introduce risk.

Awareness of risk introduces new possible contents to the agent's body of knowledge, and different bodies of knowledge make different actions available to an agent. But incorporating awareness of risk into our theory of rationality should change neither its conception of the given attitudes nor its principles of derivation or coherence.[14]

---

[14] I make a similar argument with respect to how deontological theories should incorporate risk in Tenenbaum (2017). In this case too, risk and uncertainty change not the relevant moral principles but the nature of the actions available to the agent.

9

Actions, Preferences, and Risk

9.0 Introduction

Most of the presentation of the extended theory of instrumental rationality (ETR) has assumed a background of knowledge or at least outright belief. In fact, it is a common feature of discussions of the principle of instrumental reasoning, and various "means–ends coherence" principles, that the principles are formulated in terms of outright beliefs (and intentions) rather than in terms of credence or degree of belief. This is not particularly surprising: it is unclear that there is any principle of expected means–ends coherence or any formulation of the principle of instrumental reasoning that generalizes to risky contexts. But given our claim that the principle of instrumental reasoning is the only principle of derivation, we need to provide some account of how an instrumentally rational agent acts in cases in which she is relatively ignorant of the relevant facts. One part of the strategy is simple. I argue that the rationality of an action under risk is not determined (solely) by the attitudes the agent has towards her actions under conditions of knowledge and the probabilities that attach to the possible actions the agent might end up performing in a risky situation. Rather, risk changes the nature of the actions available to us and might require that we revise our ends as we realize that certain means are not available or cannot be relied upon.[1] So, for instance, if I realize that none of the means available to me can ensure that I earn a million dollars, then "becoming a millionaire" is not a possible intentional action for me. I can perhaps engage in closely related actions ("making it likely/possible/more likely than not that I become a millionaire", or "trying to become a millionaire"), but I must revise my initial end. But even these closely related actions are in many important ways different from the original action, and the sufficient and contributory means to the new ends will have different structures.

---

[1] This is similar to the strategy I employed in trying to defend a view of how deontological theories should approach risky scenarios. See Tenenbaum (2017).

It is reasonably clear what counts as a sufficient means to my becoming a millionaire, or a contributory means to preparing for my trip to Madrid. But what is a sufficient means to trying to become a millionaire or contributory means to making it more likely that I will be in Madrid next summer? Does anything that raises the probability of my becoming a millionaire count as a sufficient means to this end? If I befriend a millionaire, I make it slightly more likely that one day I will inherit her fortune. But such an act is not, on its own and in all circumstances, the full actualization of my end of trying to become a millionaire; there are certainly better ways of trying to become a millionaire. We encounter similar issues in accounting for contributory means in this context. If I am trying to arrange a trip to Madrid for next summer, it seems to be a clear manifestation of my instrumentally rational powers to join a Spanish class, so that I will have a better time in Madrid if it all works out. But it is not obvious how this is a contributory means to *trying* to go to Madrid; after all, going to a Spanish class seems not to contribute at all to the quality of my *attempt* to go to Madrid.

This chapter will try to answer these questions by looking at the internal structure of the ends we pursue in the context of relative ignorance. And I will argue that the existence of Pareto Preferences and preferences internal to these ends, in particular in ends involving the pursuit of general means, also gives us important ways in which our theory can explain the nature of rational action under risk and uncertainty; it also allows us to accept that some form of decision theory has a crucial role to play in these contexts.

9.1 Knowledge, Ignorance, and Action

I like to go for long bike rides. As I am casually looking at my daily astronomical briefings, I find out that the distance to the moon is about 385,000 km. I think to myself: "that's a nice distance to bike; if I bike 350 km a day, it would take me just over three years to get there". As I search for my keys to the bike lock and start packing some food, I remember some facts about gravitational fields and the absence of extraterrestrial bike paths, and I realize that it would be impossible to bike to the moon. It seems that at this point it is no longer possible for me to intend to bike to the moon, or pursue the end of biking to the moon, let alone engage in biking to the moon intentionally.[2] Examples of this kind speak in favour of what is often described as

---

[2] Of course, even before I remembered it was impossible, I would not have succeeded in arriving at the moon, but this is not enough to show that I could not have been engaged in

the belief (or knowledge) condition on doing something intentionally. Of course, the version here would be a rather weak version of the principle, a version according to which you cannot intend/do what you believe/know to be impossible for you to do.[3] The strongest versions of the view, inspired by Anscombe's views on practical knowledge (Anscombe 2000), require that in order for the agent to be doing something intentionally she must know, or at least outright believe, that she is doing it.[4] Whether we accept any version of the belief or knowledge condition, it seems difficult to deny, as the radical case above illustrates, that changes in an agent's state of knowledge or belief can change the options available to the agent.

Learning that an end cannot be realized is a "degenerate" instance of the antecedent of *ETR COHERENCE*. According to *ETR COHERENCE*, a rational agent who realizes that not all her ends can be actualized at the same time abandons at least one of her ends from the smallest subset of her ends that cannot be jointly realized. An impossible end forms a singleton such that not all ends in the singleton can be "jointly" realized and thus must be abandoned. As the case above illustrates, there's often no obvious "backup" end that I can pursue once I realize that my end is impossible. There is no particular reason why I should now engage in the pursuit of biking to another distant location or struggle to find some other way to reach the moon. And even if there were such reasons, they would not be instrumental reasons; in other words, exercising my instrumental rational powers will not carry me from the abandonment of this end to the adoption of another particular end.

Possibly more common than realizing that a certain end is impossible is realizing that I do not have knowledge of any sufficient means which I am willing to take in the pursuit of my end; the best I can do is to pursue means

---

biking to the moon. As emphasized by Thompson (2008), among others, the progressive aspect is compatible with the action never being completed, and even with it not being able to be completed from an objective standpoint. Of course, there are cases in which the inefficiency of my actions makes the progressive inapplicable, but this need not be one of them.

[3] See Wallace (2001) for a defence of this version. A different kind of weak version, focusing on credences, rather than outright beliefs, is put forward by Setiya (2009). See Paul (2009) for a sceptical discussion of the knowledge/belief condition.

[4] There are also versions that connect outright belief to intention, but they are less important for our purposes. Davidson's (1980b) famous carbon copy case is often taken to be a decisive counterexample to these views. In the example, I am trying to make twelve carbon copies while writing on a page without being able to see whether I am succeeding, and doubting very much that I am. According to Davidson, if I am in fact succeeding, I am making twelve carbon copies intentionally, even though I don't believe that this is what I am doing. See Thompson (2011) for a discussion of the example that is sympathetic to the knowledge condition.

that will make it likely, or at least more likely, that I will actualize certain ends. On some approaches to practical philosophy, this is always my situation no matter which end I pursue. Given that there can be no certainty about empirical matters, we can at best pursue likely means to our ends.[5] However, we have formulated ETR in terms of knowledge, and, absent very radical scepticism, many of our actions are performed under the relevant conditions of knowledge. In particular, we assumed that whenever an agent is pursuing an end E, there is at least some sufficient means to the completion or maintenance of E such that the agent knows that these means are sufficient and is willing to take these means for the completion or the maintenance of E. If, for instance, my end is to cross the street, then, at least in the absence of radical scepticism, it seems unproblematic to assume that I know how to actualize this end. The same is true, doubtless, for cases in which there are many more potential risks of failure: Pierre Hermé knows how to efficiently pursue the end of baking a cake and J. K. Rowling knows how to efficiently pursue the end of writing a book. When Hermé is baking a pound cake, or when Rowling is writing her new fantasy series, they are acting under conditions of knowledge that, even if a sceptic could put pressure on various background assumptions, must be true in order for such an endeavour to be successful.[6] Of course, even though I would love to grace the world with a refutation of scepticism, or even provide reassurances that knowledge resists sceptical pressures, this is not something I can do here and now. I can only sheepishly acknowledge that the possibility of this kind of knowledge is a background assumption of ETR, and defensively point out that there are many companions in guilt here. It is very unclear how we would understand agency in general if radical scepticism were true; even decision theory arguably presupposes that a rational agent is in possession of some empirical knowledge.[7]

But even when I do know some sufficient means to my end, and even if I am willing to take them, I might prefer to try first some means M such that I am uncertain whether M is a sufficient means to my end. If I am fixing my bike, I might prefer to first see if I can glue the parts together with super

---

[5] This is often assumed in the literature on deontology and risk. See for instance, Fried (2012) and Jackson and Smith (2006). But, arguably, this is also an assumption of a number of Bayesian models.

[6] The relevant knowledge is naturally described as knowledge-how; I am not taking a stand on whether "knowledge-how" is propositional or non-propositional. Stanley and Williamson (2001) and Stanley (2011a, 2011b) defend the view that the knowledge in question is propositional. For criticism of their view, see Hornsby (2017).

[7] See Weatherson (2012).

glue, before I take the more time-consuming, but certain to work, option of soldering the parts together. But this does not essentially change our case. After all, I am taking sufficient means to my end of getting my bike fixed; I pursue my end of fixing the bike by employing the following, doubtless convoluted, but sufficient means: I first try to use super glue, then, if necessary, I solder the parts together. However, in some cases, there are no sufficient means that I know will achieve my end, but I do not abandon the end:[8] I try means that will likely, or at least possibly, achieve my end. So, for instance, I might realize that I know of no sufficient means to achieve my end of earning a million dollars (or that the only means that I know will achieve this end, defrauding my great-uncle, is not a means I am willing to take), but that there are some actions that I could perform that would have a good chance of achieving the end (becoming a lawyer) or that could at least make it possible (buying a lottery ticket).[9]

In some of these cases it would be strange to say that I am φ-ing if I don't know that the actions that I am undertaking suffice for achieving the end of φ-ing.[10] Here we're not concerned (at least not in the first instance) about the relation between my intentionally crossing the street and my knowledge that I am *crossing* the street. The question is whether it would be natural to describe myself as crossing the street if I were aware[11] that I did not know that I was going to arrive at the other side. Suppose that bullies are trying to prevent nerds like me from reaching the other side (if they see us, they grab us by our pants and drag us back to our side of the street), and, even though I am trying my best to avoid their capture, I know there is a serious chance that they'll stop me before I reach the other side. In such a case, it would

---

[8] As I said above, I would now be pursuing a different action, so in some sense I did abandon the end. The sense in which I do not will be clear in the following.

[9] There are cases which seem to be somewhat different. Suppose I know I would make a million dollars by becoming a plastic surgeon who caters to an exclusive clientele. I would be willing to take this path if there were no other options. However, there is also the option of becoming a cardiologist, and while I do not know that this option will provide me with a million dollars, I think it is very likely that it will. But I can only choose one specialty and I know I'll not have an opportunity to retrain. So I choose to become a cardiologist even though it carries the risk that I'll succeed in making a million dollars (obviously, there is nothing irrational in my pursuing the means to training in cardiology rather than training in plastic surgery). We'll treat such cases in parallel with cases of not being willing to take certain means; they are both cases in which I revise my end of φ-ing in favour of the end of trying to φ.

[10] This is slightly different from the Anscombean knowledge condition on intention discussed above, at least when the knowledge condition is restricted to the present progressive (that is, when it is restricted to claims of the form "if I am φ-ing intentionally, then I know that I am φ-ing"). It is closer to the belief conditions on future-directed intentions that motivate some versions of cognitivism about intention. See, for instance, Marusic and Schwenkler (2018).

[11] I leave cases of false belief and errors to the next section.

seem that I would more naturally describe my action by saying, "I am trying to cross the street", rather than "I am crossing the street". Similarly, although people who are better trained in first aid than me can say, "I am performing the Heimlich manoeuvre", I can only say, "I am trying to perform the Heimlich manoeuvre". Does the ordinary parlance of English here tell us something philosophically important about the nature of intentional action? I think so; I think that our practical rational powers must be understood through a conception of our abilities such that I can typically only set myself to do what I know I am able to do *hic et nunc*.

But I need not convince the unpersuaded reader of this claim. For our purposes, it is enough to notice that in situations in which the agent takes herself not to know that she will achieve the end of her φ-ing, the agent can be correctly characterized as *trying* to φ whether or not we accept that in all such circumstances she can also be correctly characterized as φ-ing. For the cases of knowledge, our canonical characterization of the action was "A is intentionally pursuing the end of φ-ing (or having φ-ed)". In the absence of knowledge, the canonical characterization of the action is "A is trying to φ". Since "trying" already implies that φ is intended, we do not need to use expressions such as "having the end of φ-ing". We can now say that the agent who realizes that she cannot, or is not willing, to pursue means she knows to be sufficient for her end of φ-ing must revise her ends, and among the possible acts still available to her will be the act of trying to φ. But, for our purposes, trying to φ is an essentially different action from φ-ing.[12] Thus, suppose an agent takes herself to be engaged in φ-ing, but then realizes that she does not know whether she is in a position to φ. In other words, she is not confident that she can φ. ETR implies nothing about whether such an agent must adopt the end of *trying to* φ, upon realizing she might fail to φ. Suppose I was on my way to meet Mary at her office, and I now realize that Mary might not be in her office (a common friend just reminded me that Mary takes a few days off throughout the year). Nothing about my given basic attitudes here determines whether I will, insofar as I am rational, engage in the action of trying to meet Mary at her office. Unless one is previously committed to the view that the basic attitudes are degrees of desire, this does not seem a particularly startling conclusion. It would seem possible for me to give up the end entirely upon the realization that Mary might not be in her office without thereby acting irrationally. Of course, it would also be possible for me to abandon my end of *trying* to meet Mary at

---

[12] Though, of course, one could be both trying to φ and φ-ing.

her office because I learn that the chances of success are significantly lower than I thought. I might give up trying to meet her because I learn that it is not only possible that she will be elsewhere, but actually likely to be the case. We have characterized the action of trying as a uniform action independently of the chances of success, but this need not be the case. We could talk (slightly artificially) about "likely φ-ing" or "possibly φ-ing". But I find it more natural to think of trying as having an internal structure, so that there are better and worse ways we can try to φ. If this is true, we can think that my end is often not just to try to φ, but to try to φ in an acceptable manner.

In Section 9.3, we will see what the principle of instrumental reasoning implies with respect to trying. This would be ETR's equivalent to an analysis of the rationality of acting under uncertainty. But before we move on to this discussion, we need to briefly look into how the theory treats cases of error and false belief.

9.2 Error and False Belief

We have focused so far on the relatively tame cases of ignorance and limited knowledge. But there are particularly vexing questions when the agent's instrumental powers are exercised not only under conditions of ignorance, but also under conditions of false, or even irrational, belief. Let us modify our biking to the moon example so that I do now believe that I can bike to the moon; I was persuaded by conspiracy theories that there is a safe but well-hidden bike path to the moon leaving from Chickaloon, Alaska. I believe that government officials use the path all the time, but they do not want the people to know about it, as they do not want to share access to the lovely spa they built on the moon. I carefully plan my trip, say goodbye to my family, and I start biking towards Alaska. As I engage in these actions (let us suppose I even get to Chickaloon and I am now biking on what I erroneously take to be the hidden bike path), am I biking to the moon? Is this kind of massive error compatible with being engaged (unsuccessfully, of course) in the action that I represent myself as engaged in? These are fascinating questions, but, alas, answering them does not serve our current aims. For our purposes, at least one of our canonical descriptions unproblematically applies to such a case: I can certainly describe my action as trying to bike to the moon.[13] It seems that my various pursuits (getting to

[13] There are incoherent ends such that it is not clear that we could even try to pursue the end in question. Could I try to touch the number twelve? Or to swim across asphalt? In such

Alaska; looking for the hidden path; packing dehydrated food) are the pursuit of means to this action—that is, as the exercise of my instrumentally rational powers.

Given our formulation of the principle of instrumental reasoning, many of the actions I take in the pursuit of this end will count as manifestations of my rational power. Let us make this point a bit more precise by looking at the instrumental order of some of my actions:

I am trying to bike all the way to the moon
thus
I am pursuing the end of preparing for a long bike trip
thus
I am pursuing the end of having non-perishable food for a long bike trip
thus
I am pursuing the end of packing dehydrated food
thus
I am pursuing the end of buying dehydrated food at the New Age food store

Once we get to "pursuing the end of preparing for a long bike trip", all my other downstream actions can be inferred through the principle of instrumental reasoning and thus they would qualify under ETR as manifestations of my instrumental rational powers. After all, having non-perishable food is in fact a contributory means (if not part of a sufficient means) for preparing for a long bike trip. On the other hand, preparing for a long bike trip is not in actuality a means to bike to the moon; in fact, nothing is. But we formulated the principle of instrumental reasoning so that the minor premise is the content of an agent's state of knowledge. The obvious fix is to correct the principle so that the content of the minor premise is *believed* rather than known. However, there is also another way to understand this case; namely, that the move from biking to the moon to taking any means towards this end is not a manifestation of my instrumental rational powers. That is, in such a case, I fail to exercise these powers, or my exercise is defective, much as I fail to exercise my powers of aquatic locomotion when I try to swim against a strong current or, even better, on hard asphalt.

---

cases, however, it seems correct to say that nothing I do in pursuit of such incoherent ends could count as a manifestation of a rational power.

Given my discussion of the instrumental virtues, it might seem that I am committed to accepting the first option; after all, isn't the same power that is manifested in my reasoning from this particular end (biking to the moon) to this particular means (preparing for a long bike ride) also manifested in my pursuit of any other end?[14] However, this is not quite true in this case; after all, my reasoning here does nothing to further my ends (just as my batting my arms does nothing to move me against strong sea currents). Of course, it is not my fault (or it is at best my fault only insofar as I badly exercised my powers of *theoretical* reason) that I failed to pursue my ends in this case, but this arguably only shows that the agent's failures to exercise her instrumental powers need not be her fault. More specifically, defective or failed exercise here does not necessarily indicate a defective (rather than a limited) capacity or power. This second "fix" has an important advantage over the first. On the first view, false beliefs do not speak against the fact that an agent has manifested her instrumentally rational capacities. If we allow the view to generalize and say that it never makes a difference to the exercise of practical reason whether the agent's state was knowledge or belief, then it seems that we are committed to the view that a brain in a vat could have the same powers of instrumental rationality that an unenvatted human being has, at least if our theory of mind allows brains in a vat to have beliefs that they are engaged in certain actions. Although many philosophers might find this palatable, I am not among them; in fact, I find this conclusion absurd. Practical rationality is rationality in action and thus a being incapable of acting cannot manifest any kind of practical rational powers.[15]

---

[14] There might be other reasons to keep the false belief and the knowledge case together, especially if one is trying to answer questions about the normativity of rationality. If you think that rationality itself is a virtue or that it has some intrinsic value in some way, then you might find that the same virtue or value is present in both cases. For a view congenial to this line of reasoning see Wedgwood (2017).

[15] We have been assuming that mental actions are essentially different from bodily action for the purposes of presenting ETR (see Chapter 1). Of course, if we allow mental actions then an envatted brain could have this limited form of practical rationality. One could object that a brain in a vat could still choose, decide, or form intentions, etc., and these must be *in some way* manifestations of practical rationality. I actually doubt this claim. My view is that a mental state that is detached from any possibility of action cannot be choice, decision, or intention. Or, if someone would want to keep these labels for mental states that are, within a brain in a vat, similar in respects to our intentions, decisions, and choices, then I would be happy with the conclusion that they are not manifestations of practical rationality. On a related matter, if we accepted this view, would we be able to argue that a brain in a vat also cannot manifest theoretical rational powers, given that it cannot know anything? But in most views about brains in a vat, at least as long as we allow brains in a vat to have contentful mental states, there is much

I favour the second "fix", but it is worth emphasizing that ETR does not depend on it. The final choice between these two views depends on a more general answer to the question of what a rational power or capacity is. I put forward a possible view of the nature of rational powers in Chapter 1, and this book is an attempt to provide an account of a specific rational power, but I do not attempt here to provide a definitive answer to this more general question.

9.3 Trying and Basic Risk Principles

There is a sense of "trying" that commits us to very little in the pursuit of what we're trying to do. Suppose my friend really wants to teach me how to dance the tango. I explain to her that dancing the tango is beyond my abilities and not something that I'd ever enjoy. She's sceptical about both these claims, but I insist. Finally, knowing my weakness for pecuniary incentives, she tells me she'll give me $1 if I at least *try* to dance the tango. So I make a few half-hearted attempts at the 8-Count Basic, I let her give me some tips, act accordingly, but I don't even make an effort to filter out the distracting influences of the sounds that are coming from the other room, and, after a while, I stop paying attention to her instructions and advice. My friend refuses to give me money, alleging that I "didn't really try".

I think there is a sense in which I have a legitimate claim to the money; how else would you describe all that I did other than as "trying to dance the tango"? There is a sense of trying in which almost any effort I put towards a goal counts as "trying". On the other hand, my friend is also on to something. There is a sense of "trying" in which I don't count as really trying unless I am committed to doing my best to succeed under the circumstances. It is the second sense of "trying" that matters to us; if I am allowed to rely on the guise-of-the-good thesis, I would say that in trying to ϕ, the agent regards ϕ-ing itself as good, even if she might not know whether ϕ-ing is a possible act for her. In my tango case, I did not see dancing the tango as good (either intrinsically or instrumentally); I only saw *trying to tango* itself as good.[16] Of course, this does not mean that I will do whatever is in my

that they might know (they might have knowledge of some of their mental states, of mathematics, etc.).

[16] My friend could even dispute that there is *any* sense of "trying" in which I tried. I was merely *pretending* to try. I need not settle this issue; in fact, if my friend's view is correct, then the sense of "trying" I'll be using is the only legitimate sense.

power to tango if I am trying to tango in this sense. Perhaps I'd do better if I kidnapped a tango teacher from Argentina, but my other pursuits will not permit such a thing. But understanding "trying" in this more demanding way does give us a preference ordering internal to tryings; after all, since ϕ-ing is the good I am pursuing, insofar as this activity is concerned, I'll prefer actions that will make my trying more likely to succeed over the ones that make it less likely to succeed. If trying in this way is "doing my best to succeed in ϕ-ing" then I engage in better means if the means I employ are more likely to succeed. And, of course, in cases in which a certain action X will advance all my other ends equally over another action Y except that it also makes it more likely that I will succeed in ϕ-ing when I am trying to ϕ, I will have a Pareto Preference for X over Y. This preference generates a defeasible principle; roughly, the principle says that the rational agent will take the more likely means over the less likely means, all else being equal:

[BETTER CHANCE] If doing X and doing Y are both means of trying to ϕ for an agent A, and neither doing X nor doing Y are sufficient for ϕ-ing, but doing X is more likely[17] to result in A's ϕ-ing than doing Y, and assuming that whether A does X or Y is irrelevant to all A's other ends, then insofar as A is instrumentally rational, A will X if she does either X or Y as a means to ϕ-ing.

It is worth noting that even with all the caveats, the principle is defeasible; this is a consequence of the fact that the agent has a standing permission to pursue indeterminate ends even when she needs to act counterpreferentially in light of her Pareto Preferences. The more I practice, the more likely it is that I'll be signed by Barcelona. But if I do nothing but practice, I'll not be able to pursue my end of visiting Aunt Jane regularly, even if it were true that no particular moment that I train makes a difference to my general project.

[BETTER CHANCE] is a long-winded way of formulating a rather trivial principle: *ceteris paribus*, we choose the action that is more likely to bring about the end we're trying to achieve. The formulation just tries to make clear that ETR does not need to give up on this compelling principle given

---

[17] I interpret "more likely" here to represent the relation of the agent's evidence to a possible state-of-affairs; we assume that the agent knows (at least implicitly) that this relation holds. But it makes no difference to my argument if we understand "likely" here as expressing subjective confidence.

the complications that arise in acting from this principle in the context of being engaged in overlapping extended pursuits. A similar principle also seems grounded on preferences internal to our ends. If I can engage in actions that are equally likely to realize an end that I am pursuing, but I know that one of them would realize a better manifestation of the end, *ceteris paribus*, the latter action is the action that a rational agent would pursue. If I can take singing lessons with two teachers, and in both cases, I'll be realizing my end of singing, but one is a better teacher, and if I learn with her, I'm more likely to sing better, then, *ceteris paribus*, I take lessons with the better teacher insofar as I act rationally. We can formulate the principle as follows:

[BETTER EXPECTED ACTUALIZATION]
If doing X and doing Y are both means for ϕ-ing for an agent A, but doing X is more likely to result in a better actualization of the end of ϕ-ing than doing Y, and assuming that whether A does X or Y is irrelevant to this end in any other way and to all A's other ends, then insofar as A is instrumentally rational, A does X if she does X or Y as a means to ϕ-ing.

Similarly, if two means are equally likely to result in ϕ-ing, but one of them would be a better actualization of ϕ-ing if it did result in ϕ-ing, a rational agent would pursue the means that could result in a better actualization. I'll not try to give a precise formulation of this principle as I hope it is clear that ETR can accommodate these very minimal principles. But it is also important to admit that accepting these principles leaves us still pretty far from the robust comparisons that decision theory can make, even when we relax some of its idealizations and allow for incomplete orderings.[18] Our good old friend Mary from Chapter 3, with her two ends of singing and being a marathon runner, would not get significant advice from us as soon as there is uncertainty about either end. Suppose Mary is suffering from a debilitating disease that affects both her running and her singing. She can take either the blue pill or the yellow pill, but not both (they are lethal if taken in combination). The blue pill has a .7 chance of saving her ability to sing and the yellow pill has a .3 chance of saving her ability to run. None of these minimal principles can say anything about which pill Mary should take in this case. Of course, if Mary has a reflective preference to give priority to singing

---

[18] Of course, it depends on how incomplete the ordering is. The more acceptable extensions of the agent's preference ordering are allowed, the fewer choices are ruled out by the theory.

over being a marathon runner, we can make a case in favour of singing. As she revises the minimal set of her conflicting ends in this case, if the reflective preference is held fixed, she must give up her end of being a marathon runner.

One might object that even with the help of reflective preferences, ETR's power is limited. We can see this by supposing that Mary has the opposite reflective preference in this case: she gives priority to being a marathon runner over singing. In such a case, the reflective preference does not settle the issue; it's not incompatible with the end of giving priority to marathon running that she revises her ends so as to choose a better chance of singing over a smaller chance of running marathons. But, unless Mary has much more specific reflective preferences, changes in the probabilities in the success of each will not determine that Mary should take one or the other alternative, as long as we hold fixed that the blue pill has a higher (or at least non-negligibly higher) chance of success than the yellow pill. Even in some cases in which we have only one end, we'll face a similar lack of rational constraint on possible courses of actions. A complex end like singing will have very different dimensions of better and worse actualizations—there is range, pitch, "feeling", and so forth. In cases in which we're uncertain how various actions will contribute to the degree to which various dimensions of an end are actualized, the theory will not put rational constraints on choices among actions that prioritize different dimensions.

But are these limitations really a difficulty for ETR? First, let us be more precise about the nature of the limitation. ETR does tell us what counts as rational agency in such circumstances; it simply does not constrain instru-mental rational agency as much as some might find desirable. If Mary has no reflective preferences, or gives priority to marathon running, the prin-ciple of instrumental reasoning will make either taking the yellow pill or the blue pill a rational action for her (but not taking both, given that it fails to advance any of her ends, and in fact conflicts with nearly all of them). If this is a problem for ETR, it must be because these verdicts are incorrect, because something about her given attitudes determines that she should take one pill over the other.

I don't find it particularly intuitive that there are further constraints on the rationality of Mary's actions beyond the ones identified by ETR. Of course, if you're already a realist about utility, you will be committed to the existence of these further constraints. We already saw in Chapter 3 that there are serious difficulties in trying to add degrees of desire to the basic given attitudes of the theory of instrumental rationality. Certainly, there will be cases in which Mary is committed to some more specific trade-offs; the most obvious cases are those in which she thoughtfully and stably expresses her preference for, say, taking the yellow pill in the situation above. But here there is no problem for ETR; while certain versions of decision theory will take such behaviour to express the utility of the different outcomes for Mary, ETR will ascribe to her a more specific reflective preference in such contexts. It is unclear that a theoretical advantage accrues to either view on this basis.

A more important objection would focus on the fact that ETR can impose only rather meagre coherence requirements in such situations. So, for instance, suppose Mary has a very specific reflective preference that as long as the gap between the chances of the pills being effective (p(blue pill is effective)—p(yellow pill is effective)) is greater than .4 she will take the blue pill, and if it is smaller than .4 she will take the yellow pill. According to decision theory, this type of preference is incoherent,[19] but ETR cannot deliver this verdict. But does a theory of instrumental rationality really need to rule out such attitudes to risk? Someone might argue that if Mary has this preference she is not properly weighing things by their probability; caring about the absolute differences between probabilities, rather than the ratio, must reflect a misunderstanding of the nature of probability.[20] But it is not clear that this argument can be made without presupposing that utility or degree of desire is the basic attitude.

There has been a great deal of work on our attitudes to risk. In light of the fact that our attitudes, even upon reflection, fail to approximate those

---

[19] Let R stand for the proposition "Mary will be able to run", S for the proposition "Mary will be able to sing", B for "Mary takes the blue pill", Y for "Mary takes the yellow pill", and N for "Mary takes no pill". Let us stipulate that u(N) = 0 (since utility functions are invariant to positive linear transformations, this stipulation results in no loss of generality). Assuming that the only possible outcome of her taking the pill is that either she is able to do the corresponding activity or that she is not cured of anything, then u(B) = p(S|B)*u(S) and u(Y) = p(R|Y)*u(R). To make it simpler, let's assume that .4 is her indifference point; she is always indifferent if p(S|B)—p(R|Y) = .4 (and prefers taking the blue pill if it is higher and the yellow pill otherwise). Thus, for the particular case in which p(S|B) = .5 and p(R|Y) = .1, we have.5u(S) = .1u(R), thus u(R) = 5u(S). But for the particular case in which p(S|B) = .6 and p(R|Y) = .2, we get that u(R) = 3u(S). But, of course 3u(S) ≠ 5u(S), given that we know that u(S) ≠ 0 (since u(N) = 0 and u(S) > u(N)).

[20] One might argue that we'd also need an ad hoc solution for the case in which p(R|Y) = 0 (or even approximately 0) given that, of course, Mary should take the blue pill in such a situation as long as p(S|B) > 0 (or significantly greater), even if the difference in the probabilities is smaller than .4 (given that *some* chance of singing, no matter how small, is better than no, or a negligible, chance of running). But ETR explains why this is a different case. In such situations, taking the yellow pill is not at all a means to the end of being a marathon runner. So her Pareto Preferences determine that she should take the blue pill.

demanded by orthodox decision theory, a number of philosophers have tried to provide alternative models that are more permissive to differing attitudes to risk.[21] In traditional decision theory, attitudes of risk aversion and risk seeking are understood as a function from wealth levels to utility; a convex function is risk-seeking and a concave function is risk-averse.[22] But a theory like Buchak's risk-weighted expected utility theory allows for risk-aversion and risk-seeking attitudes toward utility itself; it permits not only being risk averse to relatively low wealth levels, but risk averse to relatively low levels of utility. However, once we allow that we have such risk attitudes, then it is not clear why we could not have different risk attitudes to different ends, and different risk attitudes to different sets of ends. So I might have risk-averse attitudes with respect to my pursuit of gastronomic pleasure and risk-seeking attitudes to the pursuit of professional success, and have yet different attitudes when the prospects of gastronomic pleasure and professional success combine or collide in different ways.[23] Once we allow that one's attitude to risk is not just a function of the importance we attach to certain outcomes (or of our degree of desire for certain outcomes), but instead it can vary even while holding our degree of desire fixed, there seems to be no principled reason to require that the risk attitude will be fixed across different objects of desires, and different contexts. ETR's wide permissions with respect to acting in situations of uncertainty are no less demanding than this natural extension of a view that, unlike orthodox decision theory, allows for risk attitudes towards utility itself.

Moreover, if it is indeed true that there is something incoherent about relating to the probabilities of the outcomes in this manner, that this attitude somehow reflects a misconception about the nature of probability itself, it will arguably also be the case that Mary has a set of ends that run

---

[21] See, for instance, Buchak (2013). For criticism, see Pettigrew (2015), Thoma and Weisberg (2017), and Thoma (2019).

[22] A common form of risk aversion in this sense is a utility function that assigns a diminishing marginal utility to wealth levels.

[23] Buchak (2013), pp. 79–80 rules out the possibility of different risk functions in different domains because it has some troubling consequences for Risk-Weighted Expected Utility: (1) it does not allow that all gambles are comparable, and (2) it leaves the theory without any resources to deal with hybrid gambles (gambles in which there are outcomes belonging to different domains). But these seem to me to be problems for the theorist, not for the rationality of domain-specific risk attitudes. At any rate, we have already granted some version of (1) and (2). ETR is certainly not committed to the comparability of all gambles, and as we discussed above, cases of risk involving different ends will not impose any restrictions on choice other than the ones imposed by the agent's reflective preferences and principles like BETTER CHANCE and BETTER EXPECTED ACTUALIZATION.

afoul of *ETR COHERENCE*. After all, her end of giving priority to singing over running if the probability difference of success is higher than .4 is further determined by the more specific ways in which she gives priority to singing over running for different assignments of the respective probabilities. These more specific ends would turn out not to be consistent, at least under some further plausible assumptions. To make this point clearer, let us first suppose that you have strange obsessions with certain probabilities. You dislike the idea of pursuing a course of action whose probability of realizing your end is a non-terminating decimal. Doubtless, an unusual disposition, but instrumental rationality is mostly forgiving about the content of basic attitudes. In such a case, even decision theory will find a way to accommodate your bizarre attitudes towards risk.

The idea that there is something wrong with the person who uses the difference rather than the ratio of probabilities must be that this is *not* one of the agent's basic attitudes; the agent is mistaken in how to express in her actions her more basic attitudes to situations of risk and uncertainty. But if this is correct, then ETR also has resources to allow for the possibility that this metapreference expresses some confusion about the nature of probability. Let us assume that the agent has a reflective preference to give *some*, but not too much, priority to running. Then, one could similarly argue that an appropriate understanding of probability cannot allow this more general preference to be implemented by Mary's more specific preference to take the yellow pill if the difference is less than .4 and the blue pill if the difference is more than .4. On such a view, it is not a coherent specification of giving "some priority" to running to take the yellow pill over the blue one, when they have, respectively, a .1 and .3 chance of success, but to take the blue pill over the yellow one when they have, respectively a .3 and a .8 chance of success. Of course, whether there is such an incoherence in the agent's attitudes depends on whether we can make good on the idea that such an agent is somehow confused about the nature of probability in a way that does not presuppose accepting the axioms of some form of decision theory. But if we cannot, there is no argument against ETR here short of arguing for the cogency of the decision theory in question.

9.4 General Means and Risk

Taking the yellow (or the blue) pill serves only one of Mary's means, but in many cases we pursue means that are general means to many of our ends.

As I have argued previously, a rational agent will typically pursue such means as means to the general end of happiness or doing well as described in Chapter 1. Many of these general means generate preferences that are internal to the content of the pursuit. There is an ordering of progressively healthier existence that will generate a preference ordering for the various ways in which we might engage in the pursuit of health. However, the mere fact that health is a general means for happiness cannot, on its own, provide anything that approximates a complete ranking of possible actions in cases of complete knowledge, let alone in cases of risk and uncertainty. As we said previously, there are many dimensions of health that provide different kinds of means to my general end of happiness. There is nothing on a conception of pursuing health as a general means that will determine on its own in which contexts we give priority to longevity over cardiovascular fitness or to preserving eyesight over preserving hearing (in the sighted and hearing agent).

But things seem different with wealth. Given the general fungibility of currency, it seems that there is only one dimension in which wealth can promote the general end of happiness: its relative potential for exchange for goods. Even here, of course, the situation is not quite straightforward. There are issues of liquidity, for instance: Is it better to invest my savings in a house and get a better return or put it in the bank, where I need not wait a long time to retrieve the money? Or should I just put it under the couch so I can access it at any time? But let's leave these issues aside and assume that all my assets have perfect liquidity. Would this conception of general means result in a complete ordering? Of course, in cases of knowledge, the ordering is rather straightforward: more money is always a better actualization of the pursuit of monetary resources. Moreover, our minimal risk principles [BETTER CHANCE] and [BETTER EXPECTED ACTUALIZATION] would still apply. But it is dubious whether such a conception of general means can generate more robust requirements, and it is especially dubious whether it can restrict the agent's risk attitudes so that only the risk functions allowed by orthodox decision theory are considered to be rational. It is well known that our ordinary attitudes to monetary risk[24] are not compatible (at least under some very plausible assumptions) with orthodox

---

[24] And not just monetary risk. Framing effects, for instance, apply to non-monetary rewards as well (as in the case of the famous Asian Disease experiment, Tversky and Kahneman (1981)).

decision theory,[25] and it is not clear that this very abstract conception of the general means can rule out all these "deviant" ordinary attitudes.

As we saw in Chapter 4, my end with regard to wealth is not to pursue as much wealth as possible. Given that the unrestricted acquisition of wealth is not compatible with some of my other ends, my end must be something like "pursue enough wealth" or "pursue a reasonable amount of wealth". However, in cases in which no risk or uncertainty is involved, this end does create a quite straightforward preference ordering: the greater amount of wealth secured, the better the actualization of the end of pursuing wealth. My pursuit of wealth in situations of risk and uncertainty is different: in such situations, I need to find ways to specify my various reflective preferences. I might give high priority to realizing ends that need only a modicum of wealth, or have various ends that I would give high priority to at least "giving them a shot" even if it would require a significant amount of wealth to realize them. A conception of how to pursue expected wealth is a conception of how to pursue this rather indeterminate end that I adopt as general means for many of my ends, including such possible reflective preferences. Such a conception would be, at least in some cases, a specification of a (partial) preference ordering internal to the pursuit of this end. In other words, I could even specify how I am to pursue expected wealth as a general means to my ends by having a procedure by which I (partly) identify better and worse actualizations of this end.

A very simple conception of how to pursue expected wealth would be a maximax conception: that is, I always go for the option that has the potential to give me the highest amount of wealth, no matter how unlikely it is that this potential will actualize; for obvious reasons, this maximax conception is not found in the wild, and ETR can rule it out in most cases. After all, given the easy availability of lotteries, roulette, and so forth, we can be as confident as we want that such a conception would quickly lead the typical agent into bankruptcy. Although not in principle problematic, making decisions simply on the basis of maximizing expected wealth is also a rather rare disposition. Decision theory, restricted in its application to the pursuit of expected wealth, promises to provide a compelling specification of this end. In other words, commitment to a risk function classically understood

---

[25] For a particularly striking example, see Rabin and Thaler (2001). If you would turn down a 50/50 bet on win \$11/lose \$10 no matter what your wealth level is, then you cannot coherently accept any 50/50 bet for win \$x/lose \$100, for any x, no matter how large x is. Such examples play an important motivating role in Buchak's (2013) development of her alternative risk-weighted expected utility theory.

(that is, to a continuous function from wealth levels to utility assignments) is a significantly more plausible way of specifying this end than either the maximax procedure or the expected wealth procedure. It is certainly compatible with ETR that one engages in the pursuit of wealth in situations of risk and uncertainty in this way; in other words, it is compatible with ETR that an agent would specify how she gives priority to different levels of (expected) wealth by means of a classical risk function. Of course, this does not mean that I will always choose the action that maximizes utility whenever I engage in actions that have financial consequences. The pursuit of wealth must be taken up alongside the pursuit of my other ends, and some of my ends might be generically implicated in the range of my actions pursuing wealth. But *insofar as only the end of wealth accumulation is concerned*, my preferences would conform to the axioms of decision theory.

However, is this the only way in which a rational agent could specify this end? It depends in part on how successful we think that the usual pragmatic arguments, or arguments based on representation theorems, are when we restrict them to contexts involving only financial decisions. Are the axioms of decision theory compelling enough in such a context? Do the ways in which agents can be financially exploited (by, for instance, being liable to be turned into "money pumps" if they violate the axiom of transitivity) show that there is something wrong with preferences regarding monetary outcomes that do not conform to these axioms? I tend to think that both these questions must be answered in the negative. We know that many of our preferences regarding financial decisions violate the axioms of decision theory, and I'm not sure how one could show that ordinary agents do not count as coherently pursuing the end of wealth accumulation due to these violations.[26] We also know that sophisticated agents can avoid being exploited in the way envisaged by the pragmatic arguments,[27] so I also can't see how this conclusion could be delivered by the pragmatic arguments. Thus, I tend to think that ETR is compatible with other specifications of the end of pursuing wealth in contexts of risk and uncertainty. But I do not have any airtight arguments for or against this conclusion. At any rate, even if we reject the claim that orthodox decision theory provides the uniquely correct model for how to pursue

---

[26] For a more systematic recent argument for scepticism here, see Orri Stefanson (forthcoming).

[27] For a classical argument, see Schick (1986). For doubts that money-pump arguments can be avoided, see Rabinowicz (2000, 2001) and Dougherty (2014). For other problems with money-pump arguments, see Andreou (2016) and Thoma (2017).

expected wealth, it will clearly provide in many risky contexts a useful approximation of how we should pursue wealth. There's no serious question that decision theory can help us gain a great deal of insight in such contexts, and in some risky contexts involving other types of general means (such as, for instance, the pursuit of "expected health"). However, there is a particular context in which it seems really difficult to avoid the conclusion that ETR will be more permissive than standard decision theory in purely financial contexts. Consider a case in which the agent faces a choice between a course of action in which she has knowledge of the relevant outcomes and a choice where she does not. Let us take a situation like the Allais paradox.[28] In the Allais paradox, in the standard description of the situation, I am faced with a choice between the option of having a million dollars for certain and accepting a lottery such that I am still likely (.89) to win the same million dollars, but which also gives me a small chance of winning five million dollars (.1) in exchange for a very small chance (.01) of not winning anything. Most of us prefer the million dollars for certain. Everyone agrees that this preference is not in itself irrational, but it is, by the lights of decision theory, incompatible with the preference for a lottery that gives a .1 chance of five million dollars over a lottery that gives a .11 chance of a million dollars. However, most of us have *both* preferences. Could ETR follow orthodox decision theory in condemning this pair of preferences as irrational?

Let me start with a quibble about our understanding of the Allais paradox. On some views about the nature of empirical evidence, the Allais paradox proposes an incoherent scenario, at least as far as we humans are concerned. The Allais paradox stipulates that I should have a credence of 1 on an empirical matter; namely, that I will have a million dollars if I make the first choice. But how could a (human) rational agent assign probability 1 to an empirically contingent possibility? Does she not assign any probability to the state-of-affairs in which she will die before the prize is disbursed? Or in which the organizers will be robbed and they'll not be able to pay? Of course, we could simply assume that the credence is very high, but the problem is that the set-up depends on the credence being 1, not just very high. You certainly couldn't reproduce the results by assuming that the probability was .99 (this option would be dominated by the

---

[28] The paradox originally appears in Allais (1953).

second gamble), and it's unclear how close to 1 you'd need to be to get the effect.

I think a more plausible reading of how we understand the scenario is that we assume that we *know* that we'll make a million dollars if we choose the first option. But if that is the right description, it seems difficult to avoid the conclusion that, according to ETR, the Allais preferences are coherent. After all, as we discussed in Section 9.1, the first choice puts us in a situation in which the means available to us are essentially different. There is a type of action I can perform in the first scenario that I cannot perform in the second; namely, accept one million dollars. This option is not a case of pursuing (merely) *expected* wealth, so we're not in a situation in which the end of pursuing expected wealth is the only end involved. Thus ETR could not require in this case that the agent be guided simply by her preferences that are internal to this end.[29]

Rather than an objection to ETR, this is a welcome conclusion—at least for those of us who think that the Allais preferences are not irrational. Of course, this advantage might seem to create problems elsewhere. If someone offers to sell me, a typical middle-class agent, a ticket for a .95 chance of winning five million dollars for five dollars, would it be rationally permissible for me turn it down? The answer seems to be "no",[30] and yet wouldn't the same argument that allowed the Allais preferences make it permissible for me to turn down the offer? However, there are independent reasons why a rational agent must choose this bet that are fully compatible with ETR. Given a middle-class agent's wealth level, a $5 difference in gains makes no difference to their pursuit of wealth, so the agent has a Pareto Preference for the bet. But since this is a one-shot case, no other ends are generically implicated. Thus there are no permissions I could exercise against the Pareto Preference. Of course, if we raise the pay-off enough, then a one-shot case could make a difference to the pursuit of some of my ends. If instead of five dollars, the cost of the lottery ticket is $5000, then the potential loss is significant enough that it could make a difference. But in such a case it is no longer clear that refusing the offer is irrational; indeed, it seems permissible to turn down such an offer.

---

[29] A parallel thing could be said about the Ellsberg paradox (Ellsberg (1961)), but I leave that aside.

[30] At least under the assumption that I have typical preferences regarding money in other contexts.

In fact, I think ETR presents a compelling account of some of the alleged "biases" people exhibit in their consumer choice. It is well known that we make decisions about how much effort we are willing to spend in order to save money in terms of the percentage of the savings, rather than the absolute amount. I might think it is not worth crossing the road to get a $5 discount on my purchase of a new expensive, state of the art, computer, and yet be willing to leave my place in line at the sandwich shop to go across the street if the shop there is giving away for free the exact same sandwich that I would buy for $5 at my current location. People often justify these choices by reasoning that $5 is a rather minimal saving on the price of a computer, but a larger proportional saving (well, 100 per cent) of the price of my sandwich. For many economists, this makes little sense; after all, having an extra $5 in my bank account provides me exactly the same benefit, however the money made its way there.

However, on ETR we can see how this could be a rational pattern for a limited agent. We do not want the pursuit of wealth accumulation to take over our lives, but we also need to pursue this end through repeated small gains and savings. The pursuit of money and the pursuit of convenience or comfort are not momentary choices, but ends that extend through time, and make potentially competing demands in our pursuits. An ideally rational agent would have the virtue of practical judgment in its perfection and she could simply manage these competing ends without intermediate policies; she would end up with enough money and a satisfactory realization of the end of convenience or comfort without such intermediate policies. Unfortunately, we're not such perfect beings; our limited rationality makes it extremely hard for us to pursue these ends without intermediate policies. Making our decisions based on the percentage saved is a promising candidate to be such an intermediate policy; it would let us indulge sometimes in avoiding the inconveniences of pursuing every possible saving without letting this spread too far into our lives, given that we engage much more often in small purchases than in large purchases. Similarly, at least some instances of status quo bias or the endowment effect will seem more reasonable under ETR. People famously are willing to pay much less for an item (such as a mug) than they are willing to accept to sell it.[31] This strikes many researchers as irrational, as one should have a consistent indifference point between some sum of money at t_1 and owning a mug at t_1, a point that is insensitive to

---

[31] See, for instance, Kahneman, Knetsch, and Thaler (1990).

whether the mug was "your mug" a few moments before t_1. But the pursuit of the end of having a reasonable amount of money (as a general means for many other ends) is a different pursuit from the pursuit of kitchen items (or mementos or decorative stuff). An agent that has both these ends needs to pursue them on enough occasions, but nothing about having each of these ends require agents to buy and sell at the same price point. Of course, given the facts about free market capitalism, and the fungibility of money, and so forth, we need to be careful not to engage in repeated interactions that would undermine our pursuit of these ends. In the presence of unscrupulous vendors, economists, or psychologists, we should probably be on the lookout for the possibility that we might be vulnerable to exploitation. But only on a maximizing conception of rationality, sporadic manifestations of these "biases" are necessarily instances of irrationality.

Naturally, this is all speculative.[32] The main point is that understanding human agency as it appears in its most natural form, as the continuous pursuit of various indeterminate ends that extend through time, refashions the way in which we understand rational agency more generally; whether it can really make a difference in this particular case would require much more sustained discussion and research.

This chapter constitutes just a "first stab" at how to incorporate risk and uncertainty into ETR's framework. Obviously, there is much more to be said on the topic, but here in this chapter, my aim is to make it clear that ETR has the resources to explain instrumentally rational agency in a promising way when we extend our focus to contexts of risk and uncertainty. In fact, it can co-opt the resources of decision theory in exactly the areas in which decision theory is at its most plausible.

9.5 Conclusion

Often, when we look at contemporary literature on practical rationality, we are presented with a picture in which the exercise of rational agency seems to stop just short of any bodily movement; a chain of thoughtless causation then connects our mind to our limbs. Rational agency seems, under this picture, like the composition of stop-motion animation. The artist works

---

[32] And it is important to note that I am not claiming that different theories could not have similar explanations of this behaviour. I am just saying that this type of explanation would show this behaviour to be part of a general pattern of limited rational agency identified by ETR.

on the frozen momentary stills, and the creation of (an illusion of) movement is left to the operation of the machinery that winds them together. Tempting as it is, this picture is particularly ill-suited to accounting for human agency given its extended nature, or so I have argued. Or, less contentiously, I have tried to show how an alternative picture of extended human agency provides us with a more compelling understanding of the nature of human instrumental rationality. Of course, philosophers are not unaware of the extended nature of our agency; this is why they often stress the importance of guiding or sustaining intentions, diachronic commitments, or of future-directed decisions whose rational import reaches long beyond their coming into existence. The thrust of this book was to try to argue that this is neither enough nor needed. At least as far as instrumental rationality is concerned, we get a simpler, more powerful, and more accurate picture of rational agency if we understand the work of reason in the pursuit of our extended indeterminate ends as extending all the way to the action itself.

Although the focus of the book was on instrumental rationality, I am optimistic that this way of thinking will have important consequences elsewhere. Most obviously, there is no reason to think that the basic idea does not extend to substantive rationality as well: a rational agent in general should be thought primarily as an agent who pursues the right ends in extended action, rather than an agent who forms the right intention or makes the right decision. Further afield, I think that ETR can help us understand the nature of imperfect duties. It seems paradoxical that morality would require us to help others *some of the time*, but not always, or at least not at any time that morality does not require us to do something more important or more urgent. Moreover imperfect duties cannot be understood as duties to ensure that I bring about a certain minimum amount of a good over a certain period of time—that I, for instance, ensure that I provide every month at least a certain amount of help to others. No matter how much I have helped others recently, I still have to contact the emergency services if I am driving by the scene of an accident when everyone is unconscious; I cannot get excused of this duty on account of my past benevolent acts.[33] However, if our duty is to pursue the end of helping others, and if ETR is right about how a rational agent pursues indeterminate, extended ends, the structure of imperfect duties is no different from

---

[33] For an attempt to deal with this issue with the Kantian framework, see Stohr (2011).

the structure of the pursuit of most ends we have. Of course, these are just promissory notes; it remains to be seen whether ETR can really deliver these riches.

It seems a platitude to say that practical rationality is rationality in action, and much of what I have done in this book is to examine the consequences of taking this platitude seriously. This naïve starting point is often resisted because we are tempted by the view that our rational powers cannot be directly exercised in physical action, by the view that bodily action is guilty of intelligence at best by (causal) association. I hope that the theory I have presented here will warm us to the idea that our rational powers extend all the way to the movement of our limbs and even to what we make of the world beyond our bodies. One cannot expect to gain much sympathy by closing a book on instrumental rationality by fondly alluding to an overcited passage of Hegel. Yet I will take my chances. If all went well, this book has helped us see that, at least when practical reason is flawlessly exercised, the real is the rational and the rational is the real.

Bibliography

Adams, R. M. (2008). *A Theory of Virtue: Excellence in Being for the Good*. Clarendon Press, Oxford.

Ainslie, G. (2001). *Breakdown of the Will*. Cambridge University Press, Cambridge.

Allais, M. (1953). Le Comportement de l'Homme Rationnel devant le Risque: Critique des Postulats et Axiomes de l'Ecole Americaine. *Econometrica* 21(4): 503–46.

Andreou, C. (2006a). Environmental Damage and the Puzzle of the Self-Torturer. *Philosophy and Public Affairs* 34(1): 95–108.

Andreou, C. (2006b). Temptation and Deliberation. *Philosophical Studies* 131(3): 586–606.

Andreou, C. (2007). Understanding Procrastination. *Journal for the Theory of Social Behaviour* 37(2): 183–93.

Andreou, C. (2015). Parity, Comparability, and Choice. *The Journal of Philosophy* 112(1): 5–22.

Andreou, C. (2016). Cashing Out the Money-pump Argument. *Philosophical Studies* 173(6): 1451–5.

Anscombe, G. E. M. (2000). *Intention*. Harvard University Press, Cambridge, MA, 2nd edition.

Anscombe, G. E. M. (2005). Good and Bad Human Action. In Geach, M., editor, *Human Life, Action and Ethics: Essays by GEM Anscombe*, pages 195–206. Imprint Academic, Exeter.

Aristotle (1999). *Nicomachean Ethics*. Hackett Pub. Co., Indianapolis, IN, 2nd edition.

Arntzenius, F. and McCarthy, D. (1997). Self-torture and Group Beneficence. *Erkenntnis* 47(1): 129–44.

Arpaly, N. and Schroeder, T. (2013). *In Praise of Desire*. Oxford University Press, Oxford.

Audi, R. (1989). *Practical Reasoning*. Oxford University Press, Oxford.

Baier, A. (1971). The Search for Basic Actions. *American Philosophical Quarterly* 8(2): 161–70.

Bermúdez, J. L. (2009). *Decision Theory and Rationality*. Oxford University Press, Oxford.

Bovens, L. (1992). Sour Grapes and Character Planning. *The Journal of Philosophy* 89(2): 57–78.

Boyle, M. (2011). "Making up Your Mind" and the Activity of Reason. *Philosopher's Imprint* 11(17): 1–24.

Bradley, R. (2017). *Decision Theory with a Human Face*. Cambridge University Press, Cambridge.

Bratman, M. (1983). Taking Plans Seriously. *Social Theory and Practice* 9(2/3): 271–87.

Bratman, M. (1987). *Intention, Plans, and Practical Reason.* Harvard University Press, Cambridge, MA.

Bratman, M. (1999). Toxin, Temptation, and the Stability of Intention. In *Faces of Intention*, pages 58–90. Cambridge University Press, New York.

Bratman, M. (2007). Temptation Revisited. In *Faces of Intention*, pages 257–82. Oxford University Press, Oxford.

Bratman, M. (2009). Intention, Practical Rationality, and Self-Governance. *Ethics* 119(3): 411–43.

Bratman, M. (2012). Time, Rationality, and Self-Governance. *Philosophical Issues* 22(1): 73–88.

Bratman, M. (2018). *Planning, Time, and Self-Governance.* Oxford University Press, Oxford.

Broome, J. (1999). Normative Requirements. *Ratio* 12(4): 398–419.

Broome, J. (2001). Are Intentions Reasons? And How Should We Cope with Incommensurable Values? In Morris, C. and Ripstein, A., editors, *Practical Rationality and Preference: Essays for David Gauthier.* Oxford University Press, Oxford.

Broome, J. (2013). *Rationality through Reasoning.* Wiley-Blackwell, Oxford.

Bruckner, D. W. (2009). In Defense of Adaptive Preferences. *Philosophical Studies* 142(3): 307–24.

Brunero, J. (forthcoming). *Instrumental Rationality: The Normativity of Means–Ends Coherence.* Oxford University Press, Oxford.

Buchak, L. (2013). *Risk and Rationality.* Oxford University Press, Oxford.

Buchak, L. (2016). Decision theory. In Hitchcock, C. and Hajek, A., editors, *Oxford Handbook of Probability and Philosophy.* Oxford University Press, Oxford.

Carlson, E. (1996). Cyclical Preferences and Rational Choice. *Theoria* 62(1–2): 144–60.

Chang, R. (1997). Introduction. In Chang, R., editor, *Incommensurability, Incomparability, and Practical Reason.* Harvard University Press, Cambridge, MA.

Chang, R. (2002). The Possibility of Parity. *Ethics* 112 (4): 659–88.

Chang, R. (2017). Hard Choices. *Journal of the American Philosophical Association* 3: 1-21.

Coates, A. (2013). The Enkratic Requirement. *European Journal of Philosophy* 21(2): 320–33.

Coates, D. J. (2017). A Wholehearted Defense of Ambivalence. *The Journal of Ethics* 21(4): 419–44.

Davidson, D. (1980a). Actions, Reasons, and Causes. In *Essays on Actions and Events*, pages 3–20. Oxford University Press, Oxford.

Davidson, D. (1980b). Hempel on Explaining Action. In *Essays on Actions and Events*, pages 261–75. Oxford University Press, Oxford.

Davidson, D. (1980c). Intending. In *Essays on Actions and Events*, pages 83–102. Oxford University Press, Oxford.

Dougherty, T. (2014). A Deluxe Money Pump. *Thought: A Journal of Philosophy* 3(1): 21–9.

Dreier, J. (1996). Rational Preference: Decision Theory as a Theory of Practical Rationality. *Theory and Decision* 40(3): 249–76.

Ellsberg, D. (1961). Risk, Ambiguity, and the Savage Axioms. *The Quarterly Journal of Economics* 75(4): 643–69.

Elson, L. (2016). Tenenbaum and Raffman on Vague Projects, the Self-Torturer and the Sorites. *Ethics* 126(2): 474–88.

Elster, J. (1985). *Sour Grapes*. Cambridge University Press, Cambridge.

Engstrom, S. (1997). Kant's Conception of Practical Wisdom. *Kant-studien* 88(1): 16–43.

Enoch, D. (2006). Agency, Shmagency: Why Normativity Won't Come from What is Constitutive of Action. *The Philosophical Review* 115(2): 169–98.

Falvey, K. (2000). Knowledge in Intention. *Philosophical Studies* 99(1): 21–44.

Ferrero, L. (2010). Decisions, Diachronic Autonomy, and the Division of Deliberative Labor. *Philosophers' Imprint* 10(2): 1–23.

Ferrero, L. (2012). Diachronic Constraints of Practical Rationality. *Philosophical Issues* 22(1): 144–64.

Ferrero, L. (2017). Intending, Acting, and Doing. *Philosophical Explorations* 20(sup2): 13–39.

Frankfurt, H. (1987). Identification and Wholeheartedness. In Schoeman, F. D., editor, *Responsibility, Character, and the Emotions: New Essays in Moral Psychology*, pages 27–45. Cambridge University Press, New York.

Fried, B. H. (2012). The Limits of a Nonconsequentialist Approach to Torts. *Legal Theory* 18(03): 231–62.

Friedman, J. (2018). Inquiry and Belief. *Noûs* 53(2): 296–315.

Gauthier, D. (1986). *Morals by Agreement*. Oxford University Press, Oxford.

Gauthier, D. (1997). Resolute Choice and Rational Deliberation: A Critique and a Defense. *Nous* 31(1): 1–25.

Gert, J. (2004). Value and Parity. *Ethics* 114(3): 492–510.

Gollwitzer, P. M. (1999). Implementation Intentions: Strong Effects of Simple Plans. *American Psychologist* 54(7): 493–503.

Goodman, N. (1983). *Fact, Fiction, and Forecast*. Harvard University Press, Cambridge, MA.

Greenspan, P. S. (1975). Conditional Oughts and Hypothetical Imperatives. *The Journal of Philosophy* 72(10): 259–76.

Gregory, A. (2013). The Guise of Reasons. *American Philosophical Quarterly* 50(1): 63–72.

Griffin, J. (1997). Incommensurabiliy: What's the Problem? In Chang, R., editor, *Incommensurability, Incomparability and Practical Reason*, pages 35–51. Harvard University Press Cambridge, MA.

Hampton, J. E. (1998). *The Authority of Reason*. Cambridge University Press, Cambridge.

Harman, E. (2009). "I'll be glad I did it": Reasoning and the Significance of Future Desires. *Philosophical Perspectives* 23 (1): 177–99.

Hausman, D. M. (2011). *Preference, Value, Choice, and Welfare*. Cambridge University Press, Cambridge.

Hedden, B. (2015). Time-slice Rationality. *Mind* 124(494): 449–91.

Holton, R. (1999a). Intention and Weakness of Will. *The Journal of Philosophy* 96(5): 241–62.

Holton, R. (2004). Rational Resolve. *The Philosophical Review* 113(4): 507–35.

Holton, R. (2008). Partial Belief, Partial Intention. *Mind* 117(465): 27–58.

Holton, R. (2009). *Willing, Wanting, Waiting.* Clarendon Press, Oxford.

Hornsby, J. (2017). Knowledge How in Philosophy of Action. *Royal Institute of Philosophy Supplement* 80: 87–104.

Horty, John F. (2012). *Reasons as Defaults.* Oxford University Press, Oxford.

Hurka, T. (1996). Monism, Pluralism, and Rational Regret. *Ethics* 106(3): 555–75.

Hurka, T. (2000). *Virtue, Vice, and Value.* Oxford University Press, Oxford.

Hursthouse, R. (1999). *On Virtue Ethics.* Oxford University Press, Oxford.

Hyman, J. (2015). *Action, Knowledge, and Will.* Oxford University Press, Oxford.

Jackson, F. and Pargetter, R. (1986). Oughts, Options, and Actualism. *The Philosophical Review* 95(2): 233–55.

Jackson, F. and Smith, M. (2006). Absolutist Moral Theories and Uncertainty. *Journal of Philosophy* 103(6): 267–83.

Jeffrey, R. C. (1990). *The Logic of Decision.* University of Chicago Press, Chicago.

Joyce, J. M. (1999). *The Foundations of Causal Decision Theory.* Cambridge University Press, Cambridge.

Kahneman, D., Knetsch, J. L., and Thaler, R. H. (1990). Experimental Tests of the Endowment Effect and the Coase Theorem. *Journal of Political Economy* 98(6): 1325–48.

Kant, I. (1996). *Practical Philosophy.* Trans. M. Gregor. Cambridge University Press, Cambridge.

Kant, I. (2006). *Kant: Anthropology from a Pragmatic Point of View.* Cambridge University Press, Cambridge.

Kavka, G. (1983). The Toxin Puzzle. *Analysis* 43(1): 33–6.

Kiesewetter, B. (2017). *The Normativity of Rationality.* Oxford University Press, Oxford.

Kolodny, N. (2005). *Why be Rational? Mind* 114(455): 509–63.

Kolodny, N. (2007). How Does Coherence Matter? *Proceedings of the Aristotelian Society* 107: 229–63.

Kolodny, N. (2008). Why be Disposed to be Coherent? *Ethics* 118(3): 437–63.

Kolodny, N. (2018). Instrumental Reasons. In Star, D., editor, *The Oxford Handbook of Reasons and Normativity*, pages 731–63. Oxford University Press, Oxford.

Korsgaard, C. M. (1997). The Normativity of Instrumental Reason. In Cullity, G. and Gaut, B., editors, *Ethics and Practical Reason*, pages 215–54. Oxford University Press, Oxford.

Korsgaard, C. M. (2008). *The Constitution of Agency: Essays on Practical Reason and Moral Psychology.* Oxford University Press, Oxford.

Korsgaard, C. (2009). Self-Constitution in the Ethics of Plato and Kant. In *Self-constitution: Agency, Identity, and Integrity*, pages 100–28. Oxford University Press, Oxford.

Lavin, D. (2013). Must There Be Basic Action? *Nous* 47(2): 273–301.

Lord, E. (2017). What You're Rationally Required to Do and What You Ought to Do (Are the Same Thing!). *Mind* 126(504): 1109–54.

Lord, E. (2018). *The Importance of Being Rational.* Oxford University Press, Oxford.

Mackie, J. L. (1980). *The Cement of the Universe.* Oxford University Press, Oxford.

Maguire, B. and Lord, E. (2016). An Opinionated Guide to the Weight of Reasons. In *Weighing Reasons*, pages 4–25. Oxford University Press, Oxford.

Marcus, E. (2012). *Rational Causation*. Harvard University Press, Cambridge, MA.

Markovits, J. (2010). Acting for the Right Reasons. *Philosophical Review* 119(2): 201–42.

Marušić, B. and Schwenkler, J. (2018). Intending is Believing: A Defense of Strong Cognitivism. *Analytic Philosophy* 59(3): 309–40.

McClennen, E. (1990). *Rationality and Dynamic Choice: Foundational Explorations*. Cambridge University Press, New York.

McDowell, J. (1979). Virtue and Reason. *The Monist* 62(3): 331–50.

McDowell, J. (1995). Knowledge and the Internal. *Philosophy and Phenomenological Research* 55(4): 877–93.

McDowell, J. (2010). What is the Content of an Intention in Action? Ratio (new series) 23: 61–78.

Milona, M. and Schroeder, M. (forthcoming). Desire Under the Proper Guise. In Landau, Russ Shafer, editor, *Oxford Studies in Metaethics*, Vol. 15. Oxford University Press, Oxford.

Moran, R. and Stone, M. J. (2011). Anscombe on Expression of Intention: An Exegesis. In Ford, A., Hornsby, J., and Stoutland, F., editors, *Essays on Anscombe's Intention*, pages 132–68. Harvard University Press, Cambridge, MA.

Moss, S. (2015). Time-Slice Epistemology and Action Under Indeterminacy. *Oxford Studies in Epistemology* 5: 172–94.

Mourelatos, A. P. D. (1978). Events, Processes, and States. *Linguistics and Philosophy* 2(3): 415–34.

Müller, A. (1992). Mental Teleology. *Proceedings of the Aristotelian Society* 92: 161–83.

Nefsky, J. and Tenenbaum, S. (forthcoming). Extended Agency and the "Problem" of Diachronic Autonomy. In Bagnoli, Carla, editor, *Time in Action*. Routledge, New York.

Nehring, K. (1997). Rational Choice and Revealed Preference without Binariness. *Social Choice and Welfare* 14(3): 403–25.

Nozick, R. (1994). *The Nature of Rationality*. Princeton University Press, Princeton.

Oddie, G. (2005). *Value, Reality, and Desire*. Oxford University Press, New York.

Orri Stefanson, H. (forthcoming). Is Risk Aversion Irrational? *Synthese*: 1–14.

O'Shaughnessy, B. (1973). Trying (as the Mental "Pineal Gland"). *The Journal of Philosophy* 70(13): 365–86.

Parfit, D. (1984). *Reasons and Persons*. Oxford University Press, Oxford.

Parfit, D. (2011). *On What Matters*. Oxford University Press, Oxford.

Paul, S. (2009). Intention, Belief, and Wishful Thinking: Setiya on "Practical Knowledge". *Ethics* 119(3): 546–57.

Paul, S. (2011). Review of "Willing, Wanting, and Waiting" by Richard Holton. *Mind* 120(479): 889–92.

Paul, S. (2013). The Conclusion of Practical Reasoning: The Shadow between Idea and Act. *Canadian Journal of Philosophy* 43(3): 287–302.

Paul, S. (2014a). Diachronic Incontinence is a Problem in Moral Philosophy. *Inquiry* 57(3): 337–55.

Paul, S. (2014b). Embarking on a Crime. In Villanueva, E., editor, *Law and the Philosophy of Action*, pages 101–24. Rodopi, Amsterdam.

Peacocke, C. (2007). Mental Action and Self-Awareness (I). In Cohen, J. and McLaughlin, B., editors, *Contemporary Debates in the Philosophy of Mind*, pages 358–76. Blackwell, Oxford.

Pears, D. (1978). Aristotle's Analysis of Courage. *Midwest Studies in Philosophy* 3(1): 273–85.

Pears, D. (2004). The Anatomy of Courage. *Social Research* 71(1): 1–12.

Pettigrew, R. (2015). Risk, Rationality and Expected Utility Theory. *Canadian Journal of Philosophy* 45(5–6): 798–826.

Pollock, J. L. (2006). *Thinking about Acting: Logical Foundations for Rational Decision Making*. Oxford University Press, Oxford.

Portmore, D. (2019). *Opting for the Best: Oughts and Options*. Oxford University Press, Oxford.

Quinn, W. (1990). The Puzzle of the Self-Torturer. *Philosophical Studies: An International Journal for Philosophy in the Analytic Tradition* 59(1): 79–90.

Rabin, M. and Thaler, R. H. (2001). Anomalies: Risk Aversion. *Journal of Economic Perspectives* 15(1): 219.

Rabinowicz, W. (2000). Money Pump with Foresight. In Almeida, M. J., editor, *Imperceptible Harms and Benefits*, pages 123–54. Springer, New York.

Rabinowicz, W. (2001). A Centipede for Intransitive Preferrers. *Studia Logica* 67(2): 167–78.

Rabinowicz, W. (2008). Value Relations. *Theoria* 74(1): 18–49.

Rachlin, H. (2000). *The Science of Self-Control*. Harvard University Press, Cambridge, MA.

Ramsey, F. (1931). Truth and Probability. In Braithwaite, R. B., editor, *The Foundations of Mathematics and Other Logical Essays*, pages 156–98. Routledge and Kegan Paul, London.

Raz, J. (1986). *The Morality of Freedom*. Oxford University Press, Oxford.

Raz, J. (1999). *Engaging Reason: On the Theory of Value and Action*. Oxford University Press, New York.

Raz, J. (2005). The Myth of Instrumental Rationality. *Journal of Ethics and Social Philosophy* 1(1): 1–28.

Raz, J. (2010). The Guise of the Good. In Tenenbaum, S., editor, *Desire, Practical Reason, and the Good*, pages 111–37. Oxford University Press, Oxford.

Reisner, A. (2013). Is the Enkratic Principle a Requirement of Rationality? *Organon F* 20(4): 436–62.

Richardson, H. (2004). Satisficing: Not Good Enough. In Byron, M., editor, *Satisficing and Maximizing: Moral Theorists on Practical Reason*, pages 106–30. Cambridge University Press, New York.

Rinard, S. (2017). No Exception for Belief. *Philosophy and Phenomenological Research* 94(1): 121–43.

Russell, D. (2018). Intention as Action under Development: Why Intention is Not a Mental State. *Canadian Journal of Philosophy* 48(5): 742–61.

Samuelson, P. A. (1938). A Note on the Pure Theory of Consumer's Behaviour. *Economica* 5(17): 61–71.

Savage, L. J. (1972). *The Foundations of Statistics*. Dover, New York.

Scanlon, T. (1998). *What We Owe to Each Other*. Harvard University Press, Cambridge, MA.

Scanlon, T. (2014). *Being Realistic about Reasons*. Oxford University Press, Oxford.

Scanlon, T. M. (2007). Structural Irrationality. In Brennan, G., Goodin, R., Jackson, F., and Smith, M., editors, *Common Minds: Themes from the Philosophy of Philip Pettit*, pages 84–103. Oxford University Press, Oxford.

Schafer, K. (2019). Rationality as the Capacity for Understanding. *Noûs* 53(3): 639–63.

Schick, F. (1986). Dutch Bookies and Money Pumps. *Journal of Philosophy* 83(2): 112–19.

Schroeder, M. (2005). Cudworth and Normative Explanations. *Journal of Ethics and Social Philosophy* 1(3): 1–28.

Schroeder, M. (2007). *Slaves of the Passions*. Oxford University Press, Oxford.

Setiya, K. (2005). Is Efficiency a Vice? *American Philosophical Quarterly* 42(4): 333–9.

Setiya, K. (2007). *Reasons without Rationalism*. Princeton University Press, Princeton.

Setiya, K. (2009). Practical Knowledge Revisited. *Ethics* 120(1): 128–37.

Setiya, K. (2011). Reasons and Causes. *European Journal of Philosophy* 19(1): 129–57.

Simon, H. A. (1972). Theories of Bounded Rationality. In McGuire, C. B. and Radner, R., editors, *Decision and Organization*, pages 161–76. North-Holland Publishing, Amsterdam.

Small, W. (2017). Agency and Practical Abilities. *Royal Institute of Philosophy Supplements* 80: 235–64.

Small, W. (forthcoming). The Intelligence of Virtue and Skill. *Journal of Value Inquiry*.

Stanley, J. (2011a). Knowing (How). *Nous* 45(2): 207–38.

Stanley, J. (2011b). *Know How*. Oxford University Press, Oxford.

Stanley, J. and Willlamson, T. (2001). Knowing How. *The Journal of Philosophy* 98(8): 411–44.

Steward, H. (2012). Action as Processes. *Philosophical Perspectives* 26: 373–88.

Stohr, K. (2011). Kantian Beneficence and the Problem of Obligatory Aid. *Journal of Moral Philosophy* 8: 45–67.

Tenenbaum, S. (2003). Speculative Mistakes and Ordinary Temptations: Kant on Instrumentalist Conceptions of Practical Reason. *History of Philosophy Quarterly* 20(2): 203–23.

Tenenbaum, S. (2006). Direction of Fit and Motivational Cognitivism. In Shafer-Landau, R., editor, *Oxford Studies in Metaethics*, 1: 235–64. Oxford University Press, Oxford.

Tenenbaum, S. (2007a). *Appearances of the Good: An Essay on the Nature of Practical Reason*. Cambridge University Press, Cambridge.

Tenenbaum, S. (2007b). The Conclusion of Practical Reason. In Tenenbaum, S., *Moral Psychology*, pages 323–43. Rodopi, Amsterdam.

Tenenbaum, S. (2008). Appearing Good. *Social Theory and Practice* 34(1): 131–8.

Tenenbaum, S. (2011). Review of "Self-Constitution: Agency, Identity, and Integrity" by Christine Kosgaard. *Ethics* 121(2): 449–55.

Tenenbaum, S. (2014). The Perils of Earnest Consequentializing. *Philosophy and Phenomenological Research* 88(1): 233–40.

Tenenbaum, S. (2015). Acting and Satisficing. In Pavlakos, G. and Rodriguez-Blanco, V., editors, *Reasons and Intentions in Law and Practical Agency*, pages 31–51. Cambridge University Press, Cambridge.

Tenenbaum, S. (2017). Action, Deontology, and Risk: Against the Multiplicative Model. *Ethics* 127(3): 674–707.

Tenenbaum, S. (2018a). Reconsidering Intentions. *Nous* 52(2): 443–72.

Tenenbaum, S. (2018b). The Guise of the Guise of the Bad. *Ethical Theory and Moral Practice* 21(1): 5–20.

Tenenbaum, S. (2019). On Self-Governance Over Time. *Inquiry* 1–12.

Tenenbaum, S. (forthcoming). The Practical Irrelevance of Practical Truth. In Frey, J. and Frey, C., editors, *Practical Reason, Knowledge, and Truth: Essays on Aristotelian Themes*. Harvard University Press, Cambridge, MA.

Tenenbaum, S. and Raffman, D. (2012). Vague Projects and the Puzzle of the Self-Torturer. *Ethics* 123(1): 86–112.

Thoma, J. (2017). Advice for the Steady. PhD Dissertation. University of Toronto.

Thoma, J. (2019). Risk Aversion and the Long Run. *Ethics* 129(2): 230–53.

Thoma, J. and Weisberg, J. (2017). Risk Writ Large. *Philosophical Studies* 174(9): 2369–84.

Thompson, M. (2008). *Life and Action: Elementary Structures of Practice and Practical Thought*. Harvard University Press, Cambridge, MA.

Thompson, M. (2011). Anscombe's Intention and Practical Knowledge. In Ford, A., Hornsby, J., and Stoutland, F., editors, *Essays on Anscombe's Intention*, pages 198–210. Harvard University Press, Cambridge, MA.

Tversky, A. and Kahneman, D. (1981). The Framing of Decisions and the Psychology of Choice. *Science* 211(4481): 453–8.

Ullmann-Margalit, E. and Morgenbesser, S. (1977). Picking and Choosing. *Social Research* 44(4): 757–85.

Valaris, M. (2018). Reasoning and Deducing. *Mind* 128(511): 861–85.

Velleman, D. (1997). Deciding How to Decide. In Cullity, G. and Gaut, B., editors, *Ethics and Practical Reason*, pages 29–52. Oxford University Press, Oxford.

Vendler, Z. (1957). Verbs and Times. *The Philosophical Review* 66(2): 143–60.

Von Neumann, J. and Morgenstern, O. (2007). *Theory of Games and Economic Behavior*. Princeton University Press, Princeton.

Voorhoeve, A. and Binmore, K. (2006). Transitivity, the Sorites Paradox, and Similarity-Based Decision-Making. *Erkenntnis* 64(1): 101–14.

Wald, B. (2017). Judging the Guise of the Good by Its Fruits. PhD Dissertation. University of Toronto.

Wald, B. (2018). A New Defense of the Motive of Duty Thesis. *Ethical Theory and Moral Practice* 21(5): 1163–79.

Wald, B. and Tenenbaum, S. (2018). Reasons and Action Explanation. In *The Oxford Handbook of Reasons and Normativity*, pages 214–32. Oxford University Press, Oxford.

Wallace, J. (2001). Normativity, Commitment, and Instrumental Reason. *Philosophers' Imprint* 1(3): 1–26.

Wallace, R. J. (2013). *The View from Here: On Affirmation, Attachment, and the Limits of Regret.* Oxford University Press, Oxford.

Watson, G. (1975). "Free Agency". *The Journal of Philosophy* 72(8): 205–20.

Way, J. (2009). Defending the Wide-Scope Approach to Instrumental Reason. *Philosophical Studies* 147(2): 213–33.

Weatherson, B. (2012). Knowledge, Bets and Interests. In Brown, J. and Gerken, M., editors, *Knowledge Ascriptions*, pages 75–101. Oxford University Press, Oxford.

Weber, M. (2005). Are Terrorists Cowards? *Public Affairs Quarterly* 19(4): 331–42.

Wedgwood, R. (2017). *The Value of Rationality.* Oxford University Press, Oxford.

Weirich, P. (2004). *Realistic Decision Theory: Rules for NonIdeal Agents in NonIdeal Circumstances.* Oxford University Press, Oxford.

Wiggins, D. (1978). Weakness of Will, Commensurability, and the Objects of Deliberation and Desire. *Proceedings of the Aristotelian Society* 79: 251–77.

Williams, B. (1986). *Ethics and the Limits of Philosophy.* Harvard University Press, Cambridge, MA.

Index

For the benefit of digital users, indexed terms that span two pages (e.g., 52–53) may, on occasion, appear on only one of those pages.